MW01283211

MY STRENGTH IN ADVERSITY

A Tale of Tenacity

by

Edgar M. Moran

Copyeditor: Kary Wayson
Original Cover Concept: George Hampton
Cover Design and Illustration: Summer Ortiz
Layout: Daniel Moran

Library of Congress Control Number: 2020924746

ISBN
978-0-578-81951-8 (paperback)
978-0-578-81955-6 (eBook)

Table of Contents

Acknowledgments

Thanks to the many friends who took the time to read early drafts and give me encouraging feedback about this book. I am profoundly indebted to those who helped me in my writing, in particular Sallie Rodman, published writer and lecturer at California State University, Long Beach, who read some of these stories and helped me acquire confidence in their publication; Professor Jack Kates, founder of the International Association of Writing Teachers, who read my stories with interest. He thought that they should be published for their unique features as they truthfully relive the past; my colleagues and friends Stuart C. Gilman, M.D. and Lawrence Parker, M.D., who helped very much with their critical comments; and Daniel Moran, my oldest son, who performed the internal formatting and coordinated the publishing of this book.

Preface

A few years ago, my younger son, André, his wife, Noëlle, and my older son, Daniel, asked me to write the stories of my life. We were sitting at the dinner table on my birthday, and the atmosphere was festive. My immediate reaction was not inclined toward the idea. I thought it might be seen as presumptuous, possibly self-centered, to write "My Memoirs" — not my preference or style. They argued that the project did not have to be a chronological rendition of my life; rather, it could simply be an account of the things that have happened to me written in any order. They told me that they admired my skills as a narrator, and that they thought I should make a record of events that appeared, to them, unusual — some of them quite unique. It was not the first time that someone had suggested that I write down my stories for publication.

After some discussion, I agreed with my sons, and I toyed with the idea of writing certain events of my life as fiction — short stories — not as autobiography. Time passed, and I gave no real further thought to our conversation until one day, without any apparent event, I felt almost an urge to write about a great lesson my father once gave to me and my brother. This was a lesson that, because of my young age and the beautiful way in which my father taught it to me and my brother (as well as its moral meaning in the political climate of the time), made an everlastingly powerful impression on me. In fact, I think it was the first event that influenced my character. I wrote that story as I recalled it, and I thought at the time that it really did have to be written down. Then another story came to my mind, and I felt another inner directive to sit down and write. For several months I wrote every day for many hours. I was very happy to give my first edition of my stories to my sons on my next birthday.

A word about my writing: There have been incidents or episodes in my life that were out of the ordinary, and I think that they deserve to be told. Since early in my life, I have nurtured a passion for things well done, and this passion has exerted an overriding influence on my activities. I have not necessarily wanted to make things perfect, but I have always wanted to do, in everything, the best that I can do. That said, my writing experience prior to this book has been limited to scientific medical writing — and to a relatively large body of writing on medical care and on problems related to the organization of health care delivery. I've written on such ideas throughout my many years as a physician, researcher, and educator. The stories in this book have a different tonality than those; these are my life stories. All are true and written as objectively as possible, rendered in my best possible way.

I've written some of these stories for their historical value and others for their uniqueness. Each was a milestone in my development as an individual, as a physician, as a father, and as a loving human being. I lived through four dictatorships in Romania, and I faced persecution and many times of sheer hopelessness and hunger — both physical and spiritual — while longing for fairness and liberty. I hope with great fervor that my readers will be able to understand what has made me tick — what my life experiences have taught me, and what's given me, in times of great difficulty, the drive to carry on. It has not been easy sometimes, and I've gone through very difficult times. I am asking myself how was I able to go through all I have encountered, how was I able to survive so much and be successful. I believe now that my stories may help others muster the energy to overcome adversity and self-doubt.

Part One: Surviving the Sweep of History

How Did it All Start?

My father, Leon , was the son of Moses and Miriam. He was born in Bacău, a town in Moldavia, the eastern province of Romania. He grew up in Târgu Ocna, a small town also in Moldavia, and then later in Râmnicu Sărat, a five-hundred-seventy-five-year-old distribution center with a population of about fifteen thousand in the northeast area of Wallachia. He told my brother and me about many aspects of his life. His parents lived modestly. They ran a dry goods store which was important to the economy of the place at the time. The farmers brought their products to sell in the market and met their own needs at my grandparents' store. My grandmother, Miriam Yehudit Bat Moshe Hacohen (Maria), a rabbi's daughter, oversaw the store, because her husband, my grandfather, Moses, was dedicated to the study of the Talmud and Torah and spent his time in the local synagogue learning and teaching. Moses was highly regarded by the Jewish community of the town for his knowledge and wisdom. He was called *Rabbi* merely as a title of respect. He did not graduate from any religious school, and I believe he was an autodidact in Jewish studies. He was a mild-mannered man. Miriam was an energetic woman; she died in 1925 or 1926. At that point Leon's elder brothers, Mayer and Bercu, took over the store. They also had a sister, Clara.

Leon had a very modest adolescence. His parents told him that if he needed money, he should go out and work; he took any job that could pay a little, to the detriment of his schooling. Leon finished only eight grades of school. I think that this was the reason he volunteered for the army when he was eighteen years old. He was sent to the front when the country joined the Allies in World War I. The troops lacked leadership as well as food and water. A piece of old bread and soup of questionable nutritional value was all that a soldier could get for sustenance on the front line. When one soldier got a parcel from home, it was a holiday for the whole platoon. They drank rainwater from the roadside troughs, and many fell sick. Leon was sick with typhoid fever during the big epidemic of the time. The front hospital was rudimentary, and the doctor was at best incompetent — at worst, he was drunk. Medics once found Leon in a delirium with high fever walking in the deep snow.

Apparently, he had a strong constitution, and upon recovery he resumed his service on the front line. He was trained to use a machine gun, sent again to the front line, and fought valiantly at Oituz and Mărăşeşti, in the Carpathian Mountains of Moldavia. He was wounded when the machine gun got too hot to fire, swiveled around, and burned his forearm. King Ferdinand of Romania decorated him with the Iron Cross. Father told me and my brother how the Germans broke the front line and encircled them. The Germans were cutting the barbed wire fence behind the first front line when he heard them shouting *schnitt schneller* ("cut faster")! He was the only soldier who could understand them because he knew Yiddish, a jargon of German and Hebrew. Leon and his comrades were taken prisoners. Soon the Germans found out that he could understand them, and he was given the task of translator for the German troops, who needed food from the local farmers. (I remember a handwritten postcard sent by his captain to my grandmother informing her of the valiant manner in which her son had fought, and that he'd had the bad luck of being taken prisoner.)

When a prisoners' exchange was made, Leon was freed and sent again to the Allied front. The Romanians fought most heroically with their bayonets. Then the Germans dropped tear gas over the trenches. The gas was heavier than the air and fell into the trenches, forcing the soldiers out. They were then shot with machine guns. Horrible cruelty was used in that war as it is in all wars. Leon got out from the trenches quickly, but he wasn't able to jump out soon enough, and he developed an inflammation of the eyelids that affected him for several years after.

Following the October 1917 revolution, the Russian troops were recalled from the Eastern European front, and they also left its southern part, which was the province of Bessarabia, located along the eastern border of Moldavia. It is known that Lenin, the leader of the Red Revolution, had the idea that it would be more advantageous for Soviet Russia to disentangle itself from the war and complete the revolution at home, saying that the socialist revolution would conquer the rest of Europe in the years to come. At this point, the Romanian army entered Bessarabia as occupation troops. Leon was promoted to the rank of Sergeant Major, a rare promotion for a Jew in the Romanian Army, and was quartered in a decent house near Chişinău (pronounced Kishinău), the capital city of Bessarabia. A high school teacher who was his comrade in the army took an interest in him. He provided Leon with books on general philosophy and politics as well as classic literature. Leon read extensively, with a hunger for knowledge. For about three or four years, while in Bessarabia with the Romanian occupation army, a most important change occurred in his intellectual development and understanding of life. He became an ethicist and humane socialist quite versed in modern Western European philosophy.

He was honorably discharged in 1922, four years after the end of World War I, and he went back to his home in Râmnicu Sărat. There, his brothers invited him to join them in running their store, which at that time offered a small counter for serving drinks to the clientele. Leon said: "I fought in the 'Great War,'" (as World War I was called), "to help create a better life for the people, and I will not poison peasants with alcohol." He told us this story many times. He came out from the miseries of World War I a great idealist with socialist ideas.

So, Leon left, a bit miffed over the issue of selling alcohol to peasants and moved to Bucharest penniless. There he met some of his comrades from the military and with them started a shop for making cardboard boxes. He did not know a thing about the business of cardboard manufacturing, and he did not make more money than what he needed for his daily bread. Disappointed, he got on a train to Constanța, the large main deep-sea harbor of Romania, with the plan of getting on a ship sailing for the US, as many young men were doing at that time.

Constanța had a population of about sixty thousand, a relatively big town at that time. It was the capital of Dobrogea, a province in the southeast of Romania, between the river Danube and the Black Sea, and was the oldest continuously inhabited city in Romania. It was founded around 600 BCE by the Greeks, who called it Tomis. In 29 BCE, Tomis became a Roman colony, and its name was later changed to Constantiana in honor of Constantia, the half-sister of Emperor Constantine of the eastern Roman Empire (4th century CE). For several centuries, under Turkish occupation, it was a small fishing village. In 1878 it became Romanian, and Western interests developed its harbor, which became the largest on the Black Sea and the fourth largest in Europe. Pipelines were built by foreign corporations to carry oil from Prahova Valley, the oil-rich area of Romania. The same foreign corporations built oil refineries close to the harbor. Ships came from many parts of the world bearing imported wares, and through this harbor, Romania exported its riches (oil, lumber, and cereals). During this period, Constanța had a highly active commercial life and a cosmopolitan population.

Leon did not know a word of English, but he had a lot of confidence in himself. I have always thought that he was born to be an American because of his practical sense, his solid instinct in business, his smart concepts of how to make money, and, most importantly, because of his vision of a life made from honest hard work.

Things did not work out as he had planned, however. In Constanţa, he met a colleague from the army, a man called Kashkora, a Macedonian who convinced him to abandon his plans of moving to the US. Kashkora had bonds, which had some value, and his plan was to sell them, get cash, and make money by buying merchandise abroad, which was at a low price at that time. He liked Leon because of his confidence in himself and offered him a partnership. He saw in Leon a man who would fight every obstacle until he succeeded, a man dedicated to his tasks and his ideals.

Leon and Kashkora opened a business selling imported grocery products called "colonials" in Romania — products such as coffee, tea, cocoa, olives, olive oil, and rice, which were imported from many countries. They purchased large amounts of such products at low prices, which they paid in advance. As the prices of the products went up very rapidly, around 1923 and 1924, they reaped high profits. Somehow, Leon knew the principles of smart commerce, like buying when prices were low and selling when prices were high, and he made good money, which allowed him to enjoy a rich life.

One day, he met Dr. Leon Rosenblatt, who was the chief physician of the Syndicates' Medical Assurance Clinics in Constanţa. They became friends on the spot. Both were happy bachelors, and they started to go out together. The doctor had a sister, Catty, and introduced his new friend to her.

I don't know where the Rosenblatt family came from before settling in the small town of Babadag in northern Dobrogea. Babadag was home to a few thousand people: Romanians, Turks, Bulgarians, Russians, Armenians, Greeks, and some Jews. It was founded by Sultan Bayezid I in the fourteenth century, and it acquired some importance when Sultan Murad IV built a fortress there at the height of the Ottoman empire. The town was located at the northern border of the Ottoman empire. Dobrogea became Romanian in 1878 after the 1877 Russo-Turkish War and the Romanian War of Independence.

It seems that the Rosenblatt family did well in Babadag. The head of the family, Yeruham Rosenblatt, was a tanner, quite productive in his work of tanning leathers for goods which were in great demand in Turkey. He married Lisa Gold, a well-educated woman. I know that she was originally from Tulcea, a big town on the Danube, but I don't know more about her family. Many of Yeruham Rosenblatt's family emigrated to Uruguay in the 1920's. Lisa and Yeruham had four children: Leon, Eve, Janet, and Catty.

It was a great financial effort to provide a good education to children at that time, but the Rosenblatts were absolutely committed to education. They moved to Constanţa; Leon Rosenblatt was sent to Bucharest to study medicine. He graduated in 1913. His sisters Eve, Janet, and Catty were enrolled in the *Deutsche Evangelische Schule,* a German high school (lyceum) of high reputation because of its advanced classical curriculum. The teachers were from a religious order of German nuns.

Yeruham Rosenblatt died in 1914, and his wife Lisa died in 1921. Leon Rosenblatt opened his private office in Constanţa, and Catty took care of his office. In after-war Constanţa, life returned to normal. The city had a cosmopolitan population with many Greeks, Bulgarians, and some Turks. There was no unemployment, thanks to the active harbor and to the developing oil refineries.

Catty and her friends were at the center of the young people's society in the city. By all accounts, she was a very witty young lady, quite attractive, with a notable talent for using *mots d'esprit* (witty remarks). Her nickname at that time was "Venizelos," which was a high compliment because Venizelos was the Greek prime-minister who was highly regarded for his intelligence and wit.

When my father was introduced to Catty by her brother, she liked him because he was presentable, quite attractive, a true gentleman, well-spoken and smart. They became engaged after a short courtship. Catty asked Leon not to dance because she was not a good dancer, and Leon asked Catty not to play cards, because he knew nothing about playing cards. Later, they indeed did not dance, but Leon did play cards.

They were married on August 12, 1924. Leon was twenty-eight and Catty was twenty-three. They had their wedding ceremony in Chişinău, in the house of Eve, Catty's much beloved sister, and they spent a nice honeymoon in Vienna, Austria. There they fell in love with the city and with each other.

Jerome, my older brother, was born on September 28, 1925, a darling baby. I was born 2½ years later, on April 28, 1928. I was given the first name of Mario and the middle name of Edgar. The name Mario was given to me in memory of my deceased paternal grandmother, Maria. My parents wanted also to give me a name in memory of Mother's sister Eve. They could think only of Edgar. Fair enough.

There is a family story that I heard many times while growing up: Mother wanted very much to have a daughter, and when I was born, she asked: "What is the baby?" Father, very solicitously, answered, "Never mind, *mikutzo*," (*mikutzo*, for "the little one" in Romanian, was what he called her as a term of endearment) "You should enjoy your good health." Father did not want to tell her that she did not get the girl she wanted, but it was not a good answer, and mother realized the situation. At that time, she was mourning the loss of her older sister, Eve, who had died two months earlier of puerperal sepsis in the city of Chișinău. It appeared indeed that Mother was not particularly pleased at not having a daughter, but she loved me, as was only normal. It also appears from my parents' stories that I was not a good baby, crying almost every night. Father was working very hard at that time; he needed his sleep, and I did not make that easy for him.

My Early Childhood

For reasons that I still cannot understand, my parents thought that my brother and I should speak German, a language of culture, which my parents spoke well in addition to Romanian. They thought that we could learn Romanian "later." I have always thought that was not right, since Romanian was the language of the country in which we were born and lived. The Romanian language has its own poetry, music, and theater. It seems that my parents were influenced by friends who did not have a great respect for Romanian things in general. In my opinion, this was an unacceptable snobbism. Nonetheless, German became our mother tongue.

My parents decided to hire a German governess for us. I vaguely recall the appearance of this middle-aged lady, *die Fräulein* ("the Miss," in German), who spoke only German and was very strict with us. She was a sort of a reverse Mary Poppins, humorless and severe. No matter what we did, even in the most innocent way, she'd make a comment followed by *sonst* (meaning "otherwise"), a veiled threat. We disliked her intensely, but, for mysterious reasons, we did not muster the courage to tell our parents. Fräulein would take us to the Boulevard on the seashore, where we met other German-speaking kids of our age, and she would gossip with other governesses.

In 1931, our parents went on a cruise to Constantinople (Istanbul). While they were away, the governess did not like some joke Jerome made and wanted to punish him by hitting him with a wire coat hanger. He quickly hid under a bed, but she was able to reach him with the wire hanger, and she scratched his face. He bled a bit, but we saw immediately in his injury our forthcoming liberation from the Fräulein's tyranny. As soon as possible, we told our Uncle Leon what had happened. When our parents returned, the governess was fired. Freedom, freedom! Another governess came from Bucharest, highly recommended, but we did not develop warm feelings for her either.

When my brother started school, the teacher could not communicate with him because he did not know one word of Romanian. He was sent home with a letter from the teacher stating that he was "retarded" and inviting my mother to come to the school to discuss the situation. The next day, my mother visited with the teacher and told her that Jerome was not retarded; he just did not know Romanian. The teacher was absolutely stunned — and furious. She gave mother a stern lecture about not having taught Romanian to her children. This, in a known xenophobic country, did not sit well with my family. They immediately fired the governess and stopped speaking German with us. I recall vividly my brother coming from school, speaking with Mother in a different, strange language. I remember worriedly asking my mother: *Was sagt del Lommy?* which meant, "What does Rommy say?" (We called him "Rommy," for Jerome, and, like many young children, I pronounced my *r*'s as *l*'s.)

I learned Romanian with the help of our housekeeper's friend, Mitică Geană. He was a postman who courted Speranța, our young and beautiful housekeeper. Speranța loved my mother and charmed my childhood. Mitică, her boyfriend, knew many of fairytales that captivated me. He loved me dearly. I remember sitting on his lap and listening to Mitică and Speranța speak Romanian. I could not understand what Mitică said, but I was mesmerized by his warm voice and its cadence. I nudged my brother, asking him to explain to me what Mitică said. Jerome evaded my questions by saying "You'll understand when you'll grow up." It was simpler for Jerome to say this to me as he himself still had some difficulties understanding Romanian. When he finished his first grade, the teacher wrote: "He made good progress, but has a foreign accent."

I recall that when I started to understand the fantastic action in Mitică's fairytales and, even more so later, when I started reading such stories, I was absolutely absorbed and thrilled by the beauty of the heroes' moral characters, their valiance and chivalry and the victory of good over evil. The stories made a great impact on my imagination and possibly contributed to the foundation of my way of thinking. I did learn Romanian very fast, like all kids learn languages, a mental process that I've never understood, but admire to this day. In fact, I spoke Romanian very well without any foreign accent.

When we grew up, there were no German schools in Constanța, and both Jerome and I completely forgot the language. I have always been surprised that intelligent persons like our parents let this happen. We had to relearn German in high school. It is written in the Talmud that "Knowing another language is like living a new life."

♦

My father's business in Constanța did not do very well in the years after the Great Depression. Mother was very talented in handicraft work such as knitting, crocheting, needlepoint, and embroideries, and she suggested opening a store specializing in these handicrafts. My father was color-blind, so such a business seemed unrealistic to him. However, Mother assured him that she would take care of the clientele. They opened the store in the center of

Constanţa. The store was called "De-Me-Ka" and was an immediate success because there was no other store like it in the city. Ladies, schoolgirls, and their teachers were the regular customers; the type of handiwork sold in the store was still in fashion then.

I have a few memories of the house in which I was born. I know that it was on Carol Street, No. 24, the main street of Constanţa at that time. I recall that Jerome had a black toy horse, and I had a white toy lamb. I also remember meeting Santa Claus there on one of my first Christmases. I was not more than two and a half years old. (I know this because what I'll describe here happened in that apartment from which we moved a few months later.) Dad dressed himself in full Santa Claus regalia with a very convincing mask that had a little red bulb lit up on the tip of his nose, and he showed up when I was given my lunch. Around that time, I'd been showing very little interest in eating, and my parents were concerned. Well, well — it felt like the end of my little world when he, with a heavy voice, asked in German, "Does Mario eat well?" I looked imploringly at Mom, who smilingly replied: "Mario eats well most of the time." Sheer salvation! "Santa" was satisfied with her statement. This is all I recall about the first Christmas I can remember.

When my parents decided to move from the house where Jerome and I were born, we moved to a nice and very large apartment on Lahovary Street. It was a centrally located street that ran from the main street toward the sea. The house had a little tower in the corner which was part of my parents' bedroom, and Mother put her vanity there. The view of the sea was superb. I could see dolphins playing quite close to the seashore and I can recall their clicks and whistles. In winter, there were the loud and foreboding sounds of the sea, the waves beating the shore with fury. In spring and summer, we heard the cackling of seagulls and albatrosses. The sounds of the waves made a sort of acoustic background in my mind, which I have heard — and felt — at quiet times for most of my life. It always had a soothing effect on me.

I was about three years old when my paternal grandfather came to Constanţa for a long visit. I recall vividly that I had great fun with him when he carried me on his back almost daily. After each turn in the living room, I excitedly asked, *noch einmal, noch einmal!* (once more, once more!). At the time, I spoke only German and he spoke only Yiddish and Romanian, but we could understand each other very well. He loved me dearly. He was the only grandparent whom I got to know. I saw him again on a short visit to Râmnicu Sărat when I was eight years old. At that time, he was a frail old man, and he died soon thereafter.

◆

I was four or five years old when life became quite interesting for me. My brother and I did not go to kindergarten, and as soon as we moved to the new location, we found a few boys our age with whom we formed a little group of friends. I had just started to speak Romanian, but they were not interested in my conversation. We played outside if the weather permitted, and the most important and pleasing game was with marbles. I developed a passion for the game. There were clay balls, simple, easily breakable, and painted in various colors. There were glass balls with the colors inside in artful spiral rainbows. These came in many sizes. Those about one inch in diameter, called "the queens," were quite expensive. However, the most precious balls were the steel balls, the dream of all the boys. They were, in fact, ball bearings, about which I knew nothing. Most of them were about half an inch in diameter; they were the aristocrats of the game, the best a player could have. There was an active market for marbles. We gave ten clay balls in exchange for a large glass ball. The steel balls, "the kings," were even more difficult to get. It took about twenty clay balls to get a small, half-inch steel ball. I don't know how I became an expert in the marble game without having any money. I had a good feel for distances and played well. With a bit of luck, I managed to make a little fortune, about which I was very proud. I think that playing marbles gave me my first lesson in the moral rules of playing games with friends, namely that one must be honest and play fairly. There were boys a bit taller than me who would stretch to get closer to the target, and I knew this was not correct behavior. When I was five years old, I learned to argue about being correct and not cheating. I remember how upset I became when one boy tried to cheat.

I still regret not having a photo of my appearance as a marble player. I wore a cotton boy hat turned around on my head and short pants with pockets full of marbles. I found in an album the photograph below, which was taken by a photographer when we were wearing better attire.

With Jerome, my brother. Constanţa, 1932.

Father lost his hair quite early in life. He had been told that one could prevent such loss if one shaved the scalp in childhood. This is the reason for my shaved head at three years of age.

When I was five years old, I was accepted into the company of the older boys, partly due to the protection of my brother, but more so due to the influence of my cousin Iry, who was four years my senior. I was quite proud of his support. We'd go to the Boulevard, which was the grand promenade on the cliff along the seashore where the elegant houses and the famous casino were located. We'd venture onto the breakwater that jutted into the sea for about three hundred yards. At the end of the breakwater there was the Genoese Lighthouse, a very important spot for us because, in our imagination, being permitted to go there was a sign of maturity and social acceptance. We made friends with the fishermen, and from them we bought paper cones filled with cooked shrimp (*garides,* in Greek, the dominant language among Constanţa fishermen). Eating *garides* was a pastime with a special ritual. One had to do it slowly to make it last longer. A paper cornet cost two *lei,* about forty cents in today's American money. There we'd also try to fish, using rudimentary poles and — surprise, surprise! — we might catch some small sardines! Who was happier than I was at that time?

♦

I remember being sick with measles and a high fever. Mother, at my bedside, was told by my dear Uncle Leon that I should gargle with peroxide diluted with water. However, I didn't understand the process of gargling. Water in my mouth meant to my young mind that I had to swallow it. I remember negotiating with Mother, telling her, "I'll do as much as I can." Mother agreed, of course, but I was not able to do anything close to gargling. Feverish, sick, I could not understand what the grown-ups wanted from me. Again and again, I said, "I'll do as much as I can," until they let me forgo the gargle, and I recovered. That little story has remained a vital part of the family collection of funny-sweet stories. When I told it to my wife, Huguette, she liked it very much and said that it was the story of her "preferred philosopher" — the one who said, "I'll do as much as I can."

♦

It was routine for all the boys and girls in Constanța to go down to the beach called "Modern." It was not an elegant beach, but it was where I met all my friends, and I refused to miss a day. I was very involved there with building sandcastles with water-filled moats and dreaming of bigger, more permanent water channels. At least once a week, we went with Mother by open bus to Mamaia, the internationally known beach north of the city of Constanța. Mamaia was eight miles long. It was very well kept, with the finest sand I have ever seen, very clean and well-managed. There were nice lounge chairs and many umbrellas that I liked very much. One could walk into the sea for a long distance because the fine sea floor deepened slowly. It was fun finding a great variety of shells. The best thing was to meet Mother at the fine restaurant in Hotel Rex, where I could drink some lemonade.

I had a deep tan, and my nickname was *der Zigeuner* ("the gypsy," in German). I was also rather thin and a bit small for my age, but spry and fast. I didn't like to go to the beach when the weather was too hot, but my Uncle Leon was the arbiter of what Jerome and I were allowed to do or not do; his word on matters of health was decisive for my parents. It was also at that time that, according to Uncle Leon's recommendations, a daily tablespoon of fish oil (in winter) and daily yogurt with breakfast (in summer) were mandatory for our health. We had excellent Greek yogurt, but we did not like it.

In the center of Constanța, there was a sarcophagus and a statue of the Roman poet Ovid. In the year 8 CE, the Roman emperor Augustus exiled

Ovid to the place. It was there that Ovid wrote many of his poems. He died there eight years later, and we, the kids, played on his ancient sarcophagus. For many years, the image and sound of sea waves recalled in my mind the best place on earth — the paradise of my carefree and happy childhood.

The Casino of Constanţa on the Seashore Boulevard.

◆

Our extended family included our Uncle Leon, his wife Mary, and their daughter Lisette. Ephraim, the husband of Mother's late sister Eve, moved to Constanţa from Chişinău and remarried. His second wife was a good woman, Clara, who agreed to take care of Eve's son, Iry, who was only five years old at the time. We saw these relatives frequently. We also had some friends, all of them Jewish. Romanian anti-Semitism had caused a rupture in the social relationship between Jews and Romanians.

For some unexplained reason, vivid memories of my late Uncle Leon have surfaced lately in my mind. In fact, the second story that gave me the impulse to write this book is in my recollection of images and facts about my Uncle Leon. He was unquestionably a very colorful figure in my natal town, Constanţa, and he impressed me deeply throughout my childhood and adolescence. He was loved by many and respected by all. He inspired my brother and me, as well as three of our cousins, to learn, love, and respect the profession of medicine. We saw him as the prototype of the good doctor who helps, consoles, and occasionally cures.

As I explained earlier, Uncle Leon was my mother's oldest brother. He graduated as a Doctor in Medicine from the University of Bucharest in 1913. Just back from medical school, he faced his father's acute illness and was unable to diagnose it. (It was anthrax which killed my grandfather.) Horrified, thinking that he had not learned enough medicine, Uncle Leon went to Paris to advance his knowledge. I never could find out how he managed to live in Paris those few years — "in exile," as he thought of his stay there. His specialized in pediatrics. Upon his return to Constanța, his medical practice flourished. Catty, his youngest sister, took care of his office. Their mother died in 1921. Uncle Leon did not want to marry himself until he "took care" of his sisters (in other words, married them off), as was the custom at that time. After Eve's untimely death in 1928, her son Iry came to live with us for a while. My mother's second sister, Janet, a fun-loving and witty woman, married a man named Sam Goldberg from Albany, New York, whom she met when he visited Romania. After that, they went back to the US, and all I know is that she died in Albany of causes unknown to us.

Friends of the family told me that Uncle Leon was quite a romantic fellow. He was physically presentable, funny, witty, and full of stories, which he narrated in his unique style with a resonant voice and always with a serious demeanor. He was adored by the young ladies of the good society in Constanța of the time. He held several important positions: In the war with Bulgaria during World War I, he organized the military medical service of the Romanian Armed Forces, and in recognition for his hard work and talent, he was promoted to the rank of Major in the Romanian Army, which was a rank never attained by a Jew.

Early in his professional life in Constanța, he was appointed Chief Physician of the harbor and of the Syndicates' Medical Assurance Clinics. Cupid's arrow hit him when he met a young lady named Mary Bernfeld. She was quite attractive, full of verve, highly educated, and very well versed in English literature. They fell in love and married. They had a daughter, Rose-Lisette, who was one year older than me. Mary was not a good housewife. Uncle Leon's clientele was growing, but Mary, not interested in attending to the needs of his home office, neglected the waiting room and was brusque with patients and neglectful of their problems although she was the daughter of a well-known and well-respected practicing physician. She was a good pianist and liked to play the piano even though the house was in disarray.

As in many marriages based only on passionate love, my uncle and his wife encountered bad times, and divorce ensued. After a few years, however, they remarried because they loved each other. I learned from their experiences that romance is a great thing, but if it is not bolstered with solidarity, friendship, and a mutual interest in the practical aspects of life; if there is no compatibility between (or respect for) the lifelong mutual interests of the marriage partners, it is rather difficult to maintain a happy marriage. The second marriage failed after years of trials. From them I learned also that if a marriage is not going well, it is always better to separate rather than live with unresolvable frictions. Mary made the enormous mistake of continuously influencing their daughter Lisette against her father, which is one of the most destructive things that can happen to a family, and it had lasting negative effects on Lisette's development. A very sad story.

My Uncle Leon liked to take me with him for walks in downtown Constanța. I loved our outings. He was a very warm human being with a talent for speaking with people in their actual languages as well as their spiritual languages. In addition to Romanian, he spoke well French, Greek, Turkish, and Bulgarian. As I've said, Constanța was a cosmopolitan city, and as children we learned to mix well and feel comfortable with people of various origins. It was fun to watch Uncle Leon greeting people and to listen to how they returned his salutations. Someone might stop him to ask who I was and then exclaim *Ben Kiustange!* ("a Constanța-born boy!" in Turkish) and start off on a conversation in Turkish of which I could not understand one word. These encounters gave me some of my first impressions of the world as a civil and polite place with people of many nationalities — the world in which I grew up and which I liked very much.

We loved Uncle Leon not only because he was our mother's brother, but because he was a genuinely kind and truthful man, wise and witty, from whom we learned much about life and people. Later, as medical students, Iry, Jerome, and I listened and learned much from his stories about his experiences in medicine. He emphasized the philosophy of medical practice, the human contact of it, the love and understanding a doctor owes to a sick person. His stories were gems of philosophy, of human empathy and love. He was not a materialistic man, and he taught us that the beauty of medicine is in practicing it with or without financial reward. Such wisdom is rare.

The last years of Uncle Leon's life were very sad. During World War II, he and Mary lived together in the same apartment in Constanța, but they barely spoke to each other. After the war, the rules of the Office of Location in the so-called socialist times of Romania were such that neither of them could move anywhere. They were trapped together in their own house. Lisette was in Bucharest studying Letters and French. My family and I were also in Bucharest after World War II, and we communicated with Uncle Leon quite often, but we could not help him with his household problems. At that time, he was still practicing medicine, and some of his former pediatric patients brought their grandchildren to him. He was like a radiant sun in their lives, while his own life was very sad.

In late 1949, while I was a medical student in Bucharest, we learned that Uncle Leon was very sick with a heart condition, a poorly attended coronary insufficiency. Mother left for Constanţa on the first train. I heard that my cardiology professor, Dr. Basil Theodorescu, a highly respected cardiologist at that time, was about to go to Constanţa to give some lectures, at the invitation of the local medical society. I asked him to please see my uncle. Leon died suffering very severe angina pain, in December 1949, at the age of sixty, attended by my mother, but not by Mary. Mother was devastated. I think that Leon's death moved her closer to the idea of leaving Romania for Israel the next year.

I saw Dr. Theodorescu on his return to Bucharest, and he told me that he had been taken to Uncle Leon's bedside by the local cardiologists. He saw and examined him. There was nothing he or the other doctors could do. He was impressed by the love and esteem Leon's colleagues had for him, a man larger than life, whose memory I cherish. Uncle Leon taught me by example much of the philosophy — and the unwritten attitudes and precepts — that make a good doctor.

Growing Up

In the spring of 1934, I was almost six years old; the charming time of my early childhood in Constanța came to an end. This scared me because of its unpredictable nature. Father thought that his store De-Me-Ka would do much better in a more actively commercial city, and he opened a new store in Galați (pronounced "Ga-LATZ"), the city with the major Danube River harbor close to the famous delta. Galați had a population of about a hundred thousand and was important because of its shipyards. So, at that point the central store remained in Constanța and the new branch was in Galați, which was by far a more active commercial and industrial city than Constanța. Father did very well with the new store and rented an apartment in a good area of town, on Holban Street, No. 11. Then my parents decided that I should go and live with him because he was alone. The plan was that Mother and Jerome would stay in Constanța and come to Galați in the summer, after Jerome had finished his second grade of grammar school.

It was boring for me to be alone in Galați, where we did not have any family or friends. I spent time at my father's store. He was not talented with kids my age, but he had a staff of about ten young ladies who liked me, probably because I was polite, clean, and spoke well for my age. My birthday came soon, and loneliness was hard on me. I did not like to eat, and this was a real problem for my father, who did not know to cook. The greatest culinary event for me was when he took me to Ms. Manicatides, a Greek lady who ran a private restaurant for people who did not have family in town or did not like to go to public restaurants. One day, she prepared a popular Greek soup called *avgolemono*, which is a chicken soup dressed in egg and lemon. I really liked it. Father could not believe how much I liked to eat it, because I usually ate so sparingly. I like this soup even today, and I've learned to cook it myself.

Soon, Mother and Jerome arrived, and things went back to their normal swing. I think we did not go to Constanța that summer; instead, Jerome and I took much pleasure in exploring the large orchard behind the three houses of the complex we lived in. All the fruit trees that grew in Romania were growing there: cherries, sour cherries, apricots, peaches, plums, quinces, apples, pears, nuts, hazelnuts, and blackberry. As I was small, I could go beneath the branches and get the fruits, and I could also climb with great ease, like a little monkey, neighbors said. The most interesting fruit tree was a mulberry tree, which I had never seen before. I loved to pick its fruit in season. We had a half-size bicycle and I loved to ride on it. There was not much car traffic in

Galați, and I could ride the bike on the main street, which was bordered by the chamomile trees that perfumed the city in spring. We did not know what pollution was.

We lived in an apartment on the upper level of a house. A young couple, Boris and Clarisse Vurgaft, lived on the lower level of the house. He was a textile engineer, and she was a housewife. They did not have children. She immediately "adopted" me and liked to read stories with me, surprised that I already knew to read. I liked her very much as well, and one day, very smartly, I told Mother that, if something should happen to her and she could not take care of me, I wished Clarisse to do so. Mother smiled. I was not yet aware of the correct terms for ladies' appellations. I figured out that a young lady is called "Miss" and an older lady is called "Mistress." The marital implications of those terms did not yet occur to me. Ms. Vurgaft was young, and she had a husband. Therefore, I reckoned that it was correct to call her "the Miss with the husband." It was the logic of a young kid. Everybody was quite amused with my wording, but they did not correct me — they wanted to remain amused for as long as possible, as many adults still do today with children. In the end, I figured it out by myself.

I learned to read and write when I was five years old. For me, reading and writing was a game. I played it with great curiosity. It was the same with handwriting, but there I encountered the first big problem of my life: I could not pen letters as nicely as Jerome. He had a very regular and beautiful penmanship, which I could not imitate. Mother was very unhappy about this. She encouraged me to improve my handwriting without success until the first grade of high school when Mr. Schwartz, my first teacher of design and calligraphy, taught us cursive, rapid, and gothic writing. I loved the cursive and rapid writing, and somehow, I developed my own handwriting as people always do.

Mother decided that because I had been writing and reading, I should not go to school at age six and a half but stay home another year. I played a lot, read a lot, dreamed a lot, and visited our neighbors. I examined flowers very closely, and I was fascinated with the changes from flowers to fruits in our orchard. There were no young children around, and I needed more companionship while waiting for Jerome to come back from school and tell me stories from his classroom. I guess he exaggerated a bit or added to his stories to amuse me. We grew up in a very friendly and warm relationship that lasted many years. We played together, building forts and navies with "sieges from the sea." Of course, area rugs were the land, and the parquet floor was the sea. I loved to build things and "Meccano," a metal LEGO-type toy of the time, was my great friend and companion.

A nice story comes to my mind: I knew I was supposed to get Christmas presents. Dad said that I could have only one present because he wanted to make me understand that most kids in town were not as well-off as we were, that they were very happy if they got one present at Christmas. I did not follow his logic. He was right about the financial status of many families in town, but I was not yet able to comprehend the connection between other families' financial status and my receiving presents. I got a toy truck, all right, but the question of how boys and girls should be happy with only one present remained clouded in my mind. I understood this later.

One year later, I was in the first grade of grammar school. It was a public school, and most of the kids came from poor families or from families with modest means. My father, who was, paradoxically, a rich man with socialist ethos and political convictions, thought that the public school would be best for Jerome and me. He wanted us to make friends with kids who were less fortunate than ourselves. It was very important to him that we become sensitive and solicitous people. We learned about the significance of Christmas long before we went to school.

Starting more than one month before Christmas, we staged numerous rehearsals of Christmas songs, and we sang the Romanian version of "*O, Tannenbaum, O, Tannenbaum*" ("O, Christmas tree, O, Christmas tree"), immersed in our anticipation of the beautiful and miraculous happening, as the teacher had taught us about the coming holiday. He asked us to bring presents to be placed under a nicely decorated Christmas tree, which were to be given to us at the Christmas ceremony. I asked Mother for presents that I could bring to school, and she got some very nice cookies and a fancy roulade that I was quite happy to place under the Christmas tree at the school.

The day of the celebration came; we sang all the songs that we had so eagerly learned, and finally we got our presents. Much to my surprise, I only got a small trinket that did not make any sense to me. I had the common sense not to show my disappointment, but when I came home, I asked Mom what had happened, because I'd thought that I would get at least a part of what she gave me to put under the Christmas tree. This was my child-logic. I recall her smiling, pleasant face when she sat me down and, in a very calm and warm voice, told me that the teacher knew that I had cookies at home, and that other kids did not have as much as I did; that was the reason those kids got more beautiful presents than I did. We had brightened their holiday with the goodies that she gave me to place under the Christmas tree. I very much liked what she told me, and her explanation sank well into my mind. I took good note of this lesson, which was followed by many other lessons in the same vein which both my parents passed along to me and my brother throughout the years.

I have a tender memory of my first Passover, or *Pessach*, as the holiday is called in Hebrew. I was seven years old and Father thought that it was time for me to actively participate in the Seder ("celebration") of the holiday. I already knew the story, but now, Father told me, it was important for me to ask the "four questions" about the Passover significance, which the youngest child in the family asks the oldest man of the house, who most often is the father. The naiveté of these questions is very touching. The questions are asked at the beginning of the Seder. Well, well — the questions written in the Haggadah (the story of the Jews' exodus from Egypt) must be asked in Hebrew, and I did not know a word of Hebrew. I certainly could not refuse to comply with Father's request, but it was impossible for me to learn this text by heart. I tried very hard, but the words were foreign, and Mother could not help me because she did not know Hebrew. All my efforts were in vain, even though I had a good memory for the poems I learned in my first grade of school, and my struggle confused Mother. I was not able learn those few words in Hebrew because I could not memorize words without understanding them. This inability has followed me all my life. It was the first time I felt so frustrated. I cried because of my frustration and disappointment in myself. Mother was quite worried. Learning was never a problem for me, and she had never seen me crying because of learning difficulties. She did help me though, mostly with her calm demeanor and the soothing attitude which charmed me at my young age and helped with my growing pains. I learned the four questions only when Jerome wrote each Hebrew word phonetically in non-Hebrew characters next to the translated word. That helped me. I learned the four questions beautifully, and my parents were very proud of the way I asked the four questions in Hebrew on the night of the Seder. The festive Seder remains deeply enshrined in my heart and mind. I do honor Passover because it commemorates the liberation of my people from the tyranny of slavery in Egypt.

I started grammar school at age seven and a half, at the same public boys' school Jerome attended. He was two grades ahead of me. I took schooling very seriously and was determined to do well. I was genuinely interested in learning, but to my great surprise, and possibly with some disappointment, I found there was nothing for me to learn. I knew how to write, I knew how to read, and I was proficient in the multiplication tables. The teacher realized this and considered me the "star" of the class. I was not very good at physical exercises, though. My parents had not trained me in gymnastics or sports, as this was not the lifestyle of their time. I was well developed, and I did well in the physical program of the school, but I was not very agile.

As there was nothing new to learn, I enjoyed manual artisanal work, which was a novel pastime for me. I liked working with Play-Doh and creating figures, moving vehicles, ships, and airplanes. I liked to help many of my classmates who felt wonderstruck by the novelty of reading and writing. They had difficulties understanding new concepts in elementary natural sciences, geography, narration, and memorizing. Most of them were children of families with very modest means. They came to school poorly groomed. I recall that after the morning prayer and singing of the national anthem, the teacher would examine all the boys (there were no girls in our school) for the cleanliness of their necks, ears, and hands, and often found them unacceptable. Only a few of us were from middle-class families, and we came to school clean and properly dressed. This was the demographic mixture in the Romanian public schools at that time. It was good to be with kids of various backgrounds. Our parents talked a lot with us about haves and have-nots and about our duty to give a hand to those in need with humility and discretion. They insisted that we work hard, be humble, help others, and not expect anything in kind. It was unacceptable to talk about a good deed we had done, because that was boasting, which was not what well-educated people did. Father was very strict in his position on such matters.

Cousin Iry came to live with us. He was funny, knew a lot of things, was a good storyteller, and amused me and Jerome with stories from his lyceum in Constanța. I liked him a lot. Iry had an inquisitive mind and knew many things for his age. For instance, he had written a very touching poem in memory of his mother whom he lost when he was only four. His poem was published by his school, where he was seen as an emerging literary talent. He had the idea of publishing a magazine for children, an idea that appeared to me to be as if from another world. He wrote very well and composed the front page of our magazine, using any ad hoc topic. Iry taught me how to write the page called "Do You Know?" and to create crossword puzzles. We looked for things already published but not well known from geography, history, and natural sciences, and we came up with interesting things for students our age. This was long before the age of the internet and computers, and our literary product was received well by our colleagues. The name of our magazine was *Culture,* and we distributed it to our colleagues for what amounted to fifty cents, which we rarely received. We had fun with this for about one year.

The first two years of grammar school went by like a very nice dream. It was only in the third grade that three new things shocked my inner world. The first was Boy Scouting. I was immensely pleased with the idea of becoming a Boy Scout. Jerome had been a Boy Scout already, and I was very proud when I got the uniform. It was something new, however. Scouts were called *străjeri* (something like "guards"). We wore a white uniform and a white beret with all kinds of applied insignia. King Carol II was the *Grand Străjer,* and I liked that, as I'd grown up with a deep respect for — and almost love of — the monarchy. Little did I know at that time who the king really was as a leader and monarch. He in fact set a poor example of morality; he had his hands in all the major resources of Romania, a very rich country. I do recall that, not knowing the true acts of the king at the time, I sang the royal anthem with great affection for him. The lyrics were a derivation of "God Save the King." After all, the King of Romania was a cousin of the King of England.

♦

Before I go further on this part of my story, I must narrate an unforgettable experience: In 1936, I was 8-year-old.: King Carol II had returned from France to Romania on June 6, 1930 and assumed the throne, which was occupied until then by his child, Michael. We know now that his return was engineered by politicians and special interests in which the king became an interested party. He liked himself very much and delighted in yearly ceremonies in his honor. In 1936, he wanted a formidable festivity on a stadium in the periphery of Bucharest, called Cotroceni. Twenty-five thousand boy scouts (*străjeri*) had to perform giant games in his honor. Seven tribunes have been constructed around the stadium. Father wanted to give us the fun of a visit to Bucharest and bought tickets at the grand event at Cotroceni. For Jerome and for me this was a great event. I was a boy scout and loved the king, the *Grand Străjer* as he chose to call himself.

We traveled to Bucharest and on June 8, we went to the stadium. Our seats were occupied by some people. Father did not want to engage in any argument, and we moved along at a more distant tribune where we could find seats. The scouts started their performance and suddenly we heard a huge thundering noise and saw a tribune fell in a cloud of dust. It was the tribune where we had our tickets and which were taken from us. There was confusion around us, but it became evident that a major tragedy occurred. Hundreds were severely wounded and many died.

Father helped us get out. Ambulances, first-aid medical emergency workers and firefighters appeared and did good work. Jerome and I saw for the first time in our lives so many bloodied bodies and people killed. An unforgettable experience.

♦

The second new thing that happened when I was in the third and fourth years of grammar school was the promulgation of many anti-Semitic laws in Romania. My Romanian colleagues, the classmates who used to love me, who had tried to emulate me as the best in the class — those colleagues, whom I had so often helped, started to call me offensive names, names I hadn't heard before: kike, dirty Jew, Jesus killer. It came as a shock when my best friend, Dinu, son of a colonel, told me that he no longer could play with me because…I was a Jew. It was the first time I was called "a Jew" in that tone of hatred. I was distraught by this reversal of fortunes, and very confused, I asked Mother about the meaning of all this change. Mother told me not to pay attention and to continue to take care of my learning. This was very well, but I did want to know why. Why? Father talked to me gently and explained to me in simple terms what it all meant: that we were Romanian citizens like all people born in Romania and children of Romanian citizens. I got a clear understanding of the notion of citizenship. I also learned from him what was a religion and that although we were not practicing Jews, we had a different lifestyle than non-Jewish Romanians, that we had our own moral values, standards of behavior, and our own way of relating to other people. He emphasized that we were not different from other people because of our religion, and that I should not respond to insults with insults, but to keep a calm demeanor and not get tangled up in fights. I understood him well, but I was flabbergasted and upset. I could not avoid getting involved in some skirmishes. I was a boy and quite happy to retaliate in kind. This made me gain the physical respect of some of the rougher classmates whose human contact was expressed with their fists. One day, a classmate threw a stone that hit my forehead and I came home bleeding profusely. This scared Mother quite a bit.

The third new thing that changed my life at that time was the discovery that my beloved teacher, a man who was kind to me and who appreciated me as his "most distinguished student" (as he once wrote to my parents), was in fact a member of the Romanian fascist movement called The Iron Guard.

When the notoriously anti-Semitic government came to power, he was promoted to the rank of Inspector of the schools of the area. My parents had taught me that I must respect my teachers, and now I could see that my teacher was a Jew-hating man. I do recall my disappointment.

♦

In 1938, Romanian citizenship laws promulgated by the new anti-Semitic Romanian government of Goga and Cuza required Jews to document their right to Romanian citizenship even if they had been born in Romania, even if they were descendants of Jews who'd lived in the country for several centuries. There were three citizenship categories of the Jews: Category One was for those who had Romanian citizenship at the time of their birth, who'd fought in World War I, or who were born in Dobrogea. We fulfilled all those requirements, and Father, who was very careful with his civil acts, had ample documentation. However, it took him months in the Civil Administrative Court of Galaţi to be recognized as a Category One Romanian citizen, which, in fact, did not give us any advantage. I do recall how frustrated Father was, watching the chicanery of judges and court clerks inventing new fees, postponements, and diversions. I learned not to trust Romanians. This was only the beginning. Soon it became known that Jews in categories Two and Three, about one third of all Romanian Jews, lost all civil rights. Many suffered deportations, although they had been law-abiding citizens of Romania for many years, who had contributed substantially to the commercial, educational, health, and civil life of Romania.

♦

After completing four years of grammar school, students had to pass the examination for admission to the middle high school, a test which was called the Admission Examination. It was a competitive examination consisting of math, Romanian, and natural sciences. I was scheduled to write the exam at the high school "Vasile Alecsandri" in Galaţi, the best local school — which staffed well-known anti-Semitic professors. I ranked tenth place out of several hundred candidates. However, I started high school at the school of the Jewish community. That high school (a "lyceum," as it was called in Romania because of the strong French influence) had a fine reputation. In a national competition on academic standards, its students had the highest test results in sciences and classic studies. The school was well-built, with large classrooms, beautiful furniture, laboratories, and sports facilities.

I should briefly explain the school system in Romania at that time. Essentially, it followed the European system. It consisted of twelve years of basic education, followed by university studies if the student was qualified and wanted a higher education. The twelve years included four years of grammar school (obligatory for every child), the competitive admission examination to high school that I described above, and eight years of high school. The high school years were divided into four years of "lower level" and four years of "upper level." An aptitude examination, required after completion of the lower level, determined who could be promoted to the upper level of the high school. It was understood that students who did not aspire to a university education, those who wanted to go into non-academic professions, might stop their studies after eight years of studies — that is, four years in the grammar school and four years in the lower level of the high school (which was mandatory for all children). Disciplines like math and the sciences, Romanian, French, other languages, history, and geography were taught in more detail in the upper level of the high school. In the sixth grade, one had to choose between science or classics classes. Science classes were necessary for admission to medical school, engineering, and architecture schools of the University.

The curriculum of the lyceum was very intense in both breadth and depth and prepared well the students with a solid education. There were no colleges in Romania at that time. The full twelve years of schooling entitled students to stand the examinations for the baccalaureate. After passing the rigorous written and oral examinations for the Baccalaureate Diploma, a student was an educated person with a broad general knowledge and the ability to think critically. Such a person could apply for entry into the university, after having passed an entry exam, usually competitive.

The change from grammar to high school had a great effect on me. First, there was no longer only one teacher for all classes as we had had in grammar school. There were different teachers for the many different subjects. There was a lot of homework. I liked to study. I was a boy full of curiosity and a desire for knowledge. I wanted to understand how things worked, how the world worked. My parents were always saying "You'll know when you'll grow up." Jerome, of course, told me the same. This may explain why I wanted so much grow up, to understand "things." But the most important change was in my classmates. Most of my new colleagues came from private school; many of them had also studied at the Jewish grammar school; they knew Hebrew and were familiar with Jewish topics of which I did not know much.

Soon after the beginning of my first year of high school, I contracted scarlet fever. I had a light form of the disease, without complications, but the health regulations were very strict, and I had to be in absolute isolation at home for four to six weeks, until I had experienced a complete desquamation of my skin. It was very boring, and I was concerned because I was missing many of the new subjects: math, grammar, French, Hebrew. When I was able to go back to school, I immersed myself in my studies, and I caught up to the level of my classmates quite quickly.

I was a timid boy, very serious, very interested in learning and acquiring new knowledge, studious and a bit withdrawn. My mother was concerned because Jerome was always jovial and carefree, and I was different. She talked with me daily, trying to help me out of my timidity, and she prodded me to speak without fear. She did work with me very well indeed. I made good friends in the high school. Among them was Aurel Siegler. His mother, Anny, knew my mother socially, and she encouraged Aurel to invite me to their house. It was the first visit I made to a high school colleague. We liked each other. He did not care for school. I think now that he had attention deficit disorder, something which was not diagnosed at that time. We liked to play together, and later we became involved in crazy things that boys do to exercise their physical abilities, like athletic competitions in biking. I guess that my friendship with Aurel helped me keep a balance between serious and funny stuff.

One memorable little adventure with Aurel occurred about a year after we'd started spending time together, during wintertime. He had the idea to go to the harbor and cross the frozen Danube on foot. The Danube rarely froze. It was reported that this had occurred only once or twice in a lifetime. There were convoys of horse-driven carriages loaded with firewood from the forest on the other side of the river. There was a lot of horse-drawn traffic on the frozen Danube, which was about two thirds of a mile wide. We enjoyed walking with the drivers of the carriages. In the evening, at the dinner table, I casually narrated my exploit. A deep silence suddenly fell around the table. Jerome looked at me in horror. I felt that something was wrong. Father, understanding that I was only a twelve-year-old boy, did not punish me for something I did in my innocence. He did tell me that what we'd done was a most dangerous thing, and that I should never put my foot on a frozen river. I think after that, he did not care too much for my friend Aurel.

♦

My parents wanted us to learn French, and one day a very nice elderly lady appeared in our home to teach us French, at our parents' invitation. She was a well-regarded French teacher who did not know a word of Romanian. She spoke to us in impeccable French, of which we could understand only a few words. She told us that her name was Sophie. We disliked her because we could not understand her, but she was patient and perseverant, a talented teacher. I studied with her for five years, until the end of the war. She said that I was her best student, and I learned to speak French quite well from her. One day, she left a message for our parents and we learned that she was Sophie Levitsky, née baroness de Noldé, the daughter of a Russian general, chief of the Imperial Guard of the Tsar of Russia, who sent his daughters to Paris for their education before World War I. Her father was killed in the Bolshevik Revolution of 1917, and she and her sister did not want to return to Russia. It was unknown how she'd arrived in Romania, where she was living modestly at the time. I regret not knowing what happened to her when the Russians entered Romania at the end of World War II. I suspect that she did not do well.

At the end of 1939, our life started to turn toward major worries: the clouds of war, the increasingly anti-Semitic laws — everything around us heralded very difficult times. Only eleven years old, perplexed by what I heard almost every day, I asked questions about the changes around us, but I did not always get answers. My father explained things to me when a large group of Polish Jews arrived in Galați. They were destitute and horrified, running away from the Nazi invasion of Poland, which had occurred in September of that year. Some of them were wealthy and were selling jewelry and cars at ridiculously low prices. They were telling other Jews: "Leave, leave, save your lives!" This was one of the first lessons I learned about the horrors of war, and in particular the plight of Jews facing the Nazi onslaught in the Holocaust. Father explained to us that the Nazis were determined to destroy Jewish life. It was a scary and overwhelming prospect!

There was open discussion in the house about what might happen to us, and Father asked Mother to go to Constanța to check out the possibilities of getting on a ship that was going to Palestine. Mom did go to Constanța; Uncle Leon went with her to see many of his friends in the harbor and she got all the information she needed. The problem was not getting on a ship. The problem was that at that time the gates of Palestine were closed by the British Mandate to Europe's desperate Jews. The White Paper of 1939, issued by the British government of Neville Chamberlain, limited drastically the possibility of Jewish immigration to Palestine at a time when escape from Germany and from Europe in general could have been lifesaving. The White Paper was conceived to please Palestinian Arabs who were incited by the Mufti of Jerusalem, a notorious anti-Semite and known friend of the Nazis. It was widely known that the Mufti assured Hitler that his people, Arabs living in Palestine, would provide all the necessary logistic support to the German forces when, invading from North Africa, they reached Palestine. We could not get the British "certificate," as the immigration permit was called.

In rethinking this whole chapter of events, I realize that it made a vast impact on my mind and on my future life. It made me understand that anti-Semitism was devastating, that it originated in the human need to hate, the inability to live in peace. The Jews were falsely accused of having killed Jesus, who was a Jew. As Jews, we were subject to annihilation. These were hardly encouraging thoughts for an eleven-year-old boy. At this time, I also got the clear idea that I had a fatherland — not Romania, the country of my birth, but Palestine, as it was known before the creation of the modern State of Israel.

◆

We learned through various channels about the atrocities committed by the Soviet NKVD (the "People's Commissariat for Internal Affairs" — the fearsome Soviet secret service), who killed about twenty-two thousand Polish officers, soldiers, intellectuals, and dissidents in the Katyn Forest in Poland in early 1940. This was planned by Stalin to weaken the Polish people's resistance after the invasion of Russian forces and the division of Poland between Nazi Germany and USSR in 1939, based on the Molotov-Ribbentrop Pact. I recall the look on my parents' faces and on the faces of the parents of my colleagues. They were terrified. We, their children, lost our innocence at that time. One matures very fast under those circumstances. We lost our innocence so early and so painfully.

◆

The devastating earthquake of November 10, 1940 had as its epicenter the curb of the Carpathian Mountains (shaped as an inverse letter *L*) called Mt. Vrancea. According to what I've found on Wikipedia, this area is responsible for over ninety percent of all earthquakes in Romania, releasing over ninety-five percent of the seismic energy in that area. This was the strongest earthquake recorded in the twentieth century in Romania, 7.7 on the Richter scale. Its effects were devastating in central and southern Moldavia and in Wallachia. The death toll was estimated at a thousand people, with an additional figure of four thousand wounded, mostly in Moldavia. The earthquake occurred in the middle of the night. It was terrible. People in Galaţi had never experienced an earthquake. I don't think that my parents had ever had such an experience either. I only recall us shouting, "Earthquake! Earthquake!" We were scared stiff. The stoves in most houses were the type of tile stoves used in Europe, and most of them collapsed. Because we warmed the house with firewood in our stoves, smoke penetrated the apartment. In the early hours of the morning, Father said that he had to go to his store to see what had happened. He did not return for the next few hours, which worried us very much. The many shelves and cubbyholes for the wools in his store had fallen, and he started replacing things alone. He was a very strong man. Fires erupted throughout town from fallen petrol lamps, like in the Chicago Fire of 1871. Many people were left without roofs over their heads. The repairs and the reconstruction after this earthquake took months. I still recall the smell of burned wood which permeated our daily existence. Jews were asked to pay for most of the repairs although Jews had not caused the destruction. No questions asked. Moreover, the winds of war were on us.

Romania, after World War II. The province of Bessarabia, east of Moldavia, was ceded to USSR in 1940 and became a Soviet republic. In 1991, it acquired independence from the Soviets and became the Republic of Moldova, situated between Romania and Ukraine.

My Father's Greatest Lesson

I received one of the most powerful life lessons from my father at an early age. Its content has guided my life. It happened a few months before my brother's bar-mitzvah. What is a bar mitzvah? It is a formal ceremony, usually held in a synagogue in the presence of at least ten adult men, formally admitting a thirteen-year-old Jewish boy or girl as an adult member of the Jewish community — that is, after his or her proper indoctrination into the rituals of the Jewish religion.

There are many stories about bar mitzvah ceremony, and they vary from place to place in the world. The preparation for the bar mitzvah ceremony was known to be quite lengthy and often unpleasant because of the didactic methods employed at that time. In secular families such as ours, the father usually hired a private teacher or tutor who spent many afternoons with a day-dreaming boy teaching him things usually quite remote from the boy's immediate interests and attention. I recall watching my brother Jerome's sessions with the teacher. Because the teacher was an unpleasant person and accompanied his instruction with old-fashioned physical methods of persuasion, I was almost terrified at the thought that I would have to endure such indignity when my time will come two years later. In my mind, I secretly formulated unclear plans of escape. I talked with my brother about the entire process, and I admired his stoic approach and his "cool."

This was happening in 1938, when Jews in Romania were having a tough time because of the anti-Semitic laws that were promulgated almost every day. I clearly remember one afternoon when my father came home at an unusually early hour and asked my brother and me to sit down and listen to what he had to tell us because he had to "talk with us." Without a doubt, upon hearing that Father had to "talk with us," both Jerome and I were sure that we had done something terribly irregular, and we were very uncomfortable, to say the least.

This is what followed: Our father, who was a secular Jew, was very proud of his Jewish heritage, but a bit disenchanted with the Jewish formal religious life in our town. I distinctly remember him saying that holding the bar mitzvah ceremony at the temple and inviting other rich people to share cakes and cookies and give us presents was not what the Jewish moral teachings were about.

He then explained to us that he wanted us to understand the *meaning* of bar mitzvah. He told us that the words "bar mitzvah" mean "son" (or, "bearer") of the commandments — that is, someone who is a follower of the orders God gave us to apply to each day of our lives. He said that, by attaining the age of bar mitzvah, one was supposed to have become responsible for one's own life and deeds, and that, in the Jewish moral tradition, giving *tzdakah* ("charity," in Hebrew) is one of the most important commandments; it must be accomplished every day either by deed or by giving to the needy. He told us that the most important thing was to keep our eyes always open and to pay attention to where need exists. He told us that, according to our great sage, Rabbi Moses Maimonides (known as Rambam), there were eight ways of making good, and that the most beautiful method of performing an act of charity was to find out by ourselves where the need existed and do the needed charity without being asked, helping without expectation of recognition. In addition, one should never talk about having done a charity. He taught us the expression *matan b'seter* ("giving in secret," or "giving anonymously," in Hebrew), a concept that was dear to my father.

Father continued by telling us that he doubted that we would grow up to practice the daily Jewish religious dictates because we hadn't grown up seeing him leading a formal religious life or performing the prescribed rituals. He told us that he thought that the ceremony of bar mitzvah at the synagogue — as it was performed by the upper class of that time — was an act of vanity, conformity, performed by rich people showing off, and that it was not performed by modest or poor people. He felt that the ceremony would not provide any substantive act of mercy or helpfulness to people less fortunate than us. For him, the most important thing was to be a good person, helpful, sincere, and generous toward other people. To be true to this, he told us that he and Mother had decided not to make any home preparations for a formal ceremony at the synagogue. Instead, they wanted to ask twenty of the poorest children in town to go with their mothers, our mother, and Jerome, and we would buy for them all the clothing and school implements they needed. This would be the *tzdakah* for Jerome's bar mitzvah.

Our parents' social set had much to say about this; it was quite revolutionary. Though true to the precepts of Judaism, an act like my father described was never done, particularly not by a rich family. I presume that many of the rich Jews in town were jealous of my father's goodness. They did not think or act in the same way. I do recall that the Chief Rabbi received our father's decision with a benevolent and approving smile, as he thought the same way as my father. Our colleagues did not understand or appreciate the meaning of what my parents did.

I remember that my father's talk had a different effect on my brother and on me. My brother felt immediate relief from the annoying sessions with his teacher, while I ruminated a long time on all that I learned on that occasion. I felt an immense satisfaction in becoming familiar with the philosophy of generosity. Learning that I too could become helpful to others, I decided that I had to prepare myself to be able to do so. When my bar mitzvah time came close, there was no discussion of what should be done. It was in early 1941, when we expected Romania to go to war as an ally of Nazi Germany. It was evident that the same act of charity should be fulfilled, and it was so done.

Some events, big or small, make an everlasting impact on our lives. They mark us indelibly, regardless of our experiences. This is what happened to me while listening to Father's greatest lesson. May my own sons learn from my father's lesson and follow its precept with the same passionate integrity that it inspired in me. Blessed be my father's memory, for this has been the most powerful lesson of my life.

A Failed Exodus

World War II started in September 1939, and Romania, although historically friendly with and spiritually attached to the West, was led by an extremely reactionary government fearful of displeasing the Nazi regime. One year later, after having lost important tracts of Romanian territory to the USSR, Hungary, and Bulgaria, King Carol II of Romania was forced to abdicate, and a fascist government came to power. It became evident that Romania would go to war on the side of the Axis Alliance. The Axis pressured Romania to join. Romania had oil, which was vital to the deployment of Nazi war machinery, as well as huge resources of lumber, vast fields of wheat, and many other natural resources. As a matter of fact, Romania supplied oil and related products to Nazi Germany both before and during the war. We did not understand why the Allies did not destroy the Romanian oil fields until 1943 and 1944.

In May and June of 1941, as Romania was about to enter the war, the large Jewish community in our town suffered deep anxiety and fear. This was caused by two different factors: the geographic position of our town in the wake of a military confrontation, and the economic and political abuses expected to occur during the war. The city was very close to the river Prut, a major tributary to the Danube. The river Prut formed the border with the USSR.

Galați was the largest harbor on the Danube, where Black Sea ships brought merchandise from all over the world to be transferred to Danube-faring vessels sailing upstream through Bulgaria, Yugoslavia, Hungary, Czechoslovakia, Austria, and Germany. There were active shipyards for repairs and shipbuilding in Galați, which bustled with the activity of its prosperous economy.

There were rumors of imminent aggression from the Soviets as the result of the Romanian army joining the Nazis against the USSR. Artillery and military machinery, German as well as Romanian, passed daily through town, and the troops were greeted with enthusiasm by Romanians. People were pleased with and excited by the idea of war against the USSR and the possibility of recovering Bessarabia and Northern Bukovina, an originally Romanian province ceded to the USSR under duress in 1940, following a Soviet ultimatum. There were those, however, who could logically imagine that such aggression might trigger the Russians into entering Romania. It was during this time that I learned the power of propaganda. The poorly educated people were easily deceived by the government propaganda.

In the case of a Russian invasion, my father's position as a well-to-do merchant would not have been easy. The town's Jews, who were essentially people of the trades, were afraid. We recalled that, when the Russians entered Bessarabia in 1940, they immediately rounded up the tradespeople who were sent to labor camps in Siberia because they were considered "undesirable." In communist terminology, these people were called *burjui* (*bourgeois* or capitalists in the socialist language), and they faced a sure destiny: jail or deportation to Siberia. Very few ever returned. We also recalled that in 1940, upon ceding Bessarabia to the USSR, there was an agreement made which allowed any Romanian citizen to cross the river Prut if they opted to live with the Soviets. Many sympathizers of the socialist doctrine left Romania. We learned much later that those people were not accepted in the USSR; they were suspected of being spies, cruelly treated, and expelled to Siberia.

Stores were emptied by people who hoarded food and necessities, and the rumors of war intensified by the day. There was a frantic search for anti-aircraft shelters, and many families moved around town in search of new living arrangements. As Jews, we were marginalized, not allowed access to any anti-aircraft shelters, and the rumors in our community inflicted fear, horror, and despair upon us.

Our family lived in a nice, centrally located apartment in a good area of the city. Rules about the "living space" allowed to Jews had been decreed several months earlier, and people living in apartments with what was deemed "too much" living space were obligated to quarter military personnel. The better the apartment, the higher the rank of the military person quartered. The city's Space and Location Office quartered officers in a room in our apartment. We lived quietly with them; our interactions were polite and restrained. Mother treated the officers well and served them cookies in the afternoon with tea or coffee. This was intended to foster a civilized relationship between us rather than to win any special advantage.

One day, Mother, who was a quiet person endowed with pleasing social skills, mustered her courage, and asked the colonel who lived in our apartment at that time if it would be wise for us to move in with friends who had a cellar which might act as a good anti-aircraft shelter. The colonel did not hesitate to answer: "If I had a family, I'd move tonight." Then he grabbed his packed suitcase and promptly left us. This was enough for my parents to understand that danger was imminent and to proceed with plans to move in with our friends, the Goldstein family, who had invited us to share their underground shelter in another part of town. We took along with us only the minimum necessary, hoping that our relocation would be only temporary.

The Goldsteins lived in an old, well-built house with many rooms and a large cellar. Mr. Bernard Goldstein was the co-owner of a store of fine porcelain, a rich man by the existing standards, and a well-educated person. His wife, Mathilda, was a housewife; their daughter, Tony, nineteen years old, was a charming and sick young lady whose grave condition had not yet been diagnosed. Salo, the older son, was seventeen, a senior in high school, handsome, and a good violinist, and Freddy was sixteen, also in high school, handsome and taciturn. Jerome was almost fifteen years old, and I was thirteen years old. The Goldsteins received us with open arms; we were good friends with them, and our move there had been planned for quite some time. It was indeed timely.

The war started during the night of our move, on June 22, 1941. All hell broke loose. There were alarms, airstrikes, and bombs falling all over the town. The earth shook, walls trembled, and long-range canon fire made the night an inferno. We spent the night in the cellar, huddled together and scared. My father was the only one among us who had had the experience of an open line of fire in World War I. We kept up our spirits throughout the night. In the morning, we heard that the Romanian leader, General Ion Antonescu, had given the order: "Romanians, cross the Prut!" (as I've mentioned, the river Prut made the border with USSR). Declarations of war with the USSR and the UK were issued and widely publicized.

We were at war. The military became the supreme local authority. Posters with new orders were posted all over town. The availability of shelters was indicated. Strict rules about night camouflage were published and rigidly enforced. Many postings had to do with the new rules affecting only the Jews. We were subject to a curfew, and obligated to bring our radio receivers, cameras, compasses, maps, binoculars, telescopes, and any other optical instruments to the police headquarters. Jerome's new bicycle was requisitioned for the war effort. We were forbidden to leave town except with the special permission of the General Commander of the city, permission which was granted exclusively for medical needs.

There were daily rumors about the deportation of the Jews. Geographically, we were practically right next to the front line, and Jews were considered to be subversive, traitors, and Soviet sympathizers. Deportation meant certain death due to starvation and disease. Air bombings came upon us almost daily, and finding any modern transportation connecting us to the rest of the country became impossible when the railroad tunnel of the train line to Bucharest collapsed. The tunnel was in a little village a short distance from the periphery of our town.

It was in this extremely upsetting climate, when our lives appeared to be fated to destruction, that my parents and the Goldsteins decided that the best thing for us would be to leave town for Bucharest, Romania's capital, where Tony, who was very sick, could get a better medical diagnostic work-up. A medical certificate for Tony was obtained from the Chief Physician of the city after appropriate examinations. The official permit to leave town for Bucharest was signed by the general in charge of the area.

The local airport served only the military. None of the few cars in existence could be used by private citizens. No taxi was allowed to leave the formal boundaries of the city. The only available transport from Galați was by horse-drawn carriage to a train station located beyond the collapsed tunnel; there we could board the train to Bucharest. Our personal luggage was loaded onto an open horse-drawn carriage.

It was on a hot July day that we started our journey. The women sat on the driver's bench and on the luggage while we, the men, walked. All of us were sad to leave the town and worried about our uncertain future. We moved slowly, part of a convoy of similar carriages leaving Galați in search of shelter and security. We must have been in excellent physical shape to walk all those miles on that dusty rural road. We were also deeply concerned and scared about the unknown facing us. Soon we passed the last houses at the city's periphery. After going through fields of corn, we arrived at a barrier where military guards stopped us.

The guards stared at us for a minute or two, then asked for our identification papers. Since all of us were good citizens and had the required papers, we did not anticipate any problems. For a few minutes, all went well. But suddenly, the papers were handed to the master warrant officer in charge. He glanced at our documents, saw the "Jew" stamp on the ID papers, glared at us in a half-drunken stupor, and commanded his soldiers to arrest us.

"But we are law-abiding citizens who need to go to Bucharest for healthcare," said my father. "My friend's daughter, Tony, is gravely ill," he pleaded. "You have in your hands the specific certificate and authorization of the Chief Medical Officer of the Military District of Galați."

All this was good for naught. The warrant officer emphatically shouted, "I don't give a damn who that doctor is. Here, I am the law." Then, turning to his subordinates, he shouted: "I'll call my superiors to find out what to do with these *Jidani*. Meanwhile, lock them up in the jail." (*Jidani* was a derogatory and offensive term for Jews, like "kikes.") His hateful language did not impress or surprise us — we'd already heard it from so many others in the extremely anti-Semitic Romania of the time. However, putting us in jail seemed ominous, and we were frightened.

Our jail was a windowless wooden shed of about twelve by six feet, built of simple wooden boards. There was one door locked with a padlock. A bit of light came through the slits between the boards. My mother, Mathilda, Tony, Salo, Freddy, Jerome, and I were all pushed into this cabin. The guards locked the padlock and laughed their heads off, uttering all sorts of jokes about Jews. My father and Bernard were left outside, waiting for the warrant officer to get in touch with his headquarters.

There was no light in the shed. It was stifling hot. There was no floor, just earth, and no running water. We sat on the ground, and the women cried. We, the boys, made every effort to appear stoic. We were apparently doomed. When our eyes became accustomed to the darkness in the shed, we could see a man squatting on the floor. He was Russian. His clothing consisted of tattered pieces of what could have been a uniform. He was filthy, and his hands were tied. He smiled at us, weakly asking, *khleb, pozhàlusta, khleb* ("bread, please, bread," in Russian). We could not understand his mumblings, but Mother knew some Russian and started talking with him. He was a Russian prisoner of war who had been transferred to the place by unknown ways and circumstances. In the dim light we could see the fresh wounds he had from being beaten by his captors, who'd told him that in the morning he'd be executed because they "did not take prisoners." Horrible! Shattering! Tony cleaned his wounds. We had some dry crackers that we gave him. He took them gratefully and managed to bring them to his mouth with his tied hands. *Spasìbo* ("Thank you"), he said.

Every few hours, we were taken outside by the guards to a filthy primitive latrine. Father and Bernard remained in the warrant officer's office throughout the whole evening and night, arguing with him. The warrant officer pretended that because of the bombing the telephone lines were broken and that he could not contact his superiors in town. He emphasized that he represented the law. He asked for one million lei (the equivalent of two hundred thousand dollars in today's US money) to let us go. Certainly, we did not have this amount of cash with us. Negotiations continued throughout the night. We could distinctly hear the guards saying: "Well, well, in the morning, we'll get rid of these spies."

In the first light of the morning, while going to the latrine, we were shown the gallows in the courtyard. It was frightening! At dawn, the warrant officer, possibly more sober than he'd been the night before, started to realize that he would not get any further with his demands and threats; he accepted quite a large ransom that Father and Bernard managed to pool together and give him in cash. We were released in the morning, but he did not allow us to continue to the train station to get to Bucharest. Instead, crestfallen and shaken, we had to return to town.

Tony's health gradually deteriorated. My parents stayed with the Goldsteins every evening to provide care and moral support. They frequently had to return home rather late and faced the menaces and fines of the police for violation of the curfew rules for Jews. Tony was finally diagnosed with tuberculosis and died in January 1942. She was only twenty years old. My parents and their friends had sensed that young Tony had a serious disease that needed correct diagnosis and treatment, which was not possible in Galați at that time because of its poor medical facilities. In Bucharest, the capital, there were more knowledgeable physicians and more technically advanced hospitals. In addition, the capital was known to provide better shelter for Jews because of its rich and active Jewish community, which was more sophisticated than that in the province.

Upon our return to Galați, we entered the routine of Jewish life during World War II. Of course, we had to wear the sign of the Star of David well sewn on the fronts of our coats. Non-Jewish kids called us various offensive names, and sometimes they inflicted physical abuses. We were not allowed to retaliate.

The wife of the German consul was a client of my father's. She liked my parents, particularly my mother, who spoke perfect literary German. She told my father that we did not have to wear the Star of David. My father replied that he was very proud to wear it. He also made sure that he, my brother, and I were among the first to go out in town wearing the Star of David sewn on our jackets.

The pogrom of January 20–22, 1941 in Bucharest was a savage event enacted by the fascist Iron Guard. Its members wanted to take political power from the Romanian leader, General Antonescu, their former political comrade.

Hundreds of Jews were taken by force from their houses during the night, and many were kidnapped from the streets or from the train station. Many were killed, and their corpses were hung on the hooks of the central slaughterhouse attached to big signs proclaiming "Kosher meat." Incredible abuses happened during the days of the Iron Guard rebellion.

For some time, we did not know about the Death Trains from Iași (Jassy), the capital of Moldavia, in the summer of 1941, because this was hushed up and never reported in the newspapers. When we found out, fear became the master of our days. Fear, fear, living in fear every day. As a child, I could not understand how the publicized description of the Romanian people as jovial, generous, and hospitable could be so terribly false. Later years only confirmed the Romanians' cruelty towards Jews, and chauvinism penetrated all social strata.

Growing Up During World War II

In June 1941, I was 13 years old. Romanian troops, allied with Nazi Germany, crossed the border which was close to our city and invaded the USSR in an operation called Operation Barbarossa. Martial law and a curfew were instituted for Jews soon after the war started. Jewish men aged fifteen to forty-five were ordered to report to the police and were detained in an improvised detention center established in the building of our modern high school. I had never seen my mother crying as she did when we brought food to my father and my brother, who was then a fifteen-year-old boy. The physical conditions of the detention center were deplorable and presented a health hazard because the building did not have enough toilets or lavatories for its several hundred inmates, and the summer was very hot. After about two weeks, the local military authorities relented because they feared disease. The arrested Jews were released. However, arrests of Jews continued to occur for any imaginary infraction, usually made up to extort bribes. Father and Jerome came home a bit shaken up. Dad warned us that this would be a long saga.

All Jewish stores had to display big signs marked "Jewish store." People were asked to boycott these stores, and many who dared to continue to visit them were threatened with punishment. This was done following the model demonstrated by the 1938 German Sturm Abteilung (SA or Brown shirts) of the Nazi regime. It was an eerie time. All Jewish doctors had to change their outdoor signs to fourteen-by-ten-inch plaques reading "Jewish Physician," with a large blue Star of David painted on the white background. Jewish doctors could see only Jews in their offices or at the Jewish hospital in Galați. They could not practice at a non-Jewish hospital. All Jewish lawyers were disbarred. They took teaching posts and, in general, they experienced severe financial difficulties. All other Jewish professionals lost their licenses to practice and were eliminated from professional associations. The Jewish religion no longer qualified as a recognized religion. Later, all Jewish businesses, commercial and industrial, were "Romanized." That meant that Jews had to hand over their business to Romanians without receiving any compensation. Father and other businessmen who were deemed "necessary to the economy" continued to run their businesses, which were now the property of new owners, "Aryan" men who became their employers — that is, if they allowed men like my father to stay. This theft of ownership quickly became a national scenario, one in which the former owner, a Jew, lost his property without any compensation or recourse.

My father's lawyer, a gentile, was well connected and quite helpful. For the Romanization process, he recommended to Father his lady friend, Ms. Elisabeta Barbu, a most interesting person. She was born in an old Romanian family in the town of Sebesh, in southern Transylvania. In 1902, as a young girl, she was taken by her family to the US to visit relatives. She grew up in the States, where she received a good education and became the wife of a Mr. Nelson, chief engineer at Firestone Tires Industries. She did not have children and enjoyed a perfectly happy life in the States until, longing for her family in Romania, she came for a visit in early 1941. As was usual at that time, envious people denounced her visit, and she was arrested as an American spy. I don't know how my father's lawyer got to know her case. He was successful in saving her from her predicament with the authorities. Their relationship blossomed. She was an intelligent and beautiful woman in her forties. As the nominal new owner of my father's business, she arrived at the store every morning, very dutifully and punctually, and smoked her cigarettes and drank coffee. The business' name was changed to Elisabeta Barbu & Co. The "Co." was my father. Elisabeta (Elizabeth), was shocked by the changes in her native land. She spoke very little Romanian with a strong American accent. One day, Father asked her whether she would teach English to my brother and me. We'd already had some English lessons and could read and understand English. Elizabeth agreed, and she became my new English teacher. This worked out well throughout the wartime, and I think I made good progress. It's a pity that I do not know what happened to her at the end of World War II.

◆

After its short-lived use as a detention center for Jews, our high school building was taken over by the German High Command. Our school had to move into a private house donated to the Jewish community by a local rich family. It was in the center of the town and had many rooms, but it was not adequate for classrooms, and it housed only a few lavatories. In some classes there was no room between the desks, and we had to walk on the desks to reach our seats, leaving the imprints of our shoes with each step. Surprisingly, no epidemics occurred despite the abject sanitary conditions. There were some improvised blackboards and a few maps and charts. There was no gym, there were no science labs. We had only a small courtyard in which we set up a volleyball net. Still, our studies continued.

We were lucky to have a group of very cultured and energetic professors who were totally committed to teaching us. This was at a time when the prospect of our reaching the age of maturity was highly questionable; we were subjected to daily persecution, and destined, most likely, for death at the hands of the Nazis. However, it was the pedagogical imperative of the Lyceum of the Jewish Community to educate its young boys, and the school and its teachers endeavored to make us into "Renaissance people," the phrase they used when we entered the high school. In truth, we did not quite understand the meaning of the phrase, but we did know that our school had educated many of the best professionals in the country. Headmaster Herscovici and the teachers were dedicated to helping us become educated men of high moral character. Mr. Herscovici was a severe, dour, and highly cultured gentleman, an Oxford University graduate, and wanted to show us an example of what an educated man should be.

Our curriculum included algebra, sciences, geography, history, Romanian, French, and history of religions and of the arts in each of the eight grades of the gymnasium. We also had gym activities of sorts. In the sixth grade (the tenth grade in the American school system), we had to choose between the classic and the science paths. The focus of each of the disciplines was different from grade to grade. We had algebra and geometry in the lower level, and trigonometry and calculus in the upper-level classes. Sciences included physics, chemistry, the biological sciences (biology, zoology, botany), geology, anatomy and physiology. In the first four grades of high school (the lower-level grades), history included antiquity, the Middle Ages, modern history, and contemporary history. These subjects were repeated in much detail and with in-depth commentaries in the four grades of the upper-level high school, finishing with Romanian history.

French language was studied very seriously in Romania at that time. We studied French in each one of the eight grades of the high school. In the upper level, we studied French literature and a lot of French history (in French), as well as the geography of France. In the third grade, we started Latin and a third foreign language. My whole class opted for Italian, but German was imposed on us the following year. English was removed from the curriculum when the war started.

I was very fortunate to have Miss Schildt, a highly regarded teacher of the Romanian language. She not only taught us the syntax and correct grammar of the language, but also demanded that we express ourselves clearly and correctly — that we avoid expletives and the unnecessary words so frequently heard in American English, words such as "like," "you know," "you know what I mean," etc. She abhorred the particle "hmm," used by students and even by adults who were not sure of their wording — or simply didn't care about how they spoke. When one of us used "hmm," she would acridly interrupt him, saying "Mr. XYZ, 'hmm' does not express any thought." She asked us to be prepared to speak freely and to narrate well. It was our first exercise in rhetoric. She did have a very special dry sense of humor.

The math teacher was Mr. A. Weiss, a great mathematician, and an author of books on algebra, who taught us how to think about math and algebra. Pale and soft-spoken, a man of few words, he was proud and sure of his teaching methods and their results. I recall the day a government inspector came to check on our class, hoping to find something irregular on which he could report to his superiors in Bucharest. I was among the few called to the blackboard that day, and I answered all his questions and a bit more — quietly, precisely, and effectively, in the style of Mr. Weiss. This was a very good day for me.

Messrs. Augenstreich, senior and junior, were our French teachers in the first classes. They had a healthy sense of humor that we didn't always understand.

Rabbi Zalman taught us the history of Judaism. We did not have books on this vast topic, and there were no audio-visual techniques. He explained to us the history of the Jews and the events that had caused political and philosophical consequences over time. He was inspiring about Judaism, and he made us proud of our heritage. I learned the basics very well thanks to his beautiful teaching methods and his superb presentations.

Mr. Novak, a lawyer before the war, had been disbarred along with all the other Jewish lawyers. He knew some Latin and became our Latin teacher. He was quite a mellow sort of a man who worked to improve his own Latin while our class read Caesar's *De Bello Gallico* and Cicero's writings.

We also had Mr. Gabo, our German teacher, a Hungarian Jew who arrived in Galați as a refugee from Northern Transylvania, which had been ceded to Hungary at that time. He was very severe, and we did not like him, but we respected him. I failed a first test, and this was the most difficult report I ever had to give to my mother. She had never experienced such displeasure from me, probably because I always had high marks. In her high German culture, failing a German language test was inconceivable and inadmissible. I started to relearn German with her help, and I made good progress.

Mr. Nachmanson was our music teacher. He taught us the history of music and the different musical styles. We had a school orchestra, and he discovered that I could handwrite music very well, almost as if it were professionally printed. As there was no printed music available, I became the scribe who wrote the music for our orchestra. A pity we did not have recording instruments, only record players.

We also had Mr. Schwartz, whom we liked to tease because he didn't know how to impose his authority. In fact, he was a great teacher of design and calligraphy, disciplines that were taught seriously in our school. I know that his classes helped develop whatever artistic talent some of us had at that time; I also know that we treated him badly.

We also had two young monitors, Lupu and Deju, who knew everything in the world and could cover for any teacher. At the end of the war, Lupu, who was an attorney, married Miss Gabor, who came to us as teacher of French in the fourth grade, a charming young lady. No wonder that Lupu, a handsome young man, fell in love with her. They had a son, Radu Lupu, who became a pianist of international fame.

I wish now to narrate an episode that made a strong impression on me and on my colleagues and exerted a lasting effect on the school: In the fourth grade we had a history teacher, Mr. L., whom we did not respect because he was ill-prepared and physically abused us. One day, he had the impression that I was talking with my bench friend, something that was not allowed. In fact, we weren't talking, but Mr. L. approached us, and, without warning, he slapped the face of my friend. I could see that he intended to slap me too. I recoiled and asked him to refrain from his physical abuse. That infuriated him beyond measure.

Father had instructed us to report to him any instances of physical punishment. I told him exactly what happened, and he ordered me to leave the school before Mr. L.'s class and then return precisely in the intermission after the class. We lived close to the school, and these movements were quite easy to make. I did so for a while until the director found out, and he called a meeting of the schoolteachers and Father. Dad was at his best, arguing forcefully that no physical punishment should be allowed in the school. That message was received positively by all the teachers, and a good page of the school's history was written.

As I wrote in the section titled "Growing Up," we had to pass the aptitude test to continue our studies at the upper level. It was quite a comprehensive exam that included math, Romanian, French, geography, and history. I was in competition with two other students, both very good mathematicians. I received the highest scores and was classified as the first. This was a very joyous event for me.

There were classrooms for girls in the afternoon, in the same building. The Jewish girls had been expelled from other schools at the start of the war. Mixed boys' and girls' schools were a non-existent concept at that time. We played many tricks by leaving small *billets d'amour* for all the *dulcineas* of our imaginations. This was during the time when our hormones were starting to rev up. Although I went through puberty and opened up when I turned twelve, I was not good at flirting with girls yet. Now I see that, for me, this just had to wait a little longer. I probably wanted to become very good at it before starting such activity in earnest!

◆

In 1942, I was fourteen years old. Trains with deported Jews started to pass through the train station of Galați almost daily. They'd stop at our train station for a few hours at the urging of the city medical committee, who asked the military headquarters to allow some time for "disinfection." The Jews on these trains had been rounded up from small villages in northern Moldavia, places where their families had been living for hundreds of years. These people had not committed any crime; there was no legal contention against them. They had simply been forced to board cattle trains and told that that they were to be "relocated" but their guards did not tell where. We, however, found out that they were destined to the recently occupied territory of Transnistria, which was located between the rivers Nistru (*Dniester*, in Russian) and the river Bug, farther east in Ukraine. There were no decent amenities for life in that territory, which had been recently destroyed by the wild Romanian occupation. In retaliation against all that the Russians had committed in Bessarabia when it was ceded to them, the Romanians acted savagely in Transnistria — that is, until they realized that the destruction of so much habitable space was to their disadvantage.

The Jews on the trains were hungry, thirsty, and destitute, desperate after hours of traveling without respite. Father was the volunteer responsible for the social services of the Jewish community, and he was dedicated to helping the deportees passing through Galați. He enlisted the help of local bakeries, and they baked hundreds of loaves of bread almost every day. He asked my brother and me to help deliver the loaves of bread as well as medical supplies, warm clothing, and blankets to the people on the trains. This was very risky for us because we were not allowed to enter the train station, which was out of bounds for Jews. However, the police closed their eyes, accepting bribes in exchange for letting us do our charitable work. For my brother and me, this was our first encounter with human misery and savage persecution. At the beginning, we could not comprehend what was going on, but slowly, to our shock, we started to realize that the same fate might be ours. This realization became an obsession. Fear was on us at every moment of our lives.

Romania and the province of Transnistria (1941).

One day, I came home and found my mother terribly distraught and crying. She could not speak but made a sign to me to look out at what was happening in the street below. I have a clear visual memory of seeing there a long convoy of Jewish people carrying small suitcases, escorted by Romanian gendarmes who shouted orders. These were Jews who had run into trouble with the authorities because of denunciation (often motivated by envy), and they were being taken to the train station to be deported. Suddenly, I saw one of my colleagues, Michael Brenner, who was walking with his grandfather, a well-respected elderly man who was the owner of a manufacture of matches, an important business in Galaţi at that time. Michael was an orphan who lived with his grandfather. He was a very talented young fellow who had written a highly prized poem about his mother, whom he had lost in an accident. His poem earned literary prizes throughout the country. Our eyes connected, and he waved to me, smiling. It was the last time I saw him. We found out that his grandfather had been denounced as a "sympathizer of the Soviets," a total fabrication. His business had been confiscated, and he and Michael were on their way to deportation to Transnistria, from which they never returned. This is just one memory out of so many tragedies that happened every day at the time.

Deportation was a daily event, and we knew its outcome. Our parents explained that although Father was protected because he was "necessary to the economy," anything might happen to us at any time. Mother prepared some cotton pockets sewn on a belt into which Father put bills of US dollars and British pounds and gold coins. They explained to us that we might be deported without any notice, and that it was possible that we could accidentally get separated, as had happened to many families. In such a case, Jerome and I should carefully use the money that might save us. I still have two British sovereigns which were among the gold coins hidden in the belt I wore during the war.

◆

Deportation to Transnistria became a fixation in our mind. Nothing else mattered. When would our turn come? Who among people known to us had been deported? Without being able to listen to the radio, and with the press full of the lies of the fascist government, we were completely isolated from the world — isolated and feeling like we were jailed in Romania.

Then, belatedly, we got word of a most important event, an event that could potentially change our world: the Japanese attack on Pearl Harbor on December 7, 1941. We heard only a summary of the tragic event. We realized, however, that such a horrible attack could only result in a colossal reaction from the United States against the darkness of the Nazi world. It meant the very likely involvement of the great United States of America in the world turmoil! It was indeed a day which would "live in infamy," as President Roosevelt put it the next day. It was also a death sentence for the Axis. All of us hoped that the Pearl Harbor attack would cause an awakening in the States, and that the US would become involved in the world conflagration.

◆

There was one unforgettably sad day when my father came home tense and disheartened. Tears were streaming down his face. I had never seen him in such distress. I never saw him crying. It had been found out that the bars of shaving soaps a German soldier had sold him and other Jews in town were made from the human fat of Jews killed by the Nazis. The bars were marked with the letters *RJF*, a detail to which we'd originally not paid any attention, but he had learned that day that the letters stood for *Rein Jüdisches Fett* ("Pure Jewish Fat," in German). It meant that Jewish bodies had been used to make the soaps. Shocking. We cried, and, with great pain, we took the two bars of soap that the Germans had sold to us to the Jewish cemetery, where we buried them together with many other similar bars in a grave dedicated to the memory of our murdered brethren.

Jewish Cemetery, Galaţi, Romania. The inscription states: "Here repose the bodies of our brethren transformed to soap by the lawless followers of Hitler during World War II. Blessed be their memory."

◆

We lived on the upper level of a centrally located house. In school, I was passionate about inorganic chemistry, and my chemistry teacher encouraged my passion. One of the rooms of our apartment had a window which opened onto to a light-well, and I set up my chemistry lab table on the windowsill. I was working with my friend Abrasha (Abraham) Tzimscher, and when we warmed up some magnesium chlorate, we managed to produce a huge explosion with blinding light. Luckily, we did not get hurt, but the problem was that on the roof of that house there was a German anti-aircraft battery. This was after sundown, and the light from the explosion was seen on the roof. I was absolutely petrified when, two minutes later, I heard the entry bell and opened the door to find a German soldier who inquired into what happened. In my modest German, I told him the truth of what had happened, and, surely due to a Providential favor, the soldier looked around, realized that we were just two young nerds, smiled, saluted, and left. It took us some time to recover from our fright because we'd truly thought that our lives had come to an end.

◆

At school, in addition to our usual very serious and diverse curriculum, artisanal work was introduced — with a view toward preparing us for manual work in case we were separated from our families. Preparing us for survival became the new and very intense preoccupation of the school and of the community at large, in addition to our formal education. I enjoyed creating something with my own hands. In the bookbindery class that replaced the design and calligraphy class, I learned to bind books. They turned out well. Quite an art. I still have three books I bound at that time (André Maurois' *Histoire d'Angleterre*, Emil Ludwig's *Roosevelt*, and a dictionary). One day, looking in a magazine for children, I learned the basic plan for making stamp binders. These could not to be purchased anywhere at that time. I used blank white cardboard sheets on which I placed bands of colorless cellophane, about eight bands per page, well secured. Stamps could be placed under the bands. The binders were very showy, and I exchanged them for stamps. My parents liked my work and encouraged me to continue, probably because it assured them that I'd stay home in the afternoons. Going out was a real danger for kids of my age. It would have been a bad experience to be caught in a fight.

I became a passionate philatelist during the war. There were many active open philatelic markets, as were found in many European cities. Almost every week, I visited with the priest of the Armenian church; he was a great stamp collector. With my meager weekly allowance, I negotiated and exchanged stamps with *Popa Armeana*, (the "Armenian priest," as we called him), and I gradually enriched the stamp collection I had started when I was eleven years old. This passion resulted in a fine stamp collection. I had all the Romanian stamps except, of course, the "auroch's head," or "bull's head," from Moldavia. Printed in 1858, it was the world's first postal stamp and has a huge value. I also had the stamps Germany issued during the terrible inflation years between 1920 and 1933. My avid stamp collecting helped me learn the Greek and the Cyrillic alphabet from the printed inscriptions. My entire stamp collection was stolen from us after the war.

With the same intent of encouraging Jerome and me to stay at home rather than risk the streets during summer vacation, Mother asked us to make an area rug. We did not like the idea because we wanted to be with our friends, but our parents said that we could see our friends on Sundays, not every day. There was not very much to do during the vacation. We did not have access to a swimming pool or to sport facilities of any sort. Mother had a great talent for handicrafts. Under her guidance, on a canvas of about four and a half by three and a half feet, we drew a modern geometric and symmetrical design, and Jerome worked on the left half while I did the right half. We got the wool from Dad's store, in an assortment of the colors available. Mother showed us how to use the crochet hook, how to thread the wool, and, in particular, "not to tie too tight, nor too loose, but only as tight as necessary." We did it. It came out quite well. Mother showed us also how to make the borders and the fringes, and then we took the rug to a shop where a machine evened the height of the pile of wool. We had this and several other handmade area rugs in our houses in Galaţi and in Bucharest. My parents left Romania in 1950, and I wanted to send them at least the best of our rugs, but the Romanian authorities had interdicted the taking out of any handmade item (anything handmade was categorized as a work of art), which was simply another one of the many prohibitions of the time. I invented, however, a mode for passing the rugs under the noses of the customs officers: I wrapped the rugs around pillows, and they passed the custom inspection. My father's brother and sister agreed to take them to our parents in Tel Aviv in 1951.

◆

Father strongly recommended that we learn a profession that might save us in the case of a forced separation from them. The idea of getting separated from our parents at that time was both cruel and novel, and I recall that we could not grasp it. However, as time passed, we learned many terribly sad stories of such separations, and, even though we still could not visualize such an event happening to us, I registered at the Jewish Trades School for an electro-technical course. I took it very seriously and learned the theoretical and practical parts. I had a one-year apprenticeship with a good electrician, Mr. Lachs. He knew everything about electrical facilities, about physical plants and their proper functioning. He treated me rather poorly, but I worked with him on projects such as new motors and generators in local plants, and I got my certification as an electrician. I took small jobs, mainly doing repairs and electrical installations. One day, a lady asked me to repair her electric fan. I did a good job, and she gave me one hundred *lei*, which was the equivalent of twenty dollars in today's US money. I came home and showed my parents the shiny hundred-lei coin. They were moved to tears because they realized that at fourteen years of age, I was no longer a child.

♦

I worked very hard to break my timidity. By chance, I came across a collection of poems by a satirical poet, Ion Pribeagu, whose humorous verses I liked very much. He was not considered to be among the greatest poets, chiefly because he used his stylistic sword in his verses and this ruffled many feathers, but his poems brought a smile on the lips of many. With great ease, I learned many of his poems by heart, and I amused my family and friends by reciting them. All our friends longed for a bit of relaxation and distraction. In no time, I became the storyteller and comedian for my classmates and friends. Later I learned other poems by great poets, and people liked to listen to my passionate recitations. This practice helped me break through my timidity and gave me the sense that I could speak up and act openly without reservation because I had nothing to hide. I acquired a sense of humor that filled my persona. Friends found me "cool," and when I was a young adult, people liked my dry humor. In retrospect, I can see that reciting poems with great verve led me to the thespian arts, in which I participated some years later though my Zionist organization, and, still later, through the Radio Bucharest program of "Evening of Theater."

Relaxation and the pursuit of personal interests by members of my family consisted of family conversation and reading. The four of us read daily and intensely and discussed our readings with each other. Jerome and I read for our classical studies in school, but we also read much good literature on our own. We got to know French literature and theater quite well in the original language. I also read good translations of books by modern English and American writers. I read books by W. S. Maugham, A. J. Cronin, Pearl S. Buck, Ernest Hemingway, and I loved classical British plays. Our parents insisted that we talk with them not only about school but about everything that surrounded us, anything that made an effect on our minds. Jerome talked with Mother about every one of his relationships, and I think that she liked that. I was more reserved and talked with her about my self-doubts. She had an enormously positive influence on me, always encouraging me and saying that with the sort of work I was doing and my dedication, there is no way I would fail. She inculcated in my mind several practical principles of education, such as the ability to make myself do things that I had to do when they ought to be done, whether I liked it or not. This was hard, very hard, but it became second nature to me as well as to Jerome. Father often said, "When men really want to do something, they can move mountains." It made a great impression on me.

We had tours of the Theater of Operetta from Bucharest, which were produced quite well, with fine acting and singing. I got to know most of the operettas of Franz Lehar. I saw some ballet because the girl of my dreams at that time invited me to watch her dancing in Delibes' *Coppélia*. But the most important and influential musical event for me was the experience of attending a performance of *Carmen*, which was brought to Galați by the Opera of Bucharest, a very well-respected opera house. The music, arias, singing, lyrics, costumes, and choreography all captivated me. My ears, mind, and soul were enthralled, and I was won over for life by the magic of opera. In addition to the music and ballet, I was fully mesmerized by its artful presentations of so many themes of human behavior, human feelings and reactions to life: love and hatred, jealousy and crime, dignity and dejection, success and failure, victory and persecution, honor and humiliation.

◆

In our isolation from the world events, we could not know what had happened to the *Struma,* the ship that left Constanța for Palestine in December of 1941 with almost eight hundred Jews aboard. It was one or two years later that we learned about the tragedy. The transport was organized by a Zionist youth organization. It was very expensive to get on, and Father paid a large fee for me to be accepted onto the ship. However, just before leaving, I was removed from the list of sixty youth who made it on the ship. The MV *Struma* was a very old ship, and it sailed under a Panamanian flag. A tugboat helped its passage through the mined seawater along the Romanian shore at Constanța, but its old engine soon failed and after much difficulty, the *Struma* arrived at Istanbul. A lot of bickering ensued. The British consul stuck to the terms of the 1939 White Paper that limited the entry of Jews into the British Mandatory Palestine. They could have saved the lives of those eight hundred Jews, but they declined to do so. The Turkish government did not allow the passengers to disembark and continue their voyage. Rumor had it that only a handful of Jews would be able to travel overland. After a detention of about two months, the *Struma* was forced by the Turkish naval police to return to the Black Sea, where it was torpedoed by a Soviet submarine on February 24, 1942.

◆

In the summer of 1942, Jerome and his classmates were conscripted into "demolition squads." Under military guards and police, these young Jews, seventeen and eighteen years old, were taken to houses that had been destroyed by the earthquake of 1940. There was no wrecking machinery available in Galați at that time. The boys were ordered to complete the demolitions with only their bare hands and a few simple tools. It was very dangerous work because what was left of the houses was very precarious and unstable. Many houses, or parts of them, were crumbling spontaneously. Hundreds of boys were wounded, first aid was rudimentary and barely available, and the young conscripts were not given any protective gear.

One day, Jerome came home very pale and complaining of a severe headache. He fell on the bed, and muscle spasms and shaking chills started shortly thereafter. I recall that I tried to help him by catching his shaking limbs and holding them down firmly. He could not speak, and his stiffness almost choked his breathing. When lockjaw set in, it became clear that he'd almost certainly contracted tetanus. Doctors came, my parents were devastated, and my poor brother suffered terribly. He eventually pulled through and recovered well after a long, incapacitating illness.

♦

In late 1942, I was fourteen and a half years old when my colleagues and I were ordered by the authorities into forced labor. We had a most unusually severe winter that year with unprecedented mountains of snow, and the first floors of houses were completely blocked by the snow. Many people were stuck in their houses and panicked. As Romania did not have adequate urban services, we, the Jewish boys of the town, were ordered to clean the streets. For about three months, we worked all day removing the snow, but new snow fell. It was hard labor, and it was very cold. In the late afternoon, we went to school; we did not miss our studies. In retrospect, I realize that we owe a debt of respect and gratitude to the memory of our high school headmaster, Mr. Herscovici, who steadfastly required that we keep up our morale and continue our studies despite our physical exhaustion. All the parents backed him up and encouraged us, the student-laborers. I cannot avoid thinking that our headmaster was like Colonel Nicholson in the movie "The Bridge on the River Kwai." He showed us an unforgettable example of dignity and strength under the pressures of persecution.

♦

In the spring of 1943, a good friend asked me to take a small parcel to the place in town where his family lived because he had some duties that were going to keep him at school after hours. The place was not close to our house, but I got there without any problem; my friend's family greeted me and took the parcel from me with many thanks. Through a slightly open door I could see a young man with an arm in a sling who waved to me. He wore a leather jacket in a fashion not seen in Romania at that time. The man was an American pilot who had fallen during action and was rescued by some friends of my friends. He was moved among many homes. He had a broken arm and was in hiding at their place. The parcel I brought contained medications for him. Little by little, I began to understand that these people were part of the Romanian Underground Resistance, of which I had become vaguely aware. Being curious by nature, I was interested in learning more, and I looked at the situation like something out of the adventure and detective movies we'd watched before the war.

Gradually, I earned the trust of my colleagues who were in the Underground Resistance, and they told me more about their work. They were helping American pilots and other people who were wanted by the Nazis. They prepared new documents for them, fed them, and protected them. The most important work consisted of acts of sabotage in the harbor and the destruction of lines of communication. I learned that, in the Resistance, Jews worked hand in hand with the gentiles with whom I had not had contact during the war. I was introduced to a Zionist youth organization called *Hanoar Hazioni* ("Zionist Youth," in Hebrew), and I learned that they were preparing young Jews to emigrate illegally to Palestine, our fatherland. I liked this idea very much and became passionately involved with the ideals of reconstructing the country from which we had been exiled almost two thousand years before. I joined a "cell." My underground name was Benjamin. The underground Zionist organizations worked intensively in cooperation with the Communist Underground Resistance because at that time both aimed to help the Allies' victory. (This spirit of cooperative effort changed drastically after World War II, when the communists closed the Zionist organizations and arrested their leaders.) I was obsessed by the idea of helping the Allies win the war. Two important things I learned in the Underground Resistance: The idea of friendship (and the concept of loyalty to my friends and our ideas), and the concept of secrecy in our work. During that time, I learned that a secret shared with me was not mine but belonged exclusively to the person who confided it: I could not talk about it. Never.

Frequent police roundups occurred, with the purpose of catching undocumented people. The Romanians had learned the procedure from the Nazis: The police would close several streets at a time, and cordons of policemen would advance concentrically. They arrested all those with improper papers or Jews without the Star of David well-sewn onto their jackets. Body searches were routine. If things were not in the order dictated by police standards, the outcome could be a fine, detention, or even deportation. One late afternoon, I was carrying a little parcel for my cell of the Underground Resistance when I heard the whistling of the police raid. I was petrified, suddenly realizing that I was playing with my life. I started to run. Two policemen ran after me, and when they stopped me, one hit me with an iron bar over my right eyebrow. Blood spurted, and I was shocked when one of the policemen recognized me as the son of his benefactor, my father. "I know you. You are the son of Mr. De-Me-Ka," (the name of Father's store, by which many called him). "Why were you running? You are near your home." Indeed, we were just around the corner from my house. Gasping for air, I said, "I had to go to the bathroom," and he let me go. I almost fainted when I saw that I was free to go. Just luck. I had used an inspired lifesaving lie.

In the spring of 1944, I was sixteen years old, and I was quite well developed, muscular, and I had a fine little moustache of which I was very proud. It gave me the air of maturity that was highly desired at that age. One day, we got the shocking news of the arrest of a young man called Charlie, who was caught in an anti-Nazi activity. The Germans said that they would not "waste a bullet" on a Jew. After he was summarily "judged," he was hanged, and we were obligated to see his body hanging in public. It was shocking, but at the same time youth has such a powerful sense of one's own permanency and ability to survive! Instead of reducing or stopping my work in the Resistance, I continued my work with even more energy and passion. I wanted to fight back against the horrors of the Nazis. After school, I took packages of documents and messages to other cells, along with medications and special aerial photographs of hiding places. My most important job was facilitating communication between the cells. Communication between cells was vital to the logistics of various acts of sabotage and destruction. We could not use the telephone. I learned how to use hand grenades, and I recall that I was quite good with them mainly because of my sharp sense of distance. Finally, I could do something for our cause! My brother and my parents never knew of my underground activity during the war. I was still among the three best students in my class. It was only after the war that I found out that Father was very active in the underground organization called *Apărarea Patriotică* (the "Patriotic Defense," in Romanian). He and our headmaster, Mr. Herscovici, Rabbi Zalman, and many of the other Jewish community leaders were active in the Underground Resistance.

Later in 1944, during the long summer after we finished our school year, we were mandated to work at the airport under SS guards. It was our job to fill the huge craters made by American airdropped bombs. These craters were ten feet wide and ten feet deep. Blocks of stone, concrete, and fillers of hardened soil were spread all over. There was not very much left of the airport runways. The war scores had changed, and the German Army was in a massive retreat. The airport had to be repaired fast so that it could be used again. There were strict orders, and we worked without stopping. The heat was overwhelming, and the dust was suffocating. We were allowed only one sip of water about every four hours and could go to the toilets under guard only every six hours. We worked under stern SS guards who did not allow us to place anything over our mouths to avoid breathing the dust because they wanted to make sure that they could catch us if we spoke; speaking was totally *verboten*. Despite all the hardships of life during World War II and the food restrictions, we were in very good physical shape, and we took the hard labor as an opportunity to show off how resistant we were. . . Young males! In fact, it wasn't a kids' game, and ten hours of hard work six days a week was quite difficult. After the war, while in Israel, I heard about the financial restitution Germany made to those who were conscripted into forced labor during World War II. There was a huge program of financial restitution called *Wiedergutmachung* ("Compensation," in German). I understood the good intention behind the program, but I detested the fact that attorneys' offices made great profits from it; I've never wanted to receive money as reparation for my past sufferings as a Jew.

♦

We did not have a radio, and all we knew during the war was based on rumors passed very discreetly. We knew that, starting in 1943, the situation on the front had reversed, and a huge Russian offensive had pushed back the Wehrmacht and its Romanian ally. At the same time, we knew that thousands died every day in the Transnistria detention camps, and we prayed for them to be saved in time. In July and August of 1944, long lines of German cars and trucks carrying wounded and tired troops started to pass daily through Galați. Something started to sparkle in the air. We were happy to learn about the American bombings of the Romanian oil fields earlier that year. Finally, we thought, the Americans were destroying the source of the fuel so vital to the colossal war machinery of the Nazis: Romanian oil. Germany relied almost exclusively on Romanian oil resources, and we reckoned that the US knew this essential fact.

On August 23, 1944, around midnight, we heard an energetic knocking at the door and loud voices shouting, "Good news, good news, open the door!"

Carefully, we opened the main door, and there stood a couple of good friends, the engineer Popovici and his wife, who started to hug and kiss us. They were so excited that they could barely articulate their words. They had heard on the radio the speech of King Michael I, who had addressed the nation, saying that he'd arrested Marshal Antonescu, the Romanian leader, and that Romania was breaking its alliance with the Axis. He had declared war on Germany. The King announced that an armistice had been accepted, and he proclaimed Romania's loyalty to the Allies. He ordered the Romanian troops to turn their arms against the Nazis and to join the Allies' war effort. We could not believe it. The war had ended for us.

We went out in the middle of the night, and indeed, the streets were full of people dancing, singing, hugging, and kissing each other. There were no police in sight. None. The following morning, an eerie atmosphere permeated the city. There was not a single person in the streets, not a soul. It was unbelievable, like in some tense unreal fictional movie. No traffic, no trams, no busses. Nobody was in City Hall or in the police or fire stations. All the authorities had run away during the night and were hiding in the countryside.

Now German open cars patrolled the streets, and if there was no one in the street or around a house, they threw Molotov bottles that started huge fires. One morning, I was in the courtyard and saw the German car with the SS team approaching. We looked at each other for a few moments (which felt like hours), then they took off. We had a few unforgettable days when we felt that anything might happen. Air attacks intensified, and at night the sky was illuminated by light rockets thrown by the approaching Russian troops. The commercial district downtown was on fire.

Early one morning, while I was asleep in an anti-aircraft shelter near our house after being up all night because of the air alarms, I heard somebody shouting: "De-Me-Ka is burning! De-Me-Ka is burning!" Father, Jerome, and I ran to the store, which was quite close by. We ran through a street behind the store. Many dead bodies were scattered there, people killed by the Nazi SS who had shot at random before throwing their Molotov bottles. The houses on both sides of the street were engulfed in flames, and we ran through a tunnel of fire. We safely reached the store and were able to move some big crates of merchandise (fine embroidered curtains, high-valued needlepoint, and other artistic handmade works of art) that Dad had prepared, hoping we could save them. We moved the crates onto the sidewalk, and later in the day we got a horse-drawn carriage and used it to move them to a safe place. Unfortunately, most of the merchandise in the store burned.

The Soviet armed forces entered Galați a few days later. Some people cheered them; others looked at the Russian soldiers with reserve. I went to see them myself. They were tired and suspicious of any welcome from us, and rightfully so. They knew full well that the Romanians had been their cruel enemies until just a few days ago, and they could not trust them. Upon a close look at their vehicles, I could see the blue oval Ford badges on their trucks painted over with khaki paint. Those vehicles had been shipped by the US to the Soviets through the North Atlantic and had been unloaded in Murmansk, in northern USSR.

A period of intensified uncertainty and civil turmoil dawned upon the city and its citizens. Some known Iron Guard legionnaires were found in hiding, apprehended, summarily judged by an ad hoc committee of citizens, and executed without much ado. All sorts of committees came out of hiding. Denunciations were rampant, and it's very possible that many innocent people lost their lives. By chance, one day we saw a young man riding Jerome's bicycle, the one which had been taken from us at the beginning of the war "for the war effort." He was the son of the chief of the police. We stopped him, told him that the bicycle was ours, and asked for its return. He protested, and in no time people who heard him surrounded us. He was lucky to escape alive, and we got back our bicycle.

One day, three Russian soldiers and an officer knocked at our door and asked us to give them "the guns." Obviously, somebody who had a grudge against Mr. Constantinides, our landlord, had denounced him. He was a rich Greek shipbuilder and an avid sport-hunter who had an apartment in the same building. The Russians had been told that he had some guns, which he might indeed have had without our knowledge. With a polite smile on his face, Father tried to explain that Mr. Constantinides did not live with us, but the Russians did not understand him. Mother became livid when she understood the officer telling his men, "This one" (my father) "will stop smiling when he sees what we can do to him." She mustered her courage and in her limited Russian explained that we were law-abiding citizens, and that we were renting the house. She convinced the Russians that we were innocent, and they left.

Father was well-respected for his work in the Resistance, and I got recognition for my efforts as well. My parents were quite proud of me. Jerome could not believe that I had not shared my Underground experience with him. Despite this "glory," it was clear that there was not much we could hope for in Galați, and we decided to move to Bucharest to start a new life. Father opened a wholesale wool store in Bucharest. Jerome went to be with him and to take his baccalaureate examinations. Mother and I started packing the house for our move to the Capital. A new life of freedom awaited us in Bucharest. I was so curious to see what might happen for me and my family in the freedom we hadn't had for so many years.

Life in Freedom

Mother and I arrived in Bucharest in September 1944. Freedom! What a frenetic time! People who have always lived in freedom cannot possibly understand our feelings of freedom at that time, after the war horrors. No more persecutions, no more fear of abuse or execution. Freedom, freedom! To walk where one wants, to say or sing whatever one wants. Freedom! What an elixir of life! I cannot put into words my feelings from that time. I was a sixteen-year-old fellow full of dreams and plans with the energy to pursue them.

Bucharest, population two million, had been called "the small Paris" in the pre-war years. I could see the charm of the city, with its many European-style buildings, four and five stories tall with small balconies and small domes at the corners, large boulevards, trams and buses, theaters, cinemas, orchestra halls, and museums. What a life! It was mind-boggling! I could not get enough of walking and visiting. I knew that if one wanted to remember a city, to truly experience its atmosphere, one must walk, look, and listen. I did just that. Bucharest had suffered some destruction from the 1940 earthquake and from the American bombings of 1943 and 1944. There were many foreigners there — Americans, British, some French military personnel, and many Russian troops.

After having lost most of his merchandise, Father had started a new wool business in Bucharest. Jerome had passed his baccalaureate exams and the admission exams to the medical school and was awaiting the beginning of his classes. We stayed temporarily in a hotel. We had to look for an apartment, and Mother wanted me to walk with her and Sarah, a cousin of hers, to visit free apartments. Because of the many foreign troops and the massive immigration of people from the provinces, habitable space was at a premium. Eventually, we rented a modern apartment in a good area, with easy access to tramways and to downtown.

While waiting for the school to open, I searched for my Zionist organization, *Hanoar Hazioni,* which was the parent organization of my Underground Resistance work. It did not take much time to find them because all the youth organizations were demonstrating in the streets with flags and posters declaring their philosophies. I was well-received in the Zionist organization as a hero of the Resistance. Many *haverim* ("friends," as we called ourselves in Hebrew) had also been active in the Underground Resistance. We sang partisan songs daily. We felt victorious after the darkness of our young lives; we had struggled to survive for such a long time! I immediately became immersed in the daily activities of the Zionist organization meetings.

There was only one problem. It was regarding our walking in the streets after dark: The feeling on the streets after dark was akin to what we had felt during the war, namely extreme insecurity. After dark, it was dangerous to be out because of Russian soldiers who roamed the streets attacking civilians and sometimes raping girls. They wanted wristwatches. The soldiers who had so valiantly fought the Nazis were now drunk on vodka, stopping civilians, and shouting *davai chias* ("give the watch," in Russian). If the watch was not surrendered, they took it by force. Reporting them to the police had no effect. Although Romania was now allied with the USSR, the Soviet soldiers never forgot their own suffering under Romanian occupation earlier in the war. It seems that some Romanian troops had been even more cruel than the Nazis. We were strongly advised not to be out in the street after dark, and as winter was approaching, the days became too short for all that we wanted to accomplish.

All schools had to delay the beginning of classes. Many of the buildings were partially damaged, and there was a shortage of teachers and teaching assistants because of human losses in the war. The Jewish high schools needed major repairs after the years of neglect and abuse by the military, and many Jewish teachers had not survived the war. I could not conceive of going to a Romanian school. The persecutions and the abuses I'd experienced as a result of Romanian anti-Semitism caused me to have a deep distrust of Romanian people which I could never forget. There was also the fact that as a Jew I'd grown up with a totally different way of life: different customs, behavior, attitudes, humor, everything that makes up a social life. I'd survived the pre-war persecutions, I'd survived the Holocaust, I'd survived the sweep of history. I felt quite foreign in the country of my birth.

The high school I attended, Cultura Max Aziel, also known as "Cultura A," was centrally located in a house not built to house a high school, but that building was all that was available. Our teachers knew most of my fellow students. For me, everything and everyone was new. I found my new classmates a bit arrogant. They had not suffered much during the war; the Jewish community in Bucharest had fared much better than those in the provinces due to well-connected social relationships. Many of them were preoccupied with their appearance, and as expected for sixteen-year-old boys, attire was much on their minds. I was never preoccupied with my clothing, provided it was clean and decent. I was not interested in a gaudy appearance, but in a casual elegance. I disliked showing off, and the ways in which people tried to appear as something they were not. Most of my new colleagues did not have much interest in issues of social justice and did not appear to give much thought to their personal growth. I, on the other hand, was focused on finding answers and solutions to the questions and issues of personal growth that were central to my life at that time. However, I did meet some sophisticated boys who were sincere, devoted to their schooling, and most importantly, to a sincere exchange of ideas. They had not suffered much during the war and were interested in my experiences. I became very good friends with Sergiu Levin and his brother Alexander. They were from a wealthy family, sons of a businessman in the oil industry. Well-educated and avid for new knowledge, Sergiu was a fountain of information. He was educated by his uncle David, who was erudite in Judaica, and with whom I took some Hebrew lessons later. We learned how to develop file systems on various topics of interest. Most importantly, the three of us were active in the Zionist organization, and we spent a lot of time training new members who were originally from the provinces and had been exposed to only modest levels of modern non-Jewish culture. Our friendship ended in the early years of medical school when we developed major differences in our philosophical principles and our ideas of right conduct. Sergiu felt that he should become communist to achieve a good professional position. I could not agree with this concept, and we parted ways.

I made many new friends in my class. Most of them were not Zionists. We involved ourselves with passionate exchanges of ideas on many facets of life, as all adolescents do. This was a complex and difficult period for me, as I was trying to formulate my own ideals and ideas on life. Perhaps this was the normal evolution of a young man; on the other hand, the discussions taking place in the Zionist organization required from us a deep understanding of the problems inherent in human interaction, and they prompted serious thinking on such issues. I asked myself what sort of person I wished to become, and in what sort of world. I talked with my friends, and I read a lot. I wanted foremost to be a good and honest person who always speaks the truth. I wanted to be true to myself and to everyone, to value friendship with all my heart and loyalty, and to be generous and helpful. I became inclined toward a liberal profession, something that would allow me to live a comfortable life and the pursuit of intellectual and artistic interests while also helping people. I thought a lot about social and political life and about the principle of cause and effect in all aspects of life.

Our experience of the war taught me that tolerance is the correct human attitude towards other humans. I abhorred racism. I believed without a doubt that war was not a solution to human conflict. There had to be a way in which people could and should resolve their conflicts to arrive at mature mutual understandings in peace. I thought that, with time, based on economics, a European Union should be created. And above all, I believed in social justice and human rights.

I felt that love would come, and I sought romantic love not only for its sensual aspect, but also for a meaningful relationship. I knew that this would be possible if I was lucky enough to meet the right person. The schools were segregated by gender. Being new in town, I did not know any girls my age, except the girls in the Zionist organization.

In Bucharest, I met again my cousin Iry, who was at that time a medical student. He was also a theater critic, writing very thoughtful theater reviews for magazines and newspapers. He had a fine writing talent, was well-read, and was an interesting person. He liked my thinking, and I liked his cultured analysis of ideas and events. We became friends. He opened my taste for theater, and we saw many plays together. As a published theater critic, he had discounted tickets. After viewing a play, we would have in-depth philosophical discussions. If there is indeed a "genius of people," I must say that Romanians have a definite talent for theater and opera. They have given the world great opera singers and great theater actors. Iry and I attended the entire National Theater repertoire of classic theater, from Euripides to Ibsen to modern British and French plays. There were many theaters in Bucharest at that time, and in little more than three years of freedom (August 1944 to December 1947), I saw very many plays. I developed a great love of theater because of its ability to show us unlimited facets of ourselves and of life. I also attended a good number of operas and cultivated my taste for music, though I attended the concert halls less often because they were rather costly for my budget.

◆

I became a frequent visitor of the USA Mission in Bucharest, where I attended lectures and learned a lot about the United States. I was enthused by Roosevelt's New Deal and the Tennessee Valley Authority project. It was clear that the US had saved the fabric of Europe, but we could foresee at that time the clouds of a new conflict, which materialized soon as the Cold War, which started in 1945 and continued until 1989. On April 13, 1945, I was on my way to the USA Mission when I learned that my idol, Franklin Delano Roosevelt, had died the previous day. With his death, I had the feeling that we had come to the end of the glory of the United States. Shortly thereafter, on May 8, 1945, V-E (Victory in Europe) Day was declared. We danced again in the streets of Bucharest, under the unsympathetic eyes of Russian troops. We felt that peace would not be restored smoothly; the world had been saved by the combined effort of two totally opposed forces: The Allies, people of freedom, and the Soviets, soldiers of a dictatorship. Thousands of German soldiers tried very hard to go to the West to become prisoners of the Allies rather than of the Soviets. Many of them were captured by the Russian armed forces, and their fates remain unknown. It was a short time later, on September 2, 1945, that V-J Day (Victory over Japan) was declared, the day Japan signed its surrender on the board of USS *Missouri* in the Bay of Tokyo, after two nuclear bombs had devastated Japan.

◆

I described the curriculum of the high school (the lycée) in the story titled "Growing Up." In Galați I had finished five of the eight years of high school, and in Bucharest I registered to enter my sixth year in the Science branch. Our teachers at the Lycée Cultura were eminent career teachers. Without exception, they were highly knowledgeable and experienced in their respective subjects as well as in the humanities. Mr. S. Mony Littman, our headmaster, was much beloved by all of us. We liked his broad and deep knowledge, his experience, and his sense of humor. Talking with him was a real pleasure for us because he knew how to give each of us the respect and understanding that helped us grow.

I also loved Robert Cantar, our psychology and philosophy teacher. Quite an unusual person, he stimulated our discussions on the ego and the id, on the processes of our perceptions, and on the objective evaluation and appreciation of events as well as our feelings about them. We had many discussions on matters of psychology in the *Hanoar Hazioni* (for reasons I will explain later in the chapter called "My Zionist Work.") Mr. Cantar was the source of inspiration and clarification of the ideas that preoccupied my mind at that time. I owe him so much for helping me to develop my own methods of perceiving and analyzing reality, phenomena, and situations of life with lucid and sincere objectivity, regardless of my feelings. If I developed any creativity in my thought process, it is due in great measure to Robert Cantar. He taught me how to think about myself and about the world around me. It was at that time that I discovered the way my own mind works, that my thoughts and imagination are continuously stimulated by the questions "why" and "what if."

These questions have been with me all my life, in my learning, in my teaching, and in my research. They have created the stepping-stones of any original thought I've ever had. It was at that time, stimulated by my teachers, that I configured my personal concept of life and of the world that I would like to live in.

Mr. Raphael Fajon was a well-known algebra teacher in Bucharest at that time. He was a rotund gruff man, who held two hours of class back-to-back. In the first hour, we would listen to an interesting dissertation on any topic dictated by his imagination or by his mood that day. He made good sense, but it was not algebra. After a break, he would teach us algebra and calculus, lessons delivered rapidly and with great clarity. We were not able to establish any rapport with him, but we learned a lot of math. He had a way of speaking with a special intonation, and I was very good at imitating him to amuse my friends.

Monsieur Calmanovici, distinguished, elegant, and the speaker of impeccable French, was indeed an exemplary *Monsieur*. He liked my French pronunciation, and we had interesting conversations on French classic and romantic literature, which was the topic of our senior classes.

We had many political debates, the communists working hard to convince us that we were on a wrong path, that we should abandon Zionism and join the Communist party to build up socialism in Romania. Communist dogma was in opposition to any national movement because its main tenet was the development of an international proletariat. On the other political side, the Zionists exhorted young Jews to understand the causes of anti-Semitism and to realize that the only solution was having a country of our own. Mr. Littman wanted to appear apolitical, which was necessary for his position. Certainly, my thinking matured, thanks to my teachers in addition to my parents, and I did very well in high school.

One day, Mr. Littman called me to his office and asked me a good number of questions about my life in Galaţi during the war, about my work in the Underground Resistance, and about my Zionist ideals. It became quite clear to me that he had fond feelings for the land of our ancestors, Palestine. He suggested to me that because I knew what I wanted to do, I should not "waste my time" attending the eighth grade at the regular time. "But how could I do that?" I asked. He said that he would think about how he could help me, and shortly thereafter he called me and three of my colleagues and told us his plan. Mr. Littman advised us to skip the eighth grade by taking the eighth-grade exams immediately after finishing the seventh grade, in June and September of 1946, followed by the major examinations for the Baccalaureate in Sciences. It remained to be seen whether we could also write the admission exams at our intended universities in the fall. At that time, I was a very good mathematician, and I thought only about becoming a hydraulics engineer (working on dams and canals). We were ecstatic when we received the approval of the Ministry of Education for our plan to skip the eighth grade. During the seventh grade, we studied intensely.

We wanted to take advanced algebra and calculus lessons in private. Professor A. Hollinger, a renowned author of algebra textbooks and one of the best math professors at that time in Romania, agreed to give us private lessons. He liked our group. I learned from him not only algebra and how to solve difficult problems, but also the importance of maintaining a positive attitude while thinking about the solutions to such problems. It so happened that Professor Hollinger was proofing his new algebra textbook, and one day he asked us whether we'd look it over for printing errors. I took the proofs home, and lo and behold, I found some typographic errors which I showed to him the next day. He was very impressed and offered to pay me for proofreading his book. I declined because he was my beloved teacher, and I had done it for fun. It made me discover my ability to easily pick-up typographical errors.

We were asked to write the exams for the eighth grade at the national college, St. Sava, one of the most distinguished high schools in Romania. The school had been established in the nineteenth century for young men capable of "high studies." It had a very well-known xenophobic attitude in general and an anti-Semitic attitude. The requirements at St. Sava were very strict.

With Mr. Mony Littman and my colleagues at Lycée Cultura, Bucharest, 1945. I am the first on the left.

The four of us worked hard all summer. In June, we took the written exams, and in September we took the orals. One exam stands out in my memory. It was the exam on Romanian geography. The teacher called students to the blackboard and asked them to identify and discuss various physical features on a large map of Romania. Many of those examined that day were ill-prepared, and the teacher asked those of us waiting to be called whether we knew the answers. I answered a few questions, and then I heard the teacher addressing the class. Very upset, he chastised the group: "You, Romanians, descendants of King Decebal," (the king of the Dacs, forefathers of the nation) "you don't know a thing about your country, and a Jew knows it all. Shame on you!" I froze, thinking that I would be penalized. When my turn came up, the teacher told me that I had done well and that I didn't have to answer any more questions.

Two weeks later, we had the baccalaureate examinations, written and oral. These were comprehensive examinations. The college was focused on equipping young men with fine general educations so that they might form the new cadre of the Civil Service. I recall the oral examination in philosophy. The examining committee wanted to assess our ability to conduct a sophisticated discussion on any subject. I was standing in front of a committee of five. They gave me a few closed tickets from which I had to choose one; on the ticket was written the title of my topic. We were given ten minutes to put our thoughts together and prepare our discussion. My first topic was "Logic and Religion." I could not believe it! Here I was, an eighteen-year-old fellow, being asked to discuss a topic that had never been even mentioned in the high school curriculum. I rapidly collected my thoughts. At Lycée Cultura, we had debates on any subject, developing our reviews and discussions logically and speaking articulately, even without formal preparation on the specific subject we were discussing. I'd always thought of these discussions as a pastime, an amusing method of adventure for young people. Some of us participated to show off, and others were engaged in developing their rhetorical skills without knowing it. I realized that the committee did not expect me to know formally about an esoteric subject like "Logic and Religion." They might be Communists who were pretending to be atheists and might have, therefore, negative feelings about religion. To be sure, I started out by discussing the topic logically, talking about the appearance of religion in the life of humankind (on which I had some ideas from having studied history), and I argued that religion had fulfilled an important role in the development of humankind, our civilization, culture, and arts; I gave examples. On the other hand, the formal religions had fomented and instigated hatred and had destroyed whole peoples and cultures. I think I told them what I honestly thought about religion. I do recall that I made a good speech, and I was satisfied with my...logic. I noticed furtive smiles on the faces of my examiners. Their body language was very positive. The chief examiner then asked me to pick another topic. I picked up a new ticket upon which was written "Logic and Grammar." Again, I felt lost, but also encouraged by how I'd managed the previous topic; I recalled some lessons I'd had on the philology of Romance languages, a course that we'd taken just that year, and, using some ideas from that field and from history, I constructed an argument in favor of logic in grammar and considered the history of the appearance of grammar rules in language. I think that I did a very good job, because the members of the committee appeared to be satisfied.

♦

Since the early years of high school, I had thought of becoming an engineer. I chose the science section for the last three years of high school. I imagined engineering dams and irrigation canals. Everything appeared to be set for my professional life when, in 1944 and 1945, Jerome, who was a freshman in the medical school, started to tell me about his studies in anatomy, dissections of the human body, experiments in physiology, and microscopic views of germs, all subjects of which I knew very little. He, of course, did not intend to influence me; he was just sharing his experiences with me as he always did. I was fascinated. I started to think about whether medicine would be a better career for me because I very much wanted to help people. I reminded myself that building dams and irrigation systems would help agriculture and, by extension, the production of food for people. I thought deeply and fell into a terrible quandary. In the summer of 1946, I travelled alone to the wildest part of the Carpathian Mountains, Mt. Ceahlău, to be alone and think deeply on what I wanted and what I should do. I climbed, walked, slept in shepherds' huts, and ate with them; I thought, thought incessantly. Finally, I concluded that direct contact with suffering human beings in need of professional help was my calling and that the study of medicine could bring me professional happiness. I had learned that medicine is a "social science in its very bones and marrow." This thought surfaced in my mind and helped me make my decision. Above all, I wanted to help people in need. I came home enjoying a sense of true inner peace. My parents could not believe the outcome of my inner deliberations, but I think they liked my decision because it was based on a sincere and honest soul searching.

My Zionist Activity

In the fall of 1944, while waiting for the high school to open in Bucharest, I found that there were five Zionist youth organizations that belonged to their respective adult Zionist political parties. These organizations were based upon the principles and practice of Lord Baden-Powell's Boy Scout movement. In addition, they trained youth for emigration to Palestine (upon reaching the age of eighteen) by preparing them for farm work. As the state of Israel did not exist yet, and Palestine was under the British Mandate, these youth organizations did a great job of keeping alive the idea of creating a new Jewish state in the land of Palestine, the land of our ancestors. Some of the organizations were leftist, like *Hashomer Hatzair* ("the Young Guardian"), which wanted to build a communist society in the Jewish land; there was also *Gordonia*, a socialist movement, which wanted to build a Jewish state with collective farms in a socialist society. My organization, *Hanoar Hazioni,* was centrist and wanted a free society in a Jewish country, a society that allowed people to make their own free choice of social order. There was also *Bnei Brak,* a religious youth movement, and *Betar*, a revisionist movement, which wanted to conquer the land of our forefathers by armed force; they also thought that the Jewish state should exist on both sides of the River Jordan.

For me, this was a period of absorbing and enthusiastic work. I did not know the history of Zionism. I did know about Theodor Herzl, who lived from 1860 to 1904. He was a Viennese writer and newspaperman who was sent to Paris by his newspaper Neue Freie Presse **to** report on the famously anti-Semitic Dreyfus trial in 1894. Herzl realized the anti-Semitic roots of the Dreyfus Affair and envisioned that the only natural solution could be for Jews to return to their old country now called Palestine. He wrote *Der Judenstaat* ("The Jewish State"), published in 1896, and *Altneuland* ("The Old-New Land"), published in 1902, in which he argued that this return is possible and formulated the words that became the slogan of his view: "if you'll will this will not be a dream." Herzl was the visionary of political Zionism. I learned about the Zionist congresses, starting with the Basel Congress of 1897. I did not know about the many illustrious men who had worked passionately all their lives, even before Herzl, in favor of a Jewish state ideal, the old-new country to which Jews from all over the world could relocate or return.

While my new high school underwent repairs, I studied intensively the history and philosophy of Zionism. I began to understand the social problems of the Jewish people and studied Simon Dubnow's writings on the "social pyramid" of the Jews, a phenomenon caused by centuries of persecution. Through my studies, I understood that the assimilation of the Jews was not the solution. Rather, a restructuring of the social strata of the Jewish people (through labor, agriculture, manufacturing, and services), had to occur if the Jewish people were going to be able to form a correctly social restructure of the nation in their old-new state. The Zionist youth organizations tried to achieve this. While Dubnow did not think about the possibility of a modern Jewish state, his attitude is understandable for his time (1860 through 1941). I had a good basic knowledge of the history of the Jews and of Jewish thinking, thanks to the teachings of Rabbi Zalman in Galați, but in Bucharest I learned much more. In *Hanoar Hazioni,* I was surrounded by youth who came from more traditional Jewish families who knew much more than I did about our history and culture. Some of them were very well versed in Hebrew. I knew the Hebrew alphabet, and I could read and write Hebrew, but my vocabulary did not contain more than one hundred words. I was amazed to see how much I did not know, although we'd had a good education in Galați. As I've stated, my family was secular, and I had not been exposed to much of Judaica while growing up. It was the first time that I'd seen the "Encyclopaedia Judaica," a twenty-six-volume English-language encyclopedia of the Jewish people and of Judaism, covering topics on the Jewish world, philosophy, and culture.

It was a very busy time for me, full of intellectual and spiritual excitement. We had frequent debates among the Zionist organizations on various social and political issues, which were open to the public. However, the most acerbic debates were those with the youth of the Communist Party, who wanted to convince us that their ideas were the just ones, and that we should leave Zionism and join them because they proposed an international revolution while Zionism was only national, promoting the return of the Jews to their ancient homeland. We replied that Zionism was indeed a movement concerned with national rebirth, and that that rebirth was necessary after the Holocaust. All of us were Holocaust survivors, and our concern was for the preservation of the Jewish people and its culture. We thought that it was up to Jews to build the society that they wanted in their own country. While these debates did develop our rhetoric talent, the battles of words did not result in violent demonstrations; instead they asserted what had been ignored for so many years: The right of the Jews to possess their own corner in a world that had persecuted them throughout centuries of injustice.

I was contacted many times by young fellows of the UTC (*Uniunea Tineretului Communist,* "The Young Communists Union," in Romanian) and asked to join them. I politely declined, arguing that I'd suffered as a Jew, and that my ideal was to live in my own country, Palestine, where I could be a socialist if that would better serve my people. Little did I know at that time that the Communist Party was recording everything we said in those meetings, and that many years later I would be shown all that I had said in the years 1944 through 1946, and that I would suffer for what I had said.

The activity in the Zionist youth organization was very intense, with lectures, individual studies, writings, and recitals. To conceive of a life in common on the farms that we planned to establish in Palestine, we had to acquire a good basic knowledge of human interaction, and we did this with much care. The framework of the organization was modeled on the Boy Scouts, but without uniforms, wearing short pants, saluting with three raised fingers, not drinking any alcohol, and not smoking. We always told the truth, we were always ready to help, and we were always devoted to the cause of Zionism. I was passionately devoted to the Zionism ideals.

The National Leadership Committee was composed of three young men who had suffered during the war, when they were active in the Underground Resistance. The boys and girls of our youth organization organized their weekly activities in groups. We used a house in the Jewish quarter of Bucharest, which was given to us by the Zionist Organization of Romania. Our activities consisted of learning about Zionism, Jewish history, social and political issues pertinent to Judaism, the work of Jews in the Resistance, the geography of Palestine, major philosophical currents, and a lot of psychology from Freud, Jung, and Adler. We did not learn Hebrew, but we used many Hebrew words. On Friday evenings, we had *"Oneg Shabbat"* ("Enjoyment," or "Festival" of the Shabbat), with many Hebrew songs and recitations of patriotic poems, as well as debates and discussions on many topics close to our interests. Once a week, we held a plenary meeting, when one of the three leaders would present a well-crafted lecture.

In good Scouting spirit, the youth organizations held winter and summer camps. In December of 1945, only four months after the end of the war in Romania, *Hanoar Hazioni* held their two-week winter camp in a suburb of Brasov called Poiana Brasov, in the Carpathian Mountains. Jerome and I knew the place as a very nice vacation site which we had visited before the war, and we signed up. The trains in Romania were in terrible disarray after the war. There was no established timetable, and the trains themselves were dirty, cold, and dangerous. There was no assurance that one would depart or arrive on time.

We made it to Sinaia, in the Carpathian Mountains foothills; from there the train could not continue because of mountains of snow. We got on an open truck without any benches, and we arrived in Poiana Brasov half frozen. We tried to learn to ski. After we fell a few times, our enthusiasm faltered. Otherwise, it was a fun new experience with young boys and girls from all over the country. We discussed Zionist topics from morning till late at night. The amount of new information that came my way through lectures, talks, and intense readings was overwhelming.

The return to Bucharest from Poiana Brasov by train was an adventure. There were long stops in various places, without any notice. Instead of arriving back in Bucharest at 8:00 pm, we arrived after 1:00 am. There were no taxis or buses from the North Station, the main train station of Bucharest, and there were no rooms at the hotels near the station because all habitable space in the Capital was much restricted at that time. So, our group of about ten young fellows started walking energetically through the cold January night. We did well until we got to the center of the city, when we suddenly heard some Russians shouting *stoi* ("stop," in Russian). We ran across the boulevard into a big park. Jerome was not with us, and I could not see him, when, suddenly, in the light of a gunshot, I saw him bending over, and I thought he had been shot dead. This happened about two hundred feet from the place where the rest of us were hiding. My friends and I froze. Surely, we had lost him. We did not dare leave our place until we saw that the Russians had departed. After a few minutes that seemed like an eternity, Jerome appeared, walking as if in a daze, visibly shocked, with his scarf and winter coat open. For a few minutes, he could not speak. When he recovered, he told us that he had told the Russians he was a Jew, seeking a more decent attitude from them than what they used on Romanians. But the soldiers were not interested in his ethnicity; they demanded their usual, *"davai chias,"* and promptly took his wristwatch and all his documents. That was our second encounter with the Russian military.

◆

I cannot fathom now how I was able to keep up with my schoolwork and yet devote so much time to *Hanoar Hazioni*. In early 1945, I was raised to the level of Leader of a group of Scouts. It was an important responsibility because there were competitions, and each group wanted to excel. I worked assiduously with my group. We were assigned a group of children, about forty of them, from four to eleven years old, whom the Zionist organization had rescued from all over Europe. These children were orphans, they did not know who they were. They came from DP (Displaced Persons) camps or roaming through the fields of Europe, dirty, hungry, savage, scared, unable to speak any intelligible language. They did not know how to use the basic amenities of civilization; they performed their physical business any place inside or outside the house and ate anything that became available to them. They were wild. My group was to take care of these kids in a house rented by the Zionist organization in Bucharest, where food was prepared for them. We were to show them how to wash, dress, talk, eat, take care of their biological needs, and behave. We were also to teach them to read, write, and speak. We took care of them daily. It was a very tough job. I was in charge of the operation, and I had two good helpers, Miriam and Beruria, high school girls my age, who helped me with a rarely seen devotion and talent. Another group of Zionist youth took care of the kids in the morning when we were in school. Together, we did the work. A few months later, we were able to put the kids on a train — they were less wild by that time — and we took them to a summer camp in the village of Comandău, a lumberjack commune in the Carpathian Mountains. There we achieved major success with them, and they became quite presentable. In 1960, after fifteen years had passed, I met some of them in Israel on a kibbutz; one of them had become an actor, and two were journalists. Several were employed by the government in high-ranking positions. On a visit to Tel Aviv in 2005, I had the immense pleasure of meeting Miriam and Beruria at a reunion of *Hanoar Hazioni*. We were all deeply moved by our meeting again after so many years.

We needed money for the transportation of two young Scouts plus the rescued kids, and for the running of the camp, although the summer camp was very modest. The way to achieve this was by all of us going out into the streets of Bucharest with small paper tags stamped with our coat of arms and the inscription *Hanoar Hazioni Summer Camp, Comandău, 1945*. We pinned these on the coats of people who then could not refuse our request for donations. This sort of public collection was employed widely by many organizations in the days after the war and was unofficially approved by the authorities. One could see civilians and military personnel of various sorts walking with the tags pinned on their jackets. It was funny to see officers, both Romanian and Soviet, with our tags pinned on above their decorations. We were not shy and fully determined to succeed. I was appointed responsible for this cash-collection operation, and I had the gall to go into the offices of major corporations, explaining our project and asking for support. With a smile, I asked for money. I even visited the office of the millionaire Max Auschnitt. His secretary came out of his office with a check for five thousand *lei*, which was a huge sum (about a thousand dollars in today's value). We collected so much change that I had to get three suitcases of moderate size to carry all the cash to the *Hanoar Hazioni* headquarters in Bucharest. The people in the upper echelons of the office could not believe their eyes. We made enough money to cover our expenses and more.

In mid-July of 1945, we got on a train with the children from the DP camps. There were about two hundred and forty boys and girls in five train cars, and we waited in the North Station of Bucharest to start on our trip. As usual, there was a long wait, it was stifling hot, and there was no water. I noticed that three young Polish people, two men and an attractive young woman, who joined us on the same train car. We did not know them. They spoke only a few words of Romanian. They gave me a discreet sign that I had learned in the Resistance and I understood that they would be going with us. Suddenly, some NKVD men (the USSR Security with the blue hats) got on the train and asked for our papers. They did not have any authority to ask for our documents, and I did not like their intrusion. It seemed to me that they were after the Polish guys. I gave a sign to the DP kids and the *haverim* in my group to start a raucous noise, and the children started to cry. One of us spoke some Russian and told the Russians that the children were tired and suffering because of the heat. Fortunately, the train started to move, and the NKVD got out of our car. It became evident later that the Polish guys were partisans. They carried concealed firearms, and their relationship with the Soviets was of a rather debatable nature.

We arrived late at night at Comandău, a commune in the county of Covasna in the foothills of Mt. Vrancea. The place had recently been occupied by the Romanian army, after they had turned their arms against the Nazis. Almost all five hundred people living there were Hungarian, and they did not to speak Romanian. Even if they knew some Romanian, they said *nem tudom* ("I don't know," in Hungarian). Luckily, there were among us some who knew Hungarian, so gradually we were able to mollify the initial hostility of the locals. It was a very old mutual dislike or hatred between Hungarian and Romanian people. We made our straw bedding in a clean, unoccupied building — a former Hungarian gymnasium and set up some tents outside. There was running potable water there, and toilets, and electricity. We fell asleep without much ado.

Upon exploring the surroundings, we found a small stream of clear water, about ten feet across and not more than three feet deep. The water was crystal-clear and cold. It did not take more than a quick view of the stream before I got the idea to dam the stream with some old tree trunks so we could raise the water level up to that of a pond or swimming pool. At that time, I was fascinated by irrigation plans and water dams. I discussed my plan with those in charge of our camp, and they smiled approvingly and allowed me to take ten boys and girlscouts along with my own Scouts to help me. We worked well together, and in a few days, to the great enthusiasm of everyone in the camp, we made a fine pool. The DP kids were excited. They had never seen a pool, nor had they conceived of bathing freely. It was a well-done job, I must say, and I am still very proud of our work.

The month in the summer camp passed quickly, as happens when one is having a good time. We returned to Bucharest strong, tanned, and full of vigor. I was raised to the position of Secretary of the Bucharest chapter of *Hanoar Hazioni*, the highest rank a boy my age could reach.

Now we faced a new challenge: Somebody in the hierarchy of the organization had the idea that it might help us become better known if we put on an artistic show of quality, and presented it on the theater scene in Bucharest. A great project! We had a few talented Scouts, and we debated among ourselves our ideas for a dramatic show until a plan emerged. We thought of a fantasy, including songs, poems, and play. The whole action was to take place around a Scouts' campfire, and several imaginary scenes from our lives and from our dreams would be included. Some scenes were funny, and some were very serious and quite dramatic. The title of the show was *Medurà*, which means "campfire," in Hebrew. We needed professional help because we did not want to produce an amateurish show.

There were many such shows produced by amateur groups in Bucharest at that time. For the music, the Zionist organization hired a known conductor from the Jewish theater Barasheum, Maestro H. Schwartzmann, who also had his own small orchestra. For the dramatic part, we engaged a young actor, Ionel Atlasman-Atlas, very talented and creative, who became our artistic director. To put all this together, the organization asked me to assume the position of production director. I felt overwhelmed. Soon it became necessary for me to act as well, which I did with much energy and perhaps with some talent. All existing songs and music were taken from allowed sources; original songs and choral music were composed for the occasion.

The most intense scene in the show had to do with the problems the Zionist organization had encountered in convincing the powers of the world to recognize the political plight of the Jewish nation, which was shunned at that time from international recognition. In 1945, at the United Nations in San Francisco, a delegation of the Zionist organizations and of the Jewish communities of Europe and the USA asked, urged, and implored the UN to accept them into the formal position of Observer. This was not acceptable to the big powers, who claimed that Jewish people were "not a nation." Of course, the Jews were not a nation in the strict sense of the word because at that point we did not have our land, our territory; it had been taken from us by the Roman empire almost two thousand years before, and then by foreign powers who did not allow our return. That was precisely the reason that Zionism existed, to promote the return of the Jews to their ancestral fatherland.

Ionel Atlasman and I were inspired to use the show to present a crucial point: that the half-destroyed Jewish people wanted international recognition of our existence as the remains of a nation of historically displaced people, and of our right to exist after the Holocaust. We wrote a heartbreaking poem called "The Man of Ashes." The action of the poem began in front of the United Nations building in San Francisco, where forty-six nations were assembled. A very pompous doorman was pacing in front of the main entrance when a man appears, disheveled, dirty, in tatters, barely able to walk, as if in a daze. The doorman arrogantly asked him what he wanted, in front of the house of powerful people, and beggars were not allowed. The doorman asked the man to leave but the man answered that he will not leave, that he was "The Man of Ashes," who came from the concentration camp of Maidanek! He recounted the tragedy of the Jewish people who were murdered by the Nazis. He came in the name of those who perished in the gas chambers, and in their name, he was asking for justice and a corner in the world where the survivors of his people could find a place to live in peace. He came to represent the ashes of his people, and he uttered:

(In Romanian)	(In English)
"Deschide poarta	"Open the door
Și lasă-mă să trec.	And let me go through
Sunt omul de cenușe	I am the Man of Ashes
Venit din Maidanek!	Who comes from Maidanek!
Om de cenușe,	Man of Ashes
Eu sunt cel ce cere	I am demanding
Puțină dreptate	Some justice
După-atâta durere!"	After all our suffering!"

He said that his wife died in a detention camp when she could no longer endure it. He recalled that he had a beautiful son. He reached into his bosom and took out a handful of ashes — his burned son's ashes — which he blew out, and struck by his tragedy, loses his mind and drops dead: A very powerful fifteen minutes!

We had beautiful songs, a fine chorale, and comic scenes. The Zionist organization rented the Alhambra theater in Bucharest. It had been the theater of operettas, and it had a fine reputation, for its good acoustics, and about two thousand seats. We made a great deal of publicity with posters, four by three feet in size, announcing: *Medurà, - An Israeli Fantasy*. We posted them throughout town. The names of Ionel Atlasman, of Mr. Schwartzmann, and mine were prominently displayed. I could not believe it!

The first performance took place on December 27, 1945, in front of a full house. Ionel played the Man of Ashes and I played the doorman. People in the audience cried. Mother and her cousin Sarah sat in the front row, visibly moved, as were some Russian officers who probably understood Romanian. We gave a second show two days later, and there were many complimentary articles in the press. Although it was a production by young people, the show contained very moving and serious parts and was quite thought-provoking. The State of Israel was not yet a reality.

The success of *Medurà* was so remarkable that the directors of the Alhambra Theater bought two more showings from the Zionist organization, which were given in February 1946. At that time, Ionel Atlasman could not take part, and so I played the Man of Ashes. It was a great success again. After the show, friends asked me to recite "The Man of Ashes" again and again. It had a soul-wrenching quality that haunts me to this day because it epitomizes the essence of the Jewish national tragedy in the Holocaust. I am always profoundly moved when I recall those verses.

Sixty years later, I heard about the yearly reunions of the *haverim* from *Hanoar Hazioni* of Romania who were living in Israel. They were meeting in Tel Aviv at the time of the Dan David Prize. Dan David had been a member of *Hanoar Hazioni* in Bucharest. In 2004, when I was informed of the event, my old friends invited me to attend; they wanted to hear "The Man of Ashes" again. Unfortunately, I could not travel, but Ionel Atlasman was living in Tel Aviv at the time. He did not remember the whole poem, just the first verses, which he had written, and he asked me to send him the whole poem. After sixty years, our *haverim,* now old people, still recalled the poem.

◆

I cannot close the chapter of my Zionist activities without narrating my work in founding a group of idealist young Zionists, an experience that contributed greatly to my personal growth. In December 1944, at the *Hanoar Hazioni*'s winter camp in Poiana Brasov, Romania, I was invited by Dicsy Deutsch, one of the leaders of the organization, to join in the creation of a group of pioneers to settle in our country when it became possible. The central idea was to prepare a group of young men and women who, upon immigration into Palestine, would establish a collective farm. However, we wanted to ensure a high level of culture and intellectual pursuit in this collective. This was music to my ears, and I became immersed in the work of organizing the group.

We were supposed to choose for our lifestyle the values that we liked and agreed upon. This was a utopian ideal of a collective, with hard-working, self-sufficient members who would also work to maintain high cultural and spiritual levels. We chose the name *L'hagshama*, which meant "toward realization," in Hebrew, certainly a fancy name. As expected, we heard criticism about our being selective. We did not invite everybody to join, and we thought that this was acceptable, even by an egalitarian group's standards, because our particular vision was not shared by everybody in *Hanoar Hazioni*. Most people wanted the assurance that, once in Israel, they would have food and a place to sleep and take care of their children. To our minds, this was OK, but we wanted something more from life, and we did not think we had to abandon a life of culture and intellectual pursuit while working as farmers.

In February 1946, the Zionist organization's Centrist Party bought a farm on the outskirts of Bucharest where the *Hanoar Hazioni* Scouts of our group, the group *L'hagshama*, were to learn agricultural work. This had been the farm of a rich Romanian who was only happy to sell it quickly. Important war-battles had taken place there just a few months before. The house was in ruins, and the fields were completely neglected, with wild grass growing all over, and there were several dead horses laying around in advanced states of putrefaction. The air was fetid, though there was snow on the fields when I first visited the farm. I went there after school and on the weekends. I did this for about one year, cultivating the land, the garden, planting vegetable seeds, and learning about fertilization and watering.

My parents looked at me with curiosity, reservation, and hope. I was not thinking of university studies at that time, and they understood the seriousness of my emigration plans. I was only sixteen years old. I told them that, if allowed to emigrate, I would decide about an academic career later, after I'd fulfilled my ideal of cultivating the land of our country. After working on the farm for a few months, I became friends with Dicsy Deutsch. He wanted to start an internal bulletin, and he asked me to write a paper entitled "The Jew with a Thousand Faces." It was to be a description of Jewish life in various major communities of Europe. I reviewed the history of Jewish life under persecutions throughout the centuries-old diaspora, which was instrumental in our becoming highly productive in intellectual professions, but not in manual work. I argued that there was no inbuilt set of qualities that Jews had but that the stereotype of a European Jew had been caused chiefly by the restrictions imposed on the Jews in their exile until the Napoleonic era, which made possible the Jewish emancipation. It turned out to be a good paper, interesting and well-written. It was my first paper, and Dicsy helped me with his stimulating conversation in the evenings we spent on the farm. He never let me put an end to the story until we both agreed that it was as complete as possible. I signed the paper with my "nom de plume," Benjamin, which I'd taken as my name in the Underground Resistance. I greatly regret not having kept a copy of that paper.

There were four groups of *haverim* adopted into *L'hagshama*. One group after another had left Romania illegally through Hungary and Austria, were captured by the British military police, and, thanks to the intervention of the American Joint Committee, were placed in a DP camp in Santa Maria di Leuca, in southern Italy, at the tip of the bootheel. After Israel gained independence in May 1948, the Jewish Agency and the *Keren Kayemet l'Israel* gave those groups land to farm in the Judean mountains, close to Jerusalem. The place is called *Shoresh* in Hebrew, which means "root." For unknown reasons, the group was not allowed to keep the name *L'hagshama*. I know that the Israeli government formed a committee that dealt with the preservation of the names of biblical sites and the name *Shoresh* was known from the Bible as the name of the place given to my friends.

My studies, my medical work, and the restrictions on communications in the Romanian People's Republic made impossible any contact with my *L'hagshama* group after 1948. In 1956, after my arrival in Israel, I went to Shoresh, and I found Dicsy and his family, who remembered me well. We spent a very nice day together.

At the time of my visit in 1956, the *moshav* ("collective farm") was rather poor. There was no arable land in the mountains. The *haverim* worked daily in the orchards of the area. At the time of my visit, they were establishing a chinchilla farm. Chinchillas are small rodents originally from the western part of South America; they could be imported to Israel. Their fine fur made chinchillas very precious to the fur industry, and chinchilla fur became a lucrative export product for the young State of Israel. I thought that my *haverim* would finally do well, but the animals got jaundice and died.

Undiscouraged, they built an Olympic-sized swimming pool in their *moshav*. There was a small swimming pool in Jerusalem, but people did not like it. The pool at Shoresh, twenty kilometers from Jerusalem, was an immediate success. When I lived in Jerusalem, between 1958 and 1965, I was a frequent visitor there. The pool continues as a major attraction today. In 2015, while I was on a visit to Israel, I went to the pool hoping to visit with old friends, but no one was around. I chatted a bit with the person at the entrance, who told me that all my former friends had died. He knew some of the history of *L'hagshama.* He said that he marveled at the heroism of our youth.

At the Colentina farm, run by L'hagshama (I am the first on the left in the standing row).
February 1945

At the pool of L'hagshama, now called Shoresh, seventy years later. September 2015

♦

In 1946, after I started my studies in medicine, I was eighteen years old, too old for the Scouts. At that point, if one were unable to emigrate to Palestine, one could join the students' section of the same centrist Zionist party called *Dor Hadash* ("the New Generation," in Hebrew). Between 1946 and 1948, I participated in their activities. Because I knew the geography of Palestine quite well, I was asked to teach a course on the subject called "Palestinography," which was received well.

One evening, in February 1948, while I was giving my lecture, I noticed a skirmish in the back of the lecture hall. It was highly irregular, and I could not understand the cause. A friend came up to my lectern, and in a rapid, excited, and frightened voice told me that some hooligans had come to close us down. This was two months after the coup that had terminated the monarchy, and it was the end of any overt or official Zionist work on my part.

In rapid sequence, Zionist leaders were arrested and jailed for long and difficult terms. I never understood how I escaped arrest at that time, but on May 14, 1948, despite the danger of arrest, I went out to the streets to join people like me who were dancing and hugging in an exuberant, frenzied celebration upon learning that independence had been declared for the new State of Israel — *our* new state.

In Medical School

After the baccalaureate examinations, I wrote the admission examination to the School of Medicine and started my freshman year in 1946. There was no college between high school and university. Medical school required six years of studies. In the last two years of high school, we studied inorganic and organic chemistry, physics, and biology. In the first two years of medical school, we learned anatomy, physiology, chemistry, and medical physics. The clinical disciplines started only in the third year and continued to the end of the sixth year of medical school.

Many of my colleagues had been pushed into medical school through their political connections. The Communist Party had become a dictating force in all areas of life. It was obvious that the protégés of the Party lacked basic preparation, and everything was very difficult for them to understand. They had graduated from poor high schools with weak curricula. Motivated to help them, I developed a way of explaining anatomy and chemistry in simple and clear terms. It gave me great pleasure to see that they got it and that they could become real colleagues in terms of their ability to acquire new knowledge. It was one of my first experiences in teaching and I got great satisfaction in facilitating other people's understanding of new facts and concepts.

On the other hand, I was lucky to be associated also with colleagues who were intellectually well prepared. We read and discussed much of the good literature on medicine, which prepared us well for the difficulties of medical training. One of the first novels I read in French was Maxence van der Mersch's *Corps et Ames* ("Bodies and Souls"). We read many other novels about doctors and the practice of medicine, and we learned what it means to be a physician, the moral and intellectual obligations of caring for sick people. My brother and I had also learned from the lessons and example provided by our Uncle Leon, and we felt that we maintained a good spiritual balance between what had made us come to the study of medicine in the first place and what medicine really was. Ingrained in our minds were William Osler's words: "Medicine is an art, not a trade; a calling in which the heart will be exercised equally with the head." Our teachers were inspiring men and women, a bit severe, but interesting and stimulating. We were taught not only the substance of our curriculum (for which we had excellent teachers in basic and in clinical sciences), but, in colloquia with our professors, we also discussed the principles and philosophy of medicine and its practice. First and foremost was the ancient philosophy of Hippocrates, who wrote in his "Epidemics" about the duties of a physician: "To relate what is past, to understand what is present, and to foretell what is to come."

We were idealists. I don't think that any one of us thought of going into private practice; the idea of attaining riches was foreign to us. We learned and adopted the philosophy of the words inscribed on the main entrance of the seventh-century Hotel Dieu, a well-known and long-respected hospital in Paris:

"To cure sometimes,
To help often,
To console always."

I received high grades in the disciplines of the first year, and in the summer of 1947, after my first year of medical school, I decided to undertake a rotation on a clinical medicine service. Jerome had passed the clinical competitive examination for internship with high honors, and I went to work in the same hospital, one of the best hospitals in Bucharest, the Jewish hospital *Caritas*. I wanted to learn how to give injections and make surgical dressings. The work was also a good source of income for medical students throughout their six years of study. In the late 1940s, injections of penicillin had to be given every three hours, and medical students took jobs doing this privately and were relatively well paid. Giving injections to private patients provided me with a modest income in all the years of my medical school. I got quite a large clientele because of my caring attitude. Dr. C. Peabody, a great American physician said: "The secret of patient care is in caring for the patient." At the hospital *Caritas,* I learned just that, how to care for the patient. I was assigned to work on the pavilion dedicated to tuberculosis. I learned to make dressings on patients with pus draining from osteoarthritic tuberculous fistulae, and I will never forget the penetrating odor of the tuberculosis pus.

◆

In 1947, there was already a socialist government in Romania. That summer, we'd experienced the first big financial reform that pauperized the nation at the rate of twenty percent. Unexpectedly, it was announced one morning that all prices and salaries would be reduced by the ratio of 1:20. However, all cash money was to be exchanged at a ratio of 1:400 if one was employed on a salaried job. Unemployed people, such as people in commerce, industry, arts, or free-lance work could exchange only a small amount of their cash, and the rest of their cash, in quite substantial amounts, was lost.

Fortunately, Father had a large stock of wool, which helped us for a while, until bad times started in the following year. On the positive side, I fell in love, real love, with Lily, Aurel's sister, whom I had liked since childhood. It was as in Kafka's story: "He who seeks does not find, but he who does not seek will be found." I was found.

◆

Although the Romanian government made a greatly publicized issue of what was called "denazification," it amounted mostly to exercising revenge based on long-standing personal grudges and vendettas. On the medical school junior faculty (the assistants and instructors), there were many former "legionnaires," as the Romanian fascists were called. At the dissection tables, the instructors assigned the work in such a way as to exclude the Jewish students. We were left out from the anatomic dissection study. A solution was offered to us by the chief examiner at the Medico-Legal Institute "Mina Minovici," the Institute of Forensic Medicine of Romania. We called the man "Old Gregory." He had embalmed all the political leaders and past royalty of Romania and was known and respected for his great knowledge of anatomy. When unclaimed bodies found in Bucharest were brought to the Institute, he gave us permission to dissect the areas of our interest. When we had questions on what we found or when it did not correspond to the anatomy textbook drawings, Old Gregory helped us. With even just a glance at our work, he was able to give us the correct answers; he had a phenomenal knowledge of human anatomy. Working with him helped us learn well, and we passed the anatomy exams with great scores, much to the amazement of the instructors who had persecuted us at the dissection tables.

My friends and I tended to sit together in the hospital amphitheaters and our anti-Semite colleagues soon decided to call us the "Magen David bench." Our group included Arié Feibel, Ruth Tannenzapf (later married to Arié Feibel), Alma Reisel, Basil Pfeiffer, Ninu Casvan, Nellu Teller, Silviu Schwartz, and Niky Haimovici. The name given to our group proved quite dangerous for us later, when communist students got the upper hand in all that concerned our activity and survival.

◆

On December 30, 1947, Prime Minister Petru Groza and the General Secretary of the Communist Party, Gheorghe Gheorghiu-Dej, asked King Michael I of Romania for an audience. The king accommodated them. In short words, they told him that he must abdicate. The palace was surrounded by communist soldiers. A threat to the king's life was made. He was also told that about one thousand democratic students had been arrested and that they would be killed if he did not abdicate and leave the country within one week. We knew that Andrey Vyshinsky, the Deputy Soviet Secretary for Foreign Affairs, engineered this action, and we were told that he was present at this audience. The king had to abdicate that day, and he left Romania one week later. He was dispossessed, and his citizenship was revoked. He took residence in Switzerland. His British relatives, his cousins in the royal family of England, could not help, as their relationship with the Soviets was already quite tenuous. King Michael I was only 26 years old at that time. For me and my friends, this was the end of the liberty we felt between August 23, 1944 and December 30, 1947. Too short a time.

A new era of tyranny, secrecy, denunciations, and persecutions started — and lasted until the fall of Ceausescu, in 1989, exactly 42 years. Gradually, many of my colleagues joined the Communist Party and benefitted professionally. My brother and I found this abhorrent and decided to resist, although resistance amounted to suffering, poverty, and hunger. Fortunately, we knew many people who sought out our skills as medical students, and we were able to make some money by administering prescribed injections at the homes of the sick and by making surgical dressings for chronic wounds.

♦

Our clinical experience started in the third year of medical school, when we learned the signs of diseases, how to take a medical history, and how to make a thorough physical examination. Our teachers had an uncanny knowledge of the clinical signs of disease and their correct interpretation. The hospital work was very demanding, and I was fortunate to have excellent teachers who were great role models. We were taught to be humble and to relate to our patients in a friendly and polite manner. Our teachers were the last romantics of medicine, telling us at every turn, "Medicine is the only profession that labors incessantly to destroy the reasons for its existence." I had outstanding teachers for classes of history-taking and physical examination, teachers whom I never forgot. Physical examination is an art and a science, and I learned it well in my third year of medical school. Above all, there was the thinking around the process. I learned that, in examining a person one needs to know anatomy, biology, physiology, and pathology. However, in examining a sick patient, one also needs to learn and know life. I felt at that time that my daily exposure to learning experiences fit my interest in finding answers to my many questions regarding clinical medicine.

The clinical rotations that followed helped me develop my sense of what medicine is all about — the diagnosis of diseases as well as the philosophy of medicine. It's not a simple profession. All my work in the university hospitals focused on making correct diagnoses and arriving at the appropriate treatment in the shortest possible time.

In 1949, in the summer vacation after my third year of studies, I wanted to join friends in an attempted illegal exit from Romania that failed. I will describe this in the next chapter. Fortunately, no medical colleague or friend ever knew about this. I had learned during the war and under the Communists to keep my personal experiences strictly personal.

In the fourth year of medical school, we had clinical rotations. The only problems we had were the morning mandatory readings of the Communist Party newspaper with our colleagues before we started our hospital rounds and the long and boring political meetings that we were obligated to attend. We were required to march with thousands of people in the May 1st parade, where we had to shout "Stalin, Stalin." I found this to be disgusting. It offended my sense of human dignity. It certainly was one of the methods a dictatorship uses to move masses who do not think. I invoked a terrible sore throat, and I said that I could not speak. I don't know if the supervisors believed me, but I didn't care. It was a time of make-believe, a game of appearances, and it was crucial to avoid being detected.

I enjoyed every day of my hospital clinical work. At the base of the dome of a large lecture hall in the medical school was written, in big letters, *Solvata causa tollitur effectus* ("By solving the cause, the effect disappears"). Mighty impressive. This clicked. It summed up the rational basis of medicine. I felt very good about my choice to become a doctor.

A denunciation made against me by one of my colleagues stated that I was a Zionist, and therefore, "an enemy of the people," according to the Soviet doctrine. I was invited for a "chat" with the Committee of the Communist Medical Students. They questioned me for a full afternoon. I was in my fourth year of medical school, and my colleagues knew me as a high-ranking student. I thought long and well about my attitude, and I told them up front about all my responsibilities in the Zionist Youth. I reckoned that it would be good for me to tell them what I did because I was sure that they already knew most of it. This tactic worked out very well; they did indeed know about most of my Zionist activities, and not hiding anything helped me gain credibility with them. However, they did not know about my work in the Underground Resistance during World War II, and I had to tell them about it. Records of the Underground Resistance were not always well kept, and sometimes they were intentionally destroyed by Communists to avoid recognizing the help of many non-Communist organizations such as the Zionists, who sacrificed a lot in helping the Allies. Nor did they know anything about the thousands of saved children from the European displaced persons camps and the major effort by the Zionist organizations to help those children regain their human dignity. I sensed on the spot that the debates we'd had with Communist youth in the years 1944 through 1946 had been recorded and duly reported to the higher-ups. I told the committee that, as a Jew who had experienced his share of suffering during the war, I had all the rights to defend my dignity as a future working physician, and that I wished to live in Israel, where a new class of workers would help the world. This made good sense, and the committee was unable to counter-argue.

In the last two years of the medical school, we were obligated to read and comment on many of the classic writings of Lenin and Stalin. I knew enough Marxism, Leninism, and Stalinism to develop my proper stance: "Yes, I am a Zionist, because this means a return of the Jewish people to their ancient land, where they could build socialism or communism, whichever might be better for them, and where they could prosper in science and medicine." And: "Yes, I want to go to Israel because I have suffered as a Jew in the diaspora in many ways that are unknown to your committee."

These were good words and convincing arguments. I was "invited" several times for this type of discussion by those who wanted to convince me to join the Communist Party. I was told by the committee members that I was emphatically expected to join the Party because I was a "professional summit," a term invented by the leaders at that time to indicate that I was among the highest ranked in my class. Their logic in this regard escaped me. These meetings were carried out, essentially, as veiled threats, but they were nonetheless civilized. According to a report by a good friend who was member of the Communist Party (and who had heard the deliberations of the committee after its encounters with me), I made my points well with them and they decided to leave me alone.

I was afraid that all these meetings and threats would affect my studies, but most of the professors and lecturers did not care about the so-called socialism imposed by the USSR on Romania; they did, however, care about the quality of student learning. I did well in my clinical rotations and clinics; I think that I had a talent for clinical medicine, which was an almost natural thing for me. I knew, however, that in keeping with the political philosophy of the time, I had to pay for my independence upon my graduation in 1952.

From Lumber Hideout to Liberty

After King Michael's abdication on December 30, 1947, many new laws were promulgated in rapid succession. People were dismayed, very concerned, and scared about the fast changes imposed by the Soviet-run government. Soviet troops were present in cities, industrial places, and communication centers. They were a formidable military and political presence. The Russians disliked the Romanians, recalling the abuses of the Romanian military during the Nazi invasion six and a half years before. Romanians did not like the Russians because they remembered their taking of Bessarabia in 1940.

Freedom of expression became a thing of the past; the radio gave only the news desired and approved by the Communist Party, and arrests of innocent people became a daily occurrence. The sight of the blue hats of the Soviet security officers caused shivers. The borders were closed, and only members of the top hierarchy of the Communist Party and of the government could travel abroad. We were caught in a political jail without a chance of exit.

The habitable space in all the cities was measured and recorded by the City Hall. A couple or a person were allowed only one room of about twelve by twelve feet with access to bathroom and kitchen. Apartments were occupied by two or three families at a time — people who did not have anything in common had to share the facilities. Many interpersonal conflicts ensued and there was no recourse. No one was allowed to move from their assigned space or leave the country.

One of the first of the new identification papers instituted by the regime was the Certificate of Social Origin, which all individuals eighteen to forty-five years old were obligated to obtain at the city hall. This document was issued based on the birth certificates and marriage certificates of the individual's parents. The professions of the parents were clearly stated on these certificates and usually embellished to show a higher social or material status than was true. We did not understand the significance of this paper. It appeared to be a very benign certificate, although an unusual one. However, in the changing social values of the country, it became clear that only the parents' professions of "laborer," "blue collar worker," or "clerk" were acceptable as a "good" social origin. Otherwise, the social origin was considered "unhealthy" or "bad." If one was found to have a "bad social origin" one became destitute of any civil rights. A person so designated could not obtain a deferment for studies, and the obligatory military service could not be performed in the regular armed forces but in "work detachments," dressed in a drab grey uniform and using shovels or spades as part of the uniform, instead of guns as regular soldiers carried. These men were sent to work in the most dangerous places, wrecking houses or digging trenches for public works. Most of them were sent to do the major work of building the Danube-Black Sea Canal. Tens of thousands of political prisoners as well as young men not favored by the regime were sent to the canal, which was a death sentence because of the despicable conditions and the violence of the supervisors. Very few people who were sent to work on the canal returned to their homes. The Danube-Black Sea Canal was hallowed as the third canal after the Suez and the Panama canals, but the abuses wreaked on the innocent people who built it are not known. A well-kept national secret…

After the short stretch of life in liberty, we found ourselves in a dark network of limitations that wrapped around our minds and spirits. This new life in the Romanian People's Republic was painful and foreboding. As I've stated, the principle of the Soviet system could be summarized by a few words introduced into the Soviet philosophy by Lenin: "Who is not with us is against us." But truly, how could individuals raised and educated with western values support the dictatorial system of Bolshevik Russia?

In the summer of 1949, I was twenty-one years old and had completed my third year of studies at the University of Bucharest Medical School. There were rumors that students with "bad social origin" would be eliminated from the University. In the absence of a legal military deferment for academic studies, those individuals would be obligated to do their military service in forced labor detachments unless they could be exempted for medical reasons. A good friend recommended me to a captain who, for a modest sum, arranged for a medical certificate which declared me medically unable to serve.

Many of my friends and I, who did not want to join the Communist Party, felt that we could not envision a fair professional situation upon graduation because we were well known former Zionist activists. As I've written, during World War II we had worked hand in hand with members of the Communist Party in the Underground Resistance because we were joined at that time in the effort to defeat the Nazis; now, according the strict Soviet doctrine, we were viewed as opposed to the politics of the Socialist regime.

We looked for a way out of Romania, but there was no legal way. There was a very risky possibility of crossing the border to Hungary in the west. Only a few made it, handed from safe house to safe house by individuals well-schooled in fooling the local guards, until they got to Budapest, where Underground organizations assumed responsibility for their care and survival.

The only way out appeared to be through Yugoslavia, the southwest neighbor of Romania which, under the leadership of Joseph Broz Tito, had broken political ties with Moscow. Following the dictate of the Soviets, the Romanians had instituted an active propaganda campaign against the Tito regime, which was regarded as a "traitor of socialism" and as a "slave of American imperialism." The southern part of the border with Yugoslavia was formed by the river Danube, while the northern part was a land border which was floodlit at night by powerful lights and guarded by Romanian border patrols.

One day during this oppressive time, we learned that the uncle of my good friend Aurel had escaped in a highly unusual way: on the Danube, through Yugoslavia. In 1949, this was a new and ingenious way out of Romania, a way which hadn't been thought of by any of the millions who desired to get out from the oppressive regime. Aurel's uncle, L.S., was a political fugitive from the new "justice." He knew Yani, a barge captain, who transported lumber to Austria. L.S. paid Yani quite well, boarded his barge during a dark night, and was hidden in a space prepared by Yani between the lumber logs. He hid there until the barge arrived in Belgrade, where he jumped the barge and fled to the Israeli Embassy. From there, he made it to freedom. He wrote to his family in code that he had arrived in the young State of Israel. His story gave us a dim ray of hope. The wife's family was originally from Brăila, an important harbor on the Danube, close to Galaţi. Brăila was very important to the Danube river traffic. All the timber produced in the forests of the Romanian mountains was sent by freight trains to Brăila. There, it was cut, and the lumber was loaded onto huge barges. The volume of two, or even of three, train cars could be loaded onto one barge. The Danube barges moved against the river currents along Bulgaria in the south, through Yugoslavia in the southwest, and then through Hungary, Czechoslovakia, Austria, and Germany farther north and west. The voyage on the Danube could take two to three weeks. Despite Tito's secession from the Soviets, river traffic through Yugoslavia had not been disrupted. Lumber was a huge Romanian export of major importance to all the countries along the Danube. Escape from Romania upstream along the Danube to Belgrade, the capital of Yugoslavia, required a voyage of about four or five days.

Captain Yani, a Greek barge captain who had seen better days in his life, was an old friend of Aurel's family in the city of Brăila. He told them of his fantastic idea: He had built a livable space of about ten by six-by-six feet between the logs on his barge. There was no light in the hiding place, but it was enough space for one or two people to hide in. During the night, a person could come out from the hiding place, take a few steps on the deck of the barge, and eat and drink. In Belgrade, the starboard side of the barge was very close to the river embankment and, with a little luck, the fugitive passenger could jump out and reach a street in central Belgrade. A few words of Serbian were necessary to catch a cab and get to the nearby Israeli Embassy, which had been established after the State of Israel's declaration of independence. From there, at the appropriate time, one could make one's way to freedom under the care of the Israelis.

My friend Aurel was determined to escape Romania along this route. His parents approved of the plan without any hesitation and paid the money to Yani through their family in Brăila. Aurel and Lily got on the first train available and traveled the few hours' trip from Bucharest to Brăila to embark on Yani's barge, which was scheduled to leave in the early hours of the following morning. A friend of Aurel's, Liviu Milian, joined them. I wanted to join them too. My father, however, thought that the plan was much too risky, and we argued the whole night about its pros and cons. Finally, in the morning, Father agreed that the plan, unusual as it was, offered the only possible way out at that time. I got on a train in the morning, but I arrived in Brăila too late to get on the barge.

There was nothing I could do but to return home to Bucharest and continue my medical studies. It is difficult to describe my bitter distress at having missed a rare opportunity to get out of Romania — and at being separated from my girlfriend. The only solace I had was knowing that she and her brother would shortly be free. Long summer days passed while we waited to hear news from them. After one week, we started to fear that something was not right. It was only after three weeks that a friend of the family saw Aurel, Lily, and Liviu in a western city's train station under Romanian security guards. An intense search for them ensued. One could not get any information from the police.

When Captain Yani returned from his trip upstream on the Danube, we found out what happened. Possibly influenced by some desire for adventure or possibly wanting to be brave and show off, Aurel did not follow the original plan, and argued with Captain Yani; against his advice, Aurel jumped in the water with his sister and Liviu. They swam to the Yugoslavian shore long before the ship arrived in Belgrade and were promptly arrested by a Serbian border patrol. What a terrible error! They were young and politically innocent and did not think that they might be suspected of being Romanian spies (Romania was an enemy of Yugoslavia (Serbia) at that time). They were incarcerated, judged by a military tribunal, accused of being Romanian spies, and sent back to Romania, where they were arrested by the Romanian border patrol. I knew full well that had I been with them, I would not have allowed Aurel to jump from the boat before Belgrade.

Romanian Security wanted to make a big case against the three youth. They wanted to show them as examples of political dissidents who were "dangerous to the security of the Republic." Aurel and Liviu were condemned to three years in the infamous Jilava penitentiary (called "the Wet One") on the outskirts of Bucharest. The jail had seven floors underground, and it was known as the most inhuman detention facility in Romania; it was where the political regime in power, now the Communists, placed its enemies. It was considered a place without return. Prisoners there were forced to do heavy labor, cutting trees in the adjacent forest. I did not have much hope for Aurel or Liviu, but they were robust young men, and they survived. Many jailed men were beaten, and many died. The families of the dead found out about their losses when they received the few objects these unfortunate men had possessed. No questions were asked.

Lily, my love, was condemned to two years in jail at Mislea, a famous Romanian jail for politically dissident women. She spent one year there under terribly hard conditions. The women worked ten hours a day doing the laundry for the military, painting the buildings, and serving their masters. Rumor had it that they were occasionally raped. They did not have access to outside communications of any sort and were not allowed to write or receive letters or visitors. Lily's mother was able to visit her only once for ten minutes.

The parents of Aurel and Lily, Leon and Anny, worked incessantly with lawyers trying to reduce the sentences, blaming their children's youth and inexperience, and they did obtain a reduction of the original sentences. I became very good friends with Anny, with whom I shared many thoughts and feelings, and I helped raise her morale during the oppressive times of the Communist dictatorship.

Soon after his release, Aurel got an exit permit to leave for Israel, where he could rebuild his life. Liviu spent time in Bucharest, doing practically nothing of substance. Fortunately for other aspiring fugitives, Aurel and Lily never talked to the authorities about the actual way they had arrived in

Yugoslavia, pretending that they had simply swum across the Danube. Captain Yani's barge to freedom remained the single route of escape from Romania. I don't know if it was used by other people. His lumber hideout might have offered a way to liberty.

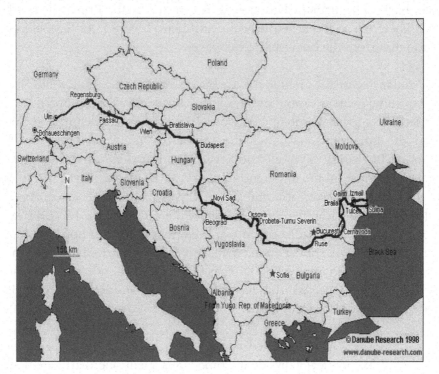

The course of the Danube River.

Tough Times in the Romanian People's Republic

In 1949, after returning from Brăila, where I'd missed what I thought of as the "opportunity of my life," I was in a terribly bad mood. I was firmly convinced that if I had been with my friends, they would not have altered the original plan, and we could have reached our liberty in Belgrade. I felt like I'd been jailed without any hope of getting free. I immersed myself in my medical studies to forget the exit plan. I noticed that my parents, while sad for me because they knew my state of mind, were content to have me back home with them. It was only normal. We resumed our life, and we began to face many major difficulties. In the previous four years, Father had developed his business. He wanted to be involved in all the phases of the production of wool yarn, so he'd acquired a spinning mill and a dying factory in addition to his wool yarn store. Quite an entrepreneur, he was well-off. However, he did not calculate well the political scene that would soon interfere with his plans. In 1948, the government started to nationalize industries, and soon he was out of any business.

The nationalization destroyed not only the owner of an industry, but also his employees. Nobody received any compensation, and the workers were sent to work in other places for lower salaries. They were told that the government was "building socialism." Corruption was rampant. In political reforms, as in any other activities, if one destroys something that is thought of as not being good any longer, one must replace what is destroyed with something new that works better and makes a better life; otherwise, chaos occurs in a social and political vacuum. This has been shown to be true many times in the history of humankind. The major problem is that revolutionaries do not always realize this truism. Ignoring it, always brings the failure of the new regime. The major deficiency of Soviet-dictated socialism in the satellite countries was that it failed to bring a better life to people; this contributed in large measure to the fall of their "socialism," which was not productive and totally unacceptable to workers of any sort.

Soon, Father lost all his enterprises, mostly because of new regulations that made it impossible to have any employees. Mother, with her practical sense and talent, got a portable loom for use at home. She started to make wool scarves, articles that did not exist on the market and were very well-liked by customers. She also designed and made small pillow covers that were sewn onto pillows. These were a great success in the few handicraft stores at that time. The demand was high. Father and I helped her daily. I learned to work on the loom and took turns with the warp and woof. We liked to make new Scottish designs for the scarves. We developed a little industry in our home, and the new income helped us survive. Mother also sold many of our porcelain bibelots, Meissen porcelain objects, Moser, Lalique, and Limoges glassware, and crystal vases. Over the years, she'd made many superb needlepoint tapestries; she was able to sell those for very high prices, as they were appreciated as works of art. Although we were closing the door on an era of living elegantly, and we did not know what was in store for us, our morale was very good, and I learned a lot about financial survival in adversity. I do recall that my family's humor and witty remarks helped us get through very difficult and austere times. I missed my girlfriend terribly.

Jerome resided at the hospital as an intern on the surgical service. He'd started to establish a fine professional reputation based on his talent as a surgeon. Our cousin Iry came to live with us until he finished his medical school courses. We were a trio of young men full of energy and wit. My father jokingly told us that we were supposed to bring home some jokes every day, and he waited impatiently for our daily harvest of jokes, mostly political. In addition to jokes, we developed a specific sort of family humor, difficult to describe: witty comments, many double entendres, always expressed with a serious demeanor and often based on exaggerations or sheer unbelievable nonsense and absurd wording. Friends and colleagues liked to visit and amuse themselves in our house (and enjoy Mother's cookies).

My brother and I enjoyed an intimate and mature relationship with our parents, in full confidence. For her part, my mother lived with four gentlemen who adored her for her love, wit, kindness, delicate attention, and helpfulness. She was a finely educated lady, intelligent and tactful, who knew how to relate to people of various backgrounds. She was a great host who prepared exquisite meals and baked cookies (known as "Catty's cookies"), which were in high demand among our friends and neighbors.

◆

One afternoon I was leaving the school with a friend. He was going to the Radio Bucharest studio. I knew that he was also a student at the Conservatory of Arts, and I asked him about his work at Radio Bucharest. The station had a program run by students called "Evening of Theater." "They need more talent. Come and try it," he said. I went with him, and he introduced me to the artistic director, Mr. Mony Gellerter, a highly respected theater director. It was explained to me that the Radio Bucharest studio needed individuals with "radiophonic" voices, which meant voices that sounded good on the radio. I learned that the natural vibrations of the human voice are perceived differently when one is listening to a radio-spoken voice than when one listens to a voice speaking through the air. To find out whether I had a good voice for the radio, I had to pass a live test on the spot. It consisted of reading a text on the microphone without any preparation. I took the text and I read it on the microphone. The director said, "You stay." Several students who were waiting in the studio for their test jumped up to congratulate me. I was confused by their reaction but they told me that it was very rare for Mony Gellerter to accept a new voice at the first reading. This is how I started my new career as speaker on Radio Bucharest.

I was the narrator who introduced the topic of a play, the *sotto voce,* who described and explained the action of various scenes. Later, I was given roles to play. This required study and rehearsals. Voice modulations and acting were the essential features of playing in radio theater. The team of students selected for "Evening of Theater" was very positive about my acting. I also spent many weekends with the best-known actors playing in classical plays. Although I had not studied theater, I acted very well, and the masters of the theater of the time, George Vraca, Ion Manolescu, and George Storin "adopted" me. I could easily imitate voices and I was good at imitating George Vraca's voice, which thoroughly amused everyone. Fortunately, Vraca did not ever hear me — because he was hard of hearing… We played a lot of Chekov and Gogol, as well as classical Romanian theater. It was great fun. In addition to the satisfactions of the artistic productivity, I was very well paid, and this helped me live for several years, until I finished my studies.

One day the political director of the program found out that I had been a Zionist and that I was interested in leaving the country. He was mighty furious and dismissed me because my ideas were unacceptable to him.

◆

Since the Communist coup d'état in December 1947, one could not ask for a passport. Only high-level members of the Party had this privilege. Nobody thought of asking for a passport or writing to the press about the restrictions on obtaining a passport, a citizen's elementary right. Those of us with histories in Zionist organizations were acutely aware of what could happen if the authorities found out that we wanted to leave the country. In early 1950, there was a rumor in Bucharest that Jews could ask for an "exit permit" to leave the country for Israel. Not a passport, but what was called a

"Certificate of Voyage," it was written in Romanian, Russian, and French, with the clear subtitle, "Without the Right of Return." In other words, a kick in the pants, losing one's citizenship. This was humiliating, but who cared? The important thing was to leave the country for all the political and social reasons I've described. The rumor about being allowed to ask for an exit permit went rapidly around among the non-communist Jewish community. Applications for that sort of exit certificate were to be made only in one place, the police headquarters in Bucharest, which was an imposing building on the main boulevard of the city, with a nefarious history and reputation. It was the place where all the political dissidents who had been arrested by any political regime were imprisoned and often tortured until their fate was decided.

Thousands of people who wanted to leave the country showed up daily and waited in long lines around the block, beginning at four o'clock in the morning. The police did not like this because it created an incontrovertible show against the so-called "happy life of socialism" right in the center of the capital. No instructions on how to apply were available until it gradually became known that we had to bring with us all the certificates of modern life: birth, marriage (if applicable), social origin, military, studies, licenses, professional, and medical and hospital certificates for chronic or disabling conditions. This was not a simple procedure. We had to complete a huge application form which asked everything about our lives since childhood: addresses of the places where we had lived, the dates we'd lived in every single place, where and why did we move, any arrest or deportation, our political activities, membership in any type of organization, our writings, speeches, and philanthropic activities. It took a wrenching three to four hours of writing, sitting there in a sort of classroom in the police headquarters. The results of the application were to be given to us "sometime." We used to say that there was "Greenwich time" and "Russian time," the latter being without a date. We had to wait, we learned to wait. Father, Mother, Jerome, and I requested our exit permits, and we started to wait.

I continued my studies and hospital work while trying to forget that there was a glimmer of hope of getting out. I also feared that my being a medical student would impede my chances of obtaining the exit permit. It was the correct assessment of the situation. About five months after requesting their exit permits, my parents got the approval. Without wasting any time, Mother went to the passport office, which was part of the security branch of the government and asked to see the director.

"Sir, I received my exit permit, but I cannot leave the country, and I wish to return it," she said.

"Why, Ma'am?" asked the officer, who was playing at being surprised by this unique experience.

"You see, Sir, my two sons are all I have. They are medical students. My husband and I will not leave the country without our sons."

"But Ma'am, you can be sure that your sons will follow in about three weeks," replied the director.

Mother accepted this promise. However, it took six and a half years for me — and seven and a half years for Jerome — to get an exit permit. I knew the system. I felt it. Younger people always sense, rather than know, a change in the general atmosphere and in the morality of a new political regime, of a new world. I sensed that the assurances of the passport office director were good for naught. There were only lies, lies on which the entire system was built. I feared for my father's safety if he and my mother were to wait for Jerome and me to receive our exit permits. The police and the security forces were gradually arresting "formers" (as industrialists were called at the time) for no reason but to extort funds which were presumed to be hidden abroad. It was vital to me that our parents' lives were secure. I convinced them to go. I suspected that Father had some funds in Switzerland, but to my surprise, he told me that he had none. We bought a hundred Israeli liras on the black market, which was enough for two months of modest living in Israel. A friend from *Hanoar Hazioni* who was working at the Israeli Embassy helped me expedite their visas. My parents left in June 1950 on the Romanian ship *Transylvania*. Mother took the separation very hard. I was also torn up by it. Did I do the right thing in convincing them to go? I felt that it had been the right thing to do, despite the heartbreak of it. Three days after they left, at two o'clock in the morning, we heard a knock on the door. There were two security men who had come to ask Dad "a few questions" — their routine for arresting people. Jerome and I played well: "Dad and Mom are visiting the family in Râmnicu Sărat and Constanța and will return in one week. Please come back."

It would have been a colossal mistake to say that they were on the *Transylvania*. They could have been taken back because they were sailing under the Romanian flag. Such things did occur. The Romanian ship *Transylvania*, with a capacity of about two thousand passengers, left the harbor of Constanța for Haifa every other week. The conditions on the ship were rather modest, but who cared about that at the time? Upon arrival in Israel, the new immigrants were accommodated in tents at Atlit, near Haifa. Atlit had been a large British camp and a detention camp for so-called illegal immigrants. Life was tough in those tents, but people were free. The State of Israel had become a reality only two years earlier, in 1948, and at that time was facing the problems of feeding and caring for thousands of immigrants from all over the world.

♦

Jerome and I started a new chapter in our life. We did not know how to cook, but we made a formal promise to each other that we would not lower our standard of living and that we would keep our apartment clean. We did keep our word. The Location Office gave one of the rooms of the apartment to a young architecture student. Two rooms were given to a big boss in the Department of the Cooperatives, Dumitru Dumitrescu. He was a politically powerful individual with whom we had a polite relationship. He and his wife Ileana gradually started to like us. She was a nice person who on occasion bought food for us from the richly supplied store of the Communist Party. She also made it possible for me to buy a new bike, which would have been practically impossible otherwise. The bike was my permanent mode of transportation.

One night, we had a unique experience. Around 3:00 am, I was awakened by a loud knock on the main door. I was surprised that our neighbors did not respond because their rooms were closer to the entry and they should have heard it. The knocking on the door intensified, and, when that got no response, it was followed by a long ringing. I woke Jerome, telling him that we had "visitors." I was sure that at that time of night it could only be Security at the door, and Jerome and I were not exactly good socialism-building citizens. I very quietly dialed the phone number of Anny Siegler, Lily's mother, who was a good friend, and said, "Harnagea came for a visit." *Harnagea* was our code name for the Security or any situations that placed us in conflict with the new dictatorship. When, finally, Mr. Dumitrescu opened the door, I clearly heard the visitors shouting, "Face the wall, hands up." We heard a noisy vociferous discussion, Dumitrescu shouting, "This is an error!" Around 5:00 am, they knocked at Jerome's and my door and inquired about what Jerome and I were doing. They did not care about us and left, taking Dumitrescu with them. It was around noon when he returned home, victorious, and disgusted because the Security was looking for an Iron Guard legionnaire with the same name who had apparently lived once on the same street. An identity error, quite costly to the agents who perpetrated it. Quite a story.

◆

In the summer of 1950, Jerome graduated as an M.D. This terminated his employment as an intern of the hospital. He refused to take the job in the remote countryside where he was sent by the communist Department of Health. We had a clear picture of what could happen to us if we lost our space allocation in Bucharest. Our living space was our best asset for getting an exit permit. It was crucial for us at that time to retain our much-coveted residence in Bucharest. We hoped that if a person with influence were interested in our living space, that could be our chance to get an exit permit. Many colleagues who took jobs in remote rural places stayed there for years, until the 1970s, when a large emigration of doctors, based on an operation called "The Buying of the Jews," took place. Jerome successfully got a job with a very modest salary working for a cooperative organization. Our cousin Iry, who had lived in our house for several years, graduated from the medical school at the same time and took a job as physician for the Security. This was a great shock for us. We'd never known of his sympathies with the communist regime. He soon left the house, and we maintained a careful, estranged relationship. I'd never imagined such an experience with him — Iry, who was like a brother to us!

Lily came home from the Mislea penitentiary physically and psychologically different. It seemed that the political prisoners were given daily barbiturates to keep them quiet. All the women lost their menstrual periods and looked puffed up. We were happy with each other until she got her exit permit in the summer of 1951. Under the circumstances, there were two possibilities: We could get married and live our lives in Romania (which we could not accept), or Lily could leave for Israel and get her precious freedom. I was close to the end of my medical schooling, and I did not have much hope of following her. The communist regime was fiercely opposed to giving exit permits to professionals. I could see that, once she was gone, it was very likely that our paths would separate, but I was ready to accept that, if she got her freedom. Therefore, she left. I missed her with a broken heart, for I had loved her very much.

All we talked about among friends was who got an exit permit. I had to become very circumspect with my relationships, and my circle of friends became quite restricted. My friend from medical school, Silvio Schwartz, and his wife Lily; Alexander Schurberg and his wife, Jeannine, a young architect; and Ms. D. Waldinger, a talented violin player in the Symphonic Orchestra of Radio Bucharest, and her sister, Magda, were my stalwart friends, people whom I trusted in every respect. I saw so many people become communists in those days, people who shouted the Party's slogans while in reality they did not care an iota about socialism or communism, that it was foolhardy to trust any of my former friends and colleagues. Leaving Romania was for me an obsession because of my passionate hatred of the dictatorship under which we lived, because of my own ideals, and because of my family who had left the country.

I maintained an intense and regular correspondence with my parents. I wrote to them weekly and I got letters from them almost weekly, except when the Censorship discarded them. I learned that it was better to write a fictitious return address and post my letters from various areas around the capital. We used code names and phrases for very personal and delicate matters.

◆

After I graduated from medical school in 1952, I was given a post in the boondocks of northern Moldavia. I got some information about the place, which was not even mentioned on most of the maps. As I wrote above, by leaving Bucharest I would have lost my room in the apartment, which was my most important asset, a living space in the city. The law was very specific and severe: One could not have two living spaces. The centrally located apartment in Bucharest was a prize-worthy location.

I went to seek advice from my beloved professor, Dr. Constantin I. Parhon, who was the founder of the discipline of endocrinology. In 1909, with Dr. Moise Goldstein, he had co-authored the world's first textbook on endocrinology. During World War II, he was the only physician in the city of Iași, in Moldavia, who took care of Jewish people. Since 1933, he had been Professor of Endocrinology at the University of Bucharest School of Medicine. In 1950, as a fourth-year medical student, I took my clinical rotation under him at the fine St. Vincent de Paul Hospital, where he ran the first School of Endocrinology. I loved this discipline because I admired the efficient regulatory action of the hormones in the body, and I liked using laboratory determinations to support clinical diagnoses. This is what I liked most in medicine at that time. Professor Parhon saw how eager to learn I was, and he was very encouraging. I had told him that, if permitted, I would like to specialize in endocrinology. At my visit, I told him that I had graduated, and that I was distraught over my separation from my parents and my fiancée, who had left for Israel. Professor Parhon had a long history of sympathy for Jews, and he understood my torment. He addressed his assistant, saying: "Edgar may be helped to join his family if we would give him a medical certificate." He wrote that I had a "depressive syndrome with anxiety" and that it was recommended that I "avoid all physical and emotional stress." He advised me to make appointments with the authorities and show them the certificate he gave me.

Now I had a solid basis for refusing to take the medical post in northern Moldavia. I could, however, work as a volunteer in the University clinics in Bucharest, which I did every morning. I was fortunate that some lecturers, who had liked me during my student years, appreciated the reasons for my refusing to take the government-dictated job and allowed me to function as an assistant without pay in the departments of medicine of the University hospitals. I made rounds with them, discussing the new admissions, and deciding on workups and treatments. This was the most important activity I could hope for while avoiding the post assigned to me. Thus, based on the medical certificate I'd received from Professor Parhon, I was able to stay legally in Bucharest and fight for my exit permit, writing letters and asking for appointments at the passport office and with various dignitaries.

I took any job that could help me make some money besides injections and surgical dressings. I was hungry for many days in a row. I will never forget the hunger pangs I suffered at that time. A lady friend made necklaces and other decorative pieces, and that gave me some ideas. I found a lathe operator who did superb work on a variety of woods. I asked him to make wood balls of various sizes with which I made necklaces. I painted the wood pieces, and I quickly learned about the porosity of different woods, their specific densities, and the quality of the polish I could get after three coats of Duco paint. I threaded about eighteen painted balls on a colored braid, and voilà, a beautiful necklace! The beads looked like stone, but they were lighter than stone. There was no plastic at the time, and everybody asked what material I used, never guessing that it was simply wood. I also noticed that there were no good-quality buttons for ladies' garments. Those had been imported from France and Germany in years past, but that was no longer the case because of the restrictions in the availability of foreign money. I designed modern buttons for jackets, blouses, dresses, and coats, and my friend Ely, the lathe operator, produced them. Then I painted them to match the color of the garment onto which they were to be sewn, and they looked like regular buttons. I mixed paints for the desired colors, and I asked a price that more than covered my expenses. In the summer, there was a big demand for buckles to be used on belts for summer dresses, and there were no items of that sort in the open market in Bucharest. I designed buckles of an appealing pattern, cut them from thin (quarter inch) plywood, sanded then, and painted them with Duco. The results were quite attractive and sold very well. I could not keep up with all the necklaces, buttons, and buckles for which I had orders. I also made hundreds of Christmas tree bells nicely decorated with glitter, and many other decorative items. I did not enjoy what I was doing in the afternoons and evenings, but I made money, a lot of money, and I was happy to send my parents eleven hundred Israeli lira, a small fortune! I did enjoy, however, what I did in the mornings at the hospital without pay. I called this period of my life "an intermezzo."

◆

Several times, I was taken from home in the middle of the night, put by force into a car, blindfolded, and brought to the police headquarters. Alone in a room with a strong light focused on me, I heard the screams of detainees in adjacent rooms. An interrogator would appear and ask me hundreds of questions about myself, about my work in the Zionist organization, about my parents and Jerome, and about fellow students and professors. There were only a few things I had to add to what they already knew, like the wartime forced labor, my work in the Underground Resistance in Galaţi, the work with the children from displaced persons camps, and the work on the L'hagshama farm in Bucharest. These were terrifying twenty-four- to forty-eight-hour-long detentions. I didn't know what they wanted until I realized they were doing it to break me. They thought that I was or might be a Zionist leader, and they wanted use me as an example of what happened to such "leaders." After my graduation from the medical school in 1952, when I refused to take the post in a remote and forsaken rural commune, a livid inquisitor banged on his table shouting repeatedly, "You are an enemy of the people!" To which I repeatedly replied (not shouting): "No, I am not, and I have respectfully showed you that I am not." I kept telling the Security officers that I wanted to go to Israel because my family was there, that I could build socialism there if that was what the people wated. One day, despairing after a long interrogation and many threats, I lost my temper, raised my voice and said to the interrogating officer: "I don't know where you were during the war, but you definitely don't know what was to suffer as a Jew at the hands of a Nazi." He let me go home.

Each Romanian government department had a Soviet minister with whom the Romanian minister had to confer with and agree on every major decision. I was arrested three times by the Security. The methods of the Romanian Security ("Securitate," in Romanian) were copied from the methods of the Soviet NKVD. Many said that Romanians added more brutality and sadism. The Securitate was a frightening department. Its employees created terror that engendered the decay of Romanian life until 1989 — and beyond. I could argue that it broke the national spirit.

I read a lot besides medicine: biology, history, natural resources, and political economy. In my senior year of high school, I'd taken a good class on political economy and sociology, and my work in the Zionist organization included much study of those disciplines in relation to Jewish problems such as the causes of anti-Semitism, the social restructuring of the Jewish people in Israel, and the future and the survival of the country through the agricultural culture of the desert (the Negev), water irrigation, and seawater desalinization. With a good background in history, I became interested in the natural resources of the world and their impact on the development of society. It was evident that natural resources had attracted human settlement since the oldest times. Humans, being social animals *("zoon politikon,"* in Aristotle's language), formed the first societies and economies, which created all the political developments in human history. Everything in the human history of the world has been caused by the need for and the exploitation of natural resources. In final analysis, all major events in our history have been caused by having or not having the necessary resources.

I found much intellectual solace in learning Hebrew. Since the days of my intense activity in the Zionist Youth Organization, I'd felt that using Hebrew terms for many of our functions was a rather superficial way of using Hebrew, and I wanted to relearn it as the language of my people, to be used in Israel where I would live one day… One day I got to know the best Hebrew teacher in Bucharest, David Faibish, a learned Hebraist who had written the best Hebrew-Romanian dictionaries. Here I'd like to write a little about my work with David: He was a jovial and optimistic middle-aged man, quite witty and curious, intense, and filled with the desire to learn. Among his interests were issues of biology and medicine. We soon found ourselves discussing such matters about which I could teach him, and we both had a good time. But this did not help me learn Hebrew. However, he did teach me something that helped me learn Hebrew later, and I think that it was the key to learning Hebrew, a language which is so different from Romance and Germanic languages. The structure of the Hebrew verb moves everything in Hebrew, as in any other language. I learned from David the meaning of the seven forms of conjugation. It made Hebrew truly easy to learn. I had a very pleasant encounter with David in 1980, when I was living in the United States and I was visiting Israel. We met on a bus ride in Tel Aviv. I was very moved by our meeting. We spoke in Hebrew, and David complimented me, saying that he was surprised to hear my "correct and bright Hebrew." I replied without hesitation that I'd "learned it from the Master of the Hebrew language."

Getting My Exit Permit

In the summer of 1953, we held the World Festival of Youth and Students, a great event that brought to Bucharest thirty thousand young men and women from a hundred and eleven countries. The event was organized by the World Federation of Democratic Youth, a left-wing youth organization.

It is worth mentioning that for many years the Bucharest stores were empty. There were no farmers' markets, which were unacceptable to the government. People bought their modest nourishments on the black market, which was quite active, or from relatives farming on the outskirts of the capital. However, during the night preceding the official opening of the event, all kinds of merchandise appeared in the store windows as if by magic: bread and butter, cheeses, all sorts of meats and fish, vegetables, fruits and marmalades, chocolates, candies, and fruit that we had not seen in years, like bananas and pineapples. Other stores displayed rich assortments of wools and silks and yarn and clothing. The city was in great fervor. Everybody went out shopping, and the foreign youth were able to see for themselves the apparent abundance of the good life in the Socialist Republic of Romania. This was a typical Soviet propaganda method. A few careless citizens talked freely with some foreigners, telling them about the realities of our lives, which were quite different than what was being advertised. They were promptly arrested and detained. Those "foreigners" were in fact Security agents disguised as visitors. What imprudence on the part of those naïve Romanian citizens!

During the festival there were shows put up by every delegation: British, French, Italian, Dutch, German, and even American. One must realize that since 1947 we had not seen a single American or British movie. No news from the West was able to filter through the Censorship. No art nor science from the West, nothing made beyond the "Iron Curtain," reached us. We were completely and firmly isolated. This was the Moscow method of conquest. We knew that the movie *Gone with the Wind* was among the last American movies brought to Romania before World War II, and its distribution had been halted by censors. Now we had plenty of good American and British movies. Now we were able to see Italian neorealist movies. It was great fun. Yehudi Menuhin came to visit his teacher, George Enescu. They had not seen each other for many years. I was able to attend their concert, Menuhin playing Beethoven's violin concerto and Enescu conducting. We were emotionally overwhelmed.

◆

The winter of 1954 started with a huge snowstorm that covered the city under ten feet of snow. The whole city was paralyzed. Nothing could move. There was nothing to eat but herring fish that the city's mayor had imported from Norway a few days before the storm. We worked hard to clean the streets so that the supply of foods could resume. We were hungry in the cold weather. It was a winter to remember…

Jerome decided to take a post that became available in a commune near the city of Iaşi, the capital of Moldavia, ten hours by train from Bucharest. The commune was called Răducăneni, and it had a population of five thousand. There he established a very nice general hospital with a well-equipped operating room, a facility that was quite unique for the size of the commune. He was very well regarded by the town's people. We did not inform the Location Office that he had left Bucharest because, in fact, he shared his living space with me, and therefore he had not vacated a living space of his own. I've described the fear of losing our Bucharest living space; the loss of it would have presumably jeopardized our chances of obtaining an exit permit.

Most Jews got their exit permits and left for Israel in the early 1950s. There were no more mass exits after 1952. In my perception, those who were denied the permit appeared to be doomed. I thought that my only chance of persuading the authorities would be to persevere with my request for a permit. I had a few thoughts:

Nothing takes the place of perseverance.

Talent does not take its place. (Nothing is more common than unsuccessful folks with talent.)

Genius does not take its place. (Unsuccessful genius is almost proverbial.)

Education does not take its place. (The world is full of educated derelicts.)

Perseverance and determination alone are omnipotent. They alone get things done.

After my conversation with Professor Parhon, I repeatedly asked the passport office for an audience. I wrote countless memoranda. When I was received by the director of the passport office, he didn't acknowledge my greeting. He was reading his newspaper, did not raise his head above it, and did not ask me to speak. I asked for permission to talk about my case. He did not listen to me, and when I stopped talking, he said: "You'll get our reply." After a few days, I received yet another postcard with the disgusting statement that my petition for an exit permit had been resolved: "Negative."

I made appointments with various officers of the passport office, but I realized that it was only a waste of time. They enjoyed humiliating me. Finally, in 1956, I got an audience with Dr. Petru Groza, who had become the President of the Republic. He said that he remembered me from years back when I was a medical student. He'd made an impromptu visit to the school, and my colleagues had asked me to make a welcoming speech. I made a nice introduction on the spot. At my audience with him in 1956, Dr. Groza wanted to appear to be nice to me, but he was a politician, and he hectored me on the value of "building socialism in the Romanian People's Republic." I had not come for that.

A visit with Gheorghe Gheorghiu-Dej, the Secretary General of the Romanian Communist Party, was much more effective. Gheorghiu-Dej was a true communist who had suffered many years of jail because of his political convictions. He had quite a good reputation among the people because he was thought of being an honest person. Surprisingly, he did listen to me and asked a few questions about my work and about my father's work in the Romanian Underground Resistance during the war. He was interested in my work with the "children of Europe." After a few days, I got my exit permit. I could not believe it! I held in my hands the letter informing me that my request of January 1950 had finally been approved. After six and a half years of trials and tribulations, after having received seventeen "negative" responses to my repeated requests, my wish had finally been granted.

I had only a few days to gather all the required papers. After all my past experiences, I decided to keep my departure an absolute secret. I knew what human jealousy could create. One of many difficulties made by the authorities was getting a certificate from all seven fiscal sectors of Bucharest stating that I did not have any unpaid taxes. I ran through all those offices and obtained the necessary documents. While doing this, I was also able to help some elderly people who were bewildered by the complicated process.

At that time there was no travel to Israel by ship, and travel by air would have been too costly. At the Israeli Embassy I was told to get a train ticket to Vienna, and that the Jewish Agency would meet me at the Vienna train station and fly me to Tel Aviv. I prepared my luggage in haste. I was allowed only forty-four pounds of personal items, only fifteen family photos, and no landscape photos. No gold items. Only one fourteen-karat gold nib on a fountain pen. No jewelry. No works of art. The suitcase was thoroughly checked by the Customs Office at the North Station in Bucharest and sealed. On the night of October 6th, I arrived at the station. Jerome and six trusted friends were with me; I departed on the train towards my new life.

I fell asleep on the train, exhausted by the week of tense preparations and fear, fear of having another encounter with the Security officials. Suddenly, somebody shook my elbow. Frightened, I opened my eyes, and I saw all the travelers worriedly looking at me and a stern Hungarian customs officer saying something I could not understand. Politely, I said: *nem tudom magyar* ("I don't know Hungarian"). Somebody helped translate that the customs officer wanted to examine the contents of my suitcase. He was upset with me; he thought that I had been trying to ignore him by making myself look asleep. When there was no problem with the contents of my suitcase, he saluted politely.

We passed the Hungarian-Austrian border at two o'clock in the morning, and I realized that it was the first time in my life that I was a free man. It took such a long, painful time to gain my liberty! Tears of joy streamed down my face. Adios, Romania, country of my birth, my happy childhood, and my painful growing up. My country of persecution and terror — Adios!

A New Life in Israel

After an overnight train ride, I arrived in Vienna. I found out that I was part of a group of seven people from Romania who had gotten exit permits. At that time, there was only a trickle of emigration out of Romania. I was the only young person, and my co-travelers were interested in who and how much I had paid for my permit. They could not believe that I hadn't paid for it. The Jewish Agency (the *Sochnut,* in Hebrew) people met us at the station, but to my surprise, there were also a few men representing the HIAS (Hebrew Immigrant Aid Society). They wanted to sponsor me if I wanted to go to the US. I did not want to discuss that path, and I stayed with the *Sochnut* people. They took me to Hotel Schiller, a quaint hotel where I had my first good breakfast in liberty. The *Sochnut* gave me thirty schillings (about three dollars) and asked me to come back to the hotel in the evening. Thirty schillings at that time could buy a modest amount food for one day. It was not known when the El Al plane would come to take us. The *Sochnut* men thought that we would have to wait two or three days. I reckoned that, with a good hotel breakfast in the morning and one or two delightful little Viennese breads during the day, I would be able to visit all that was possible in Vienna until the El Al flight. I did not waste time and was soon on my way with a small city plan in my pocket. I carried recollections of my parents' stories about the beauty of Vienna, and I had read quite a bit about the city.

With a few explanations about the bus system, I got to the Hofburg and visited the former imperial palace and the Imperial Treasury. My parents had brought home a nice album from Vienna with photos and explanations of the palace, the memory of which now helped me comprehend and admire the imperial crowns and regalia. Across the Ringstrasse, with great emotion, I visited the *Kunsthistorisches Museum* (the National Art Gallery), the main Austrian art collection, which is very rich. There had been an art museum in the royal palace in Bucharest, which included some Impressionist paintings, but the exhibits in Vienna's National Art Gallery were more than impressive to me: I spent the day there visiting a major art museum for the first time in my life. I had to leave my visit of the adjacent *Naturhistorisches Museum* (the Museum of Natural History) for the next day. After a walk on the Ringstrasse, admiring the *Rathaus* (the parliament buildings) and the famous Opera, I did not want to look too much at the windows of the *Sachercafé*, the renowned café, and I went to visit the St. Stephan Cathedral, the *Stephansdom* as it is called in Vienna. This was the first Gothic cathedral I'd ever visited. It was too late to climb the tower, and so I returned to the hotel.

Next day, I resumed my sightseeing. A young man, whose name I don't remember, insisted on joining me. He was also from Romania, had arrived in Vienna before me, and was also waiting for the El Al plane to go to Israel. The etiquette of the time and place required us to refrain from asking personal questions. I didn't like him insisting on going with me, but I did not see any danger in accepting his company. He had some Austrian money, which was a reason for feeling suspicious of him. We visited the *Naturhistorisches Museum*, about which I knew some facts, and we marveled at the exhibits. I took my companion to the *Kapuziener Kirche* (Church of the Capuchins) and its imperial crypt, where the sarcophagi of the emperors and empresses of Austria-Hungary are located. There are also more than a hundred sarcophagi of members of the Habsburg family there. My parents had also brought home from Vienna a beautiful album of the sepulchral art of the Austrian imperial family and aristocracy, which had impressed me in my childhood and made me eager to see it in person.

We paid a visit to the Café Demel; I let him invite me there because, after all, I was his unpaid guide, and I must say that what Café Demel knows to do with pastries is worth a visit. After our return to the hotel, we were informed that we would be leaving on a special El Al flight in two days. That meant that we had another full day in Vienna. With my new travel partner, I went to visit Sigmund Freud's house, and then we spent the afternoon in the Prater. Fall in Vienna has a rare charm. I have great memories of that great romantic city. I promised myself that I would return, and I did so seventeen years later with my wife, Huguette, and our two boys, Daniel and André.

The following morning, on October 10, 1956, with great emotion, we went to the airport and boarded the special El Al flight. I realized only then that we were a relatively large group of people who'd came from many places in Europe to Vienna for the El Al flight to Israel. During the flight, we were entertained by young flight attendants, and we sang partisan and Israeli songs. I remember that one of the flight attendants who spoke Romanian wanted to introduce me to the democracy in Israel. He said:

"If you don't agree with the government or Israeli politics, you can go to the Mograbi Center (the center of Tel Aviv at that time) and shout 'David Ben-Gurion is an idiot.'" For fun I asked: "Would this help?" There was no further conversation.

The few minutes in the air while we were crossing the Israeli space to the Lod (Lidda) Airport, as it was called at that time, were very emotional for me.

For so many years I'd wanted to see this, and finally I was getting to live it. I was a twenty-eight-year-old man arriving in his eight-year-old country. I prayed for the country and for my successful rebirth. Once I had deplaned, the first thing I saw was an Israeli policeman, a man in a uniform on whose epaulet I could decipher two Hebrew words: "Israeli Police." An Israeli policeman! One should understand that we never saw a Jewish policeman in Romania or in any European country. The saying was, "Police is not a profession for a Jew." But now we had our own country, which had been reborn with the correct social structure, and that included Jewish policemen.

We walked onto the tarmac, and when I was close to the airport building, I could see my parents on the balcony among the people waiting. I raised my hand to wave to them, and I dropped a portable thermos which friends had given me. *Mazal tov!* (Good luck!). This is what we say as a good wish while breaking glass. Hugging my parents after six years of separation was unreal. Father looked quite well, but Mother had swollen eyelids that made her look much older. Friends told me later how much she had cried because of our broken family. The first thing she asked me was, "When will Jerome come?" I assured her that he'd come soon. "How soon?"

My parents had lived through very difficult times in Israel, from poverty to the glimmer of a better life. They had worked very hard and lived with many deprivations. They had not wanted to stay in the tents of the Atlit Immigrants Camp where they placed on their arrival in 1950, when thousands of immigrants were arriving in the two-year-old State of Israel. With the hundred Israeli lira that Father bought in Bucharest before their departure, they went to Tel Aviv and rented a room in an apartment in the northern part of the town, on Gordon Street. Mother took a job as a housekeeper for a nice old Israeli family with whom she spoke German. Father had various jobs of heavy work. He finally got a job as an accountant for the big company called Tzinorot, which was in the huge business of irrigation pipes. He did not last long there because he wanted to "get back into the commercial circuit," as he liked to put it. With some of their savings and the eleven hundred Israeli lira that I'd transferred to them from Romania, he opened a store for knitting wool. He had the courage to buy on credit, which brought him the admiration of the tradespeople in Tel Aviv — and Mother's fear, because he did not have much money to pay it back. He needed to sell his wool rapidly to satisfy the payments that came due. He was never late with a payment though, and this established his sterling reputation. Forced by these financial constraints and because of his own commercial philosophy ("lower the price, get a small gain, sell fast, and sell much"), his business became competitive, and he started to attract a clientele. Still, there was not enough cash flow. He spent many sleepless nights on account of this. Mother and I were with him, but we could not loosen his financial straitjacket.

Mother was always very economically resourceful, and she again got a portable loom on which she started producing small pieces like pillowcases, about twenty inches by fourteen inches in size, like she'd done in Bucharest. These were a novelty on the Tel Aviv market, and they sold more rapidly than she could make them. This was a real relief to their strained budget. When I arrived, my parents were living in one room of an apartment. They had a convertible sofa, an armoire, a dining table with four chairs, a Frigidaire, and the portable loom on which Mother worked when not helping Father at his store.

It is very difficult to describe those times. It was very unusual for a young physician to get an exit permit from Romania. Parents of people my age visited every day asking not *whether* I'd bought my exit permit, but *from whom*. Their logic was strange, but I understood it because I knew my own parents' pain caused by our separation. Such cruelty from the Romanian government! Some would say that the Romanians just wanted to get the most they could from "their" Jews. In fact, they *did* end up "selling" their Jewish citizens, as it was termed later, when they gave thousands of passports to Jews going to Israel. I did the best I could by telling the truth to all these distraught parents, that I did not give money, and that if I could have given money, I would have done it also for my brother. This convinced them that I was honest in my replies to them. I encouraged them to persevere in writing to all the authorities of the Romanian People's Republic, as I had done.

I met up again with many friends from my youth. It was great fun. Lily was married and had two little boys. Her parents had gotten their exit permits and were living with her in Tel Aviv. My best friend Aurel was married to a beautiful lady, and they had a new baby. Aurel had recently bought a car, and he wanted to work for a passenger transport company. To break the car in, as was the routine at the time, he invited his parents and me to go with him to Haifa, sixty miles from Tel Aviv. This was a fine opportunity to visit Haifa, and I was very happy for my luck. After a day or two, he invited me again, this time to go to Beer Sheva in the south, and again we had a very nice day. On the way to Beer Sheva, we visited a Bedouin tribe that lived in tents. We were invited to have coffee inside, as was their tradition. I drank my coffee and thanked the host, but I could feel that there was a heavy silence in the big tent, and I looked around to find out what was going on. Aurel regarded me with a desperate look. He tried to give me a sign that I should burp, and I thought that he was crazy. I finally understood, and I made a pseudo-burp. Then, I heard all our Arab hosts saying in a chorus *Sahten habibi, sahten.* ("Enjoy it friend, enjoy it"). This was my first experience with an Arab custom. It is one of the stories that amused my sons when they were in their teens, and the reason is obvious.

♦

I arrived in Israel two days after the Qalqilya police station event, when the Israeli Defense Forces launched an attack on the Qalqilya police station in retribution for the many Arab Fedayeen incursions into Israel and their killings of innocent people. This was a period of major tension, with Arab infiltrations from the West Bank reported daily. Arab intruders killed single workers they found in citrus groves during the dark. They cut off the genitals or the ears of the murdered persons to prove that they have committed their heinous act and receive their pay. Most horrible acts! I could not understand Hebrew at that time, but I could sense the worry in the atmosphere. David Ben Gurion's impassioned speeches inspired the Israeli people to develop confidence in their rights as a nation and the courage to resist aggression.

It was a difficult time for Israel. A massive concentration of Egyptian troops and war material were detected in the Sinai at the border with Israel. Nasser ordered the closure of the Suez Canal, which was vital to the navigation routes and the international commerce of many countries. The anticipation of war dominated our lives. It was powerful, foreboding. A blackout was ordered, and we respected it punctiliously. It was unbelievable how dark the Tel Aviv streets became overnight.

On October 29, 1956, Operation Kadesh — or the Sinai Campaign — began. I woke up in the morning to the well-known sound of the alarm. Mother was at Father's store. I looked into the next-door kindergarten, and a teacher told me, *Es ist doch Krieg!* ("There is war, though," in German). My parents lived in the north part of Tel Aviv, which at that time was called the "German colony" because German was the second language spoken there. The teacher knew that I did not speak Hebrew and wanted to alert me to the news. So, we were at war. I quickly went to Father's store and told my parents that I must volunteer for the military service. At the recruitment office, I asked to serve in the armed forces but without knowing Hebrew, it was difficult for me to be useful on the front. I was sent to the front hospital, which was at the Beer Yaakov Government Hospital, not far from Tel Aviv. I worked there with a very good orthopedic surgeon, originally from Warsaw, who had trained in London, and who spoke English and French. I knew radiology quite well, and that helped me in my daily work. The war lasted only a few days, and I continued working there for about two weeks. There were no casualties because of Operation Kadesh. I had terrible migraine headaches which were triggered by *khamsin*, a Santa Ana-type of dry wind and atmospheric depression which came from the Jordanian desert.

With Operation Kadesh finished, I returned to Tel Aviv, free and without a lira in my pocket. One day, I met a young lady whom I'd helped in the fiscal offices of Bucharest when we were filling out the difficult documents required by the Passport Office for our exit permits. We were very glad to see each other again in better circumstances. She asked me why I did not go to an *ulpan* ("studio," in Hebrew), a place to learn Hebrew. I did not know anything about such schools, but I did not let grass grow under my feet — I went right away to the *Sochnut,* where friends from *Hanoar Hazioni* helped me register for entrance to an *ulpan.* I was accepted at the *Ulpan Motzkin* in Bat Galim, a quaint place in the outskirts of Haifa. Friends in Tel Aviv told me that I didn't need to learn Hebrew in an *ulpan,* that I would learn it from day-to-day practice. I did not share their opinion. I wanted to learn Hebrew and learn it well because it was the language of my country.

The *Ulpan Motzkin* was located in a house with several large rooms for classes and several smaller rooms and cabins where the students were accommodated in rather spartan conditions. We were interns, meaning that we slept and ate there and learned Hebrew all day long for six months. This program of learning Hebrew as an intern had been established by educators and had been shown to be a very successful intensive method of learning the language. The students were newly arrived immigrants from the four corners of the world. One could have heard twenty different languages spoken during the intermissions, but we were required to refrain from speaking our native languages. I had a hard time with the realization that it would take me a long time to learn to speak Hebrew in the way I could speak Romanian or French. The teachers were required to speak only Hebrew with the students. We had a young teacher, Ben Zvy. We knew he was originally from Romania, but he never said one word in Romanian. One day, he saw me sitting in the class bench, deep in my thoughts. He asked me what was the matter, and I responded in my halting Hebrew that it had taken many years of studying other languages to reach the level of facility with them that allowed me to express complex thoughts, and now I saw that it would take me an eternity to gain the same ability in Hebrew. He then used an old Romanian proverb to say that, at the end of the day, each one of us will show his or her real capabilities. This idea uplifted me, and I did make good progress in Hebrew.

I joined the *Hovevey Hateva* ("Friends of Nature"), with whom I took many tours in the Galilee. I got to know all of Galilee and its history and physical nature. One day, we found the ruins of the synagogue of *Korazim*, a fourth-century community; there were basalt arcades which were spread out in the high wild grass. (I was immensely moved when I saw the same black basalt arcades exhibited with pride in the Israel Museum in Jerusalem in 1965.)

Trains passed all night long just a few yards from the little cabin I shared with two other men at the *ulpan*. The trains carried oil, oil products, and war materials left by the Egyptian army in the Sinai. The Nasser regime of Egypt had massed a colossal amount of military stuff in the Sinai, and their armed forces had abandoned it all in their hasty retreat during the Operation Kadesh.

◆

I wanted to help my parents get an apartment, which could not be bought, only rented, after payment of "key money." This amounted to eighty-five hundred Israeli lira, which represented a very big sum. However, as a new immigrant, I could be approved for loans in various amounts for long periods of time and at a very low interest rate. Father was not too optimistic about my success. However, after meeting with many bank directors, I obtained loans in the total amount we needed for their apartment, which was a major feat (eighty-five hundred Israeli lira was the equivalent to about four thousand dollars at that time). With this money, in the spring of 1957, my parents paid the key money for the apartment on Frishman Street, No.11, in Tel Aviv, where we lived happily. It was quite centrally located and near to Father's business on the same street.

When I arrived in Israel, French was my second language, and I read and understood English well. During my first year in Israel, I studied intensely the lifestyle as well as the social and political realities of the country. I was quite aware of many of the problems of our new Jewish State, but there was much more to learn. Israel was my fatherland, not by birth, but spiritually and emotionally it was nevertheless my fatherland. I found that my friends from Romania had changed, they had become materialistic and had little political interest, if any. I talked with many other people. I was interested in the opinions of those who had been there a long time before I arrived. They were those who had endured the difficulties of building a modern state under the perfidious mandate of the British empire. The history of the return of the Jews to their fatherland is well documented. Regardless of the two millennia of living scattered throughout the world, Israel was the place my people claimed as their place in the world.

Because of my political convictions, I thought that once I arrived in Israel, my old-new country, I would be able to actively participate in helping it attain its full potential. However, the political reality of the country made newly arrived immigrants feel like outsiders. This was because the entrenched Mapai Party (the Socialist Party) determined the course of political life in Israel. Those who had arrived in the country a long time before World War II were the leaders of the decision-making process; new immigrants were supposed to be the followers. We had enormous respect for David Ben Gurion, but there were also other opinions, and the Centrist Party (*Klalzioni*) held different views about Israel's economy, its organization of life and labor, and its relationship with the Arabs and the rest of the world. The country was eight years old and not yet self-sufficient. It was coming out from a long period of national austerity, during which food had been scarce. Children and sick people had first rights to available food. These difficulties helped create the new Israeli nation.

Shortly after I arrived in Tel Aviv, I received an invitation to attend a political meeting organized by the Mapai Party, which was dedicated to helping new immigrants become aware of the social and political problems of the country. I was curious about what we, the new immigrants, could do to help. There were few speakers at the meeting, and all we were told was to register with the party and be good followers. What a terrible mistake. In their political arrogance, it did not occur to the organizers of the meeting that the invitees were people with political experience and knowledge, with very developed political ideas, ideals, and skills. Instead of trying to find out what we were thinking, our impressions and thoughts, they patronized us. It was the beginning and the end of my search for the opportunity to participate in any political activity in Israel. I asked a lady who appeared to be a political leader at that meeting how long one was I considered to be an *ole hadash* ("new immigrant"). Without any hesitation she replied, "Twenty years." I thought she was kidding me, but she was quite serious. I told her that immigrants bring new blood, and that it would be advantageous for her party to listen to what the new immigrants might have to say, but she cut me off, retorting that they (the Mapai Party) knew it all, and that all they needed was membership and votes. What a pity! It was that sort of political arrogance that led to the demise of the Mapai Party several years later. It was the Mapai's members' consensus at that time that the ruling party was the Mapai Party and that their socialist views would organize the new State of Israel. Well, well, not all the new immigrants thought that way.

The population of Israel was about 1.3 million. It had grown from six hundred and fifty thousand at the time of the Declaration of Independence, on May 14, 1948. Most Israelis were immigrants, and there has never been a place in the world where so many languages were spoken and written. The *sabra* (people born in Israel) were a minority. The native Israeli people called themselves *sabra* because they thought themselves like the cactus fruit called *tzabar* in Hebrew: They were rough and thorny outside but sweet inside, they thought and said. Hebrew was spoken widely; there were good newspapers, theater, and by all the rules and realities of life, Hebrew was the language of the land. However, there were many people who, for one reason or another, never learned Hebrew or knew only a little of it, and they were helped by people around them when they needed to make themselves understood. The idea of not being able to express myself fully was unacceptable to me, and that was the reason that I joined the *ulpan* without delay and studied passionately, learning Hebrew quickly and quite well.

The most important social problem I perceived at that time, quite vexing for me as well as for many others, was the segregation of the society by national origin. The largest communities of immigrants were from tsarist Russia, Lithuania, Poland, Romania, Germany, and from Iraq and North Africa. It was generally agreed that the immigration of Jews from Russia brought the best human resources from the point of view of creativity, language, ability to face the difficulties of a deserted land, and persevere and made the poor soil fertile again. There had not been immigration of Jews from the USSR since the Russian revolution of 1917. There were many Jews of Lithuanian origin equally well integrated into the new Israeli life.

Among the Polish immigrants there were both old-timers and those more recently arrived from the socialist republic. It was quite evident that the old-timer Polish Jews were well integrated, had good jobs, and were successfully Israeli from all points of view. The more recently arrived seemed to display a more pragmatic and egocentric attitude, and I noticed that they labelled people by their countries of origin, which was not important in my opinion. They did not get along with German Jews, calling them all sorts of unpleasant names. They held the same negative attitude toward Romanian Jews, whom they labelled "thieves," and Sephardi immigrants, whom they called "good for nothing." Such contumely could not help creating a nation.

At the turn of the nineteenth century, Romanian Jews established the first settlements in the Galilee (*Rosh Pinna*) and along the central coastal plain (*Zichron Ya'akov* and *Rishon le-Zion*), all of them thriving settlements. However, after World War II, the Jews allowed to leave Romania for Israel were not Zionists or professionals. Most of them were without definite professions. I have mentioned that the communist regime did not permit professional Jews to leave Romania after the war. Those allowed to go to Israel were businessmen or people without jobs. However, the State of Israel needed people able to work the land or in definite professions, and the new Romanian *aliya* (Hebrew for immigration to Israel) did not provide many of this sort of citizens until the 1970s, when professionals were allowed to leave Romania if they paid ransom money to the Romanian government.

German Jews brought to Palestine many well-prepared individuals — professionals and men of science. They became renowned academicians and professors under the British Mandate and were, in general, very well integrated into the Israeli way of life, although many of the German Jews who came in the 1930s had trouble learning Hebrew. German Jews were not particularly fond of Polish Jews, and the feeling was mutual.

The most acute demographic problem was related to the Sephardic Jews. They came from Iraq and North Africa, where their ancestors had lived an integrated lifestyle for centuries. They spoke very good Hebrew and practiced different rituals than the Sephardic rituals I knew of in Romania. The most important differences between them and the Ashkenazi Jews were their morals and life values. They were from two separate worlds; the Ashkenazi Jews were Western European with mentalities and values totally different from those of the Sephardic Jews. From the point of view of the customs and requirements of modern civilization, the Ashkenazi were more competitive and had better jobs than their Sephardic brethren who mostly worked for low pay. In addition, there was an overt discrimination against Sephardic Jews, very painful for a person like me who'd grown up in a racialized society and had suffered persecution based on my ethnicity. And now, to see this in my own country, Israel? It was tough for me to witness or accept. Gradually the problem of the disenfranchisement of the Sephardic community in Israel became a publicized national conflict which resulted in major political changes in the 1970s.

And of course, there was the problem of the Arabs who lived in the land of Israel. There were about one million Arabs living in Israel at the time of Israel's Declaration of Independence in 1948. They were the descendants of Arabs who invaded the land from unknown parts of the world in the seventh century. The Jewish community had been weak at that time and could not oppose the Arab settlements. The Byzantine empire (330-1453) as well as the Ottoman empire (1453-1920) did not make any effort towards developing the land. World War I, with the Sykes-Picot Agreement (1916), the Balfour Declaration (1917), and the San Remo Resolution (1920) resulted in the establishment of the British Mandate and the limitation of Jewish immigration, which was in fact contrary to the spirit of all the agreements of World War I. If Jewish immigration to Palestine had been permitted at that time, the Holocaust could have been avoided.

Throughout centuries, there had been peaceful relationships between the Arabs and Jews in Palestine — that is, until the institution of the British Mandate in 1920, which was interested only in fomenting antagonism and dissent between the Jews and the Arabs, the old *divide et impera* idea of governance.

Historically, there had been a tradition of mutual respect for property and religious tolerance maintained between the Arabs and the Jews. It was a known fact that when the war erupted after the Declaration of Independence and the creation of the State of Israel in May 1948, the pro-Nazi Mufti Party incited the local Arabs to run away while Israelis went through Arab neighborhoods asking them to stay and live together with them peacefully. Many Arabs listened to the Mufti, who was a friend of Hitler, and they ended their lives in squalor in the UNRWA displaced persons' camps in Jordan. It is a well-documented fact that none of the Arab properties in Israel were taken by Jews. They were maintained as Arab properties by the office of the *Apotropos,* the custodian of Arab properties that managed them on behalf of Arab owners. It was obvious to me at that time that in the heat of the war of 1948, the problem of the Arabs staying or leaving had not been assessed well or dealt with fairly. What was not well thought out or simply ignored at that time haunted the existence and peace of Israel in the years to follow. It was clear to me and to many apolitical people that a two-state solution would have been normal. With the help of the world powers and the Jewish community, the Arabs could have been endowed to live prosperous and comfortable lives in their own state side-by-side with the Jewish State of Israel.

From a socio-economic point of view, Israel had a unique system: two poles of social economy. There was the agrarian Israel, well-established and prosperous, and there was a small burgeoning capitalist Israel. From the time of the first wave of immigration, the first form of Israeli settlement was farming. By necessity as much as by ideology, the farms were collective enterprises, known as the *kibbutz*, which was the best example of a communist agrarian settlement, or the *moshav*, which was of two types, depending on their inner economic structures. It was not only the real hard labor, the sacrifice, and the continuous fight with nature and with soil that had been neglected for centuries — these settlements raised a new sort of Jews, the Israelis. These were very solid men and women, tenacious, honest, and dedicated to the *Yishuv*, as the Jewish community in the Palestine of that time was called. In fact, most of the political leaders during the first thirty or forty years of Israel's existence had been *kibbutzniks* or *moshavniks*, and they almost invariably served the country to its best benefit and progress. Men and women of character, tenacious people of sacrifice and moral integrity: I knew the type; in our Zionist youth organization we had been imbued with the dogma of the necessity of rebuilding our country and ourselves, and that this rebuilding had to start with the farmland, where the nation's food was produced. The aim was to become self-sufficient, and we were educated in that spirit and toward that ideal.

One had to remember that only eight years before my arrival, new immigrants were fed with bread made in the country from flour that was partially imported, and with yogurt and cheese brought in from the US. Vegetables and fruits were not plentiful, and preference was given to feeding the children. There was very little meat for adults, and everything was procured with rationed points. But things evolved rapidly, and in less than twenty years Israel became an agricultural exporter of the first rank.

There was, perhaps necessarily, also a small burgeoning capitalist movement consisting mostly of trade shops and small industry. The most important industry was, of course, the construction of homes for thousands of new immigrants. In 1950, when my parents arrived, new immigrants were placed in tents, as I have already described. But by the mid-1950s, people wanted houses. These houses, called *shikun*, were simply built, without much preoccupation for stylistic beauty, in complexes of dozens or even hundreds, depending on the place. Tel Aviv itself had been built on dunes of sand in 1909. At that time, the founders did not know to build *shikunim*, and the new city was built to model European cities.

The country had hundreds of *shikunim* in villages and in cities. It was a great feat to take possession of a *shikun* because there was a long wait for the completion of new constructions. As usual in any country, the construction of homes has the greatest impact on a variety of industries, from furniture and furnishings to kitchen appliances. These items started to be produced in Israel, to the great pride of the Israeli consumers. It was a most encouraging thing to hear people remarking that a household item had been manufactured in Israel. They said it with evident pride: *tozeret Israel* (product of Israel). Gradually, of course, many industries developed and produced various wares, first world-famous pharmaceuticals, and plastic wares that are still prime articles of export.

I had some difficulty understanding the healthcare delivery system, and I needed to get oriented. I was amazed by the fact that friends and colleagues could not describe it to me in a way that I could understand. For historic reasons, the principal health care provider was a branch of the most powerful *Histadrut* (Labor Union), called *Kupat Holim* ("the Sick Fund," in Hebrew). Kupat Holim had first class hospitals like the Beilinson Medical Center in Petach Tikva, and many clinics where most Israelis in need of medical attention went — and complained bitterly about the service received. In truth, the Kupat Holim hospitals offered first-quality service, but one could not say the same about many of its clinics.

Then there was also the government health care network, with excellent hospitals like the Chaim Sheba Medical Center at Tel HaShomer (near Tel Aviv); Rambam Hospital in Bat Galim (near Haifa); and fine hospitals in Jaffo, Beer Yaakov, and Poriah, in Galilee, as well as some clinics, mostly adjacent to the hospitals. In a development stage at that time was a new insurance-backed plan called Maccabi, which was quite appealing to people because its doctors apparently spent more time with the members of this healthcare plan than did the doctors of Kupat Holim. Some municipalities had their own hospitals. This was the case in Tel Aviv and in Haifa. The Souraski (formerly Ichilov) Medical Center in Tel Aviv was a modern hospital with state of the art medicine.

Finally, there was the famous Hebrew University-Hadassah Medical School in Jerusalem, which was the unquestionably supreme national medical authority, which boasted a long history of employing excellent physicians. Many of these physicians had served at the old location on Mount Scopus, where the university and the medical center had started in 1918 and 1939, respectively. At the end of the War of Independence, in 1949, the university and the medical center on Mt. Scopus, east of the Old Jerusalem were vacated, and the entire area became a demilitarized zone under the guard of young Israelis. Nothing could be removed from the buildings there. It was a pity because the large library of the Hebrew University could not be used. The hospital services were then relocated to various buildings in the new part of Jerusalem. The hospitals were well equipped and provided active consulting services in all medical and surgical specialties. However, the buildings housing the clinical services were inadequate. Graduating doctors were obligated to serve one year in a remote place, usually a *moshav* or a *kibbutz* far from the cities. It was generally accepted that if one had a serious condition requiring hospitalization, the medical care was excellent, but the ambulatory care was not always satisfactory.

One day, a friend whom I met on a weekend I spent in Tel Aviv told me that, while I was learning Hebrew in the *ulpan*, several hundred Polish physicians had arrived from Poland, and they were taking the few work positions available. I got the message; I left the *ulpan* about a month before its end and went for job interviews. I was very well received. Every physician I met was impressed with my proficiency in Hebrew, but there was a hurdle in the way of my immediate employment, which was explained to me by each of the chiefs I met for a position in their respective programs: I was obligated to serve one year as a physician in the Israel Defense Forces (IDF). This service was due after an immigrant's first year in the country, a year during which new immigrants had free time for "absorption." If I were to be given a position as a junior staff physician and then was called to serve in the IDF after my free year, I would be missed by the hospital team. It was better to start my life as a physician with the obligation of military service. I had to ask to be accepted for my due military service earlier, without the normal deferment, which in my case would have lasted until October 1957. In other words, I had to ask to volunteer. I recall addressing the committee that had to accept my request to volunteer. I asked in very polite Hebrew if I could "express a preference for the branch of service." They appeared to be quite pleased by my ability to speak Hebrew. "Which service do you prefer?" they asked. "I'd very much like to serve in the Navy" I replied. "Why in the Navy?"

Then I told them the story of my life: born in Constanţa on the shores of the Black Sea, loving the sea, etc, etc, etc. I am sure that they just wanted to hear this new immigrant speaking Hebrew after only a few months in Israel, and my reasoning for serving in the Navy did not impress them. It so happened that there was a position available for a physician on one of the Navy ships, and I got it! Almost in the ninth heaven, I registered with the Navy office, came home, packed my small luggage in the military bag the Navy gave me, and I was ready to start my military service for my country.

On the Israeli Navy Service

I was very happy to serve in the Navy. I respected the Israel Defense Force, the utmost guarantee of the State of Israel's existence and independence. I left on the train to Haifa, a one-and-a-half-hour trip at that time. I had to report to the base in Bat Galim, in the periphery of Haifa. There I was given my work uniform, a light grey-blue color, and an officer's hat.

I was appointed Medical Officer on the destroyer *Eilat* under the command of Captain Menachem Cohen. There was a sister ship, the *Jaffo*. Both were built in England at the beginning of World War II and were bought by Israel in 1955. They were very well equipped, each with four long-range guns, eight torpedo launchers, anti-aircraft guns, sonar, and four anti-submarine depth charges. The officers' quarters were quite elegant; their beds had leather upholstery. There was a fine dining room, which could be transformed into a fully equipped operating room. The ship had a very nice infirmary with two well-built suspension beds and a good supply of first-aid medications. The kitchen was strictly kosher because Jewish culinary rules were respected in the IDF. In Operation Kadesh, an Egyptian frigate, named *Ibrahim El Awal* ("Ibrahim the First") was captured by Jaffo and Eilat, was renamed *Haifa*. During the naval battle, the crew had rebelled against their officers, arrested them, and raised a broom on the chimney as the traditional Navy sign of surrender.

INS Eilat K-40. (INS stands for Israel Navy Ship and K stands for the Hebrew Kravy, which means battle or fight)

The officers of the INS *Eilat* had been trained in England and were very competent. Most of them were *sabras*. They were totally dedicated to their jobs and took great pride in their ship. I learned so much from them, not only about Navy work, but about themselves, their families, their feelings, and their human philosophies as proud young men, born in freedom. I liked Captain Menahem Cohen very much. Very confident in his abilities, with equanimity and good common sense, he was venerated by the crew who called him *gibor* ("hero") of naval operations.

The daily routine was quite simple. When in the harbor, the sailors looked for any medical reason to get out of their daily work assignments, while at sea they were never sick. My medical assistant was well trained. He reviewed the complaints of the sailors and referred to me those with problems that he could not resolve. Serious cases were transported to the fine government hospital *Rambam*, located in Bat Galim, close to the harbor. After we finished seeing all on the sick list, I had time to write my reports, which was a bit difficult. I had to write in very polished Hebrew while I was still learning it. It was in the Navy that I made substantial progress in my Hebrew by having many conversations and writing a lot. I also had time to watch and learn the activities on the ship which were quite interesting when we were out at sea.

On the *Eilat* we had some difficult medical situations that I was able to resolve with some luck. I recall a day at sea when I heard a big raucous noise outside my clinic. It was the *rav samal rishon* (Petty Officer, 1st class) who appeared to have a foreign body in his eye. His pain was intense. Upon examination, I found a particle of coal smoke in the shape of a needle that gotten into his cornea. I had some Pantocaine (local ophthalmic anesthetic) in the pharmacy, and as soon as the drops of Pantocaine took effect, the pain subsided. The sailor thought that I was a great doctor and wanted to leave my clinic. "Not so fast," I said. I still had to remove the foreign body from his cornea, a medical procedure I'd never performed in medical school. I feared that I would not be able to extract that particle of smoke from the sailor's cornea without leaving a scratch. Because the sea was rough and the ship was rolling badly, I had to call the bridge and ask the Captain to change course so that we could avoid big rolls. I used a slightly wetted swab with a gentle move, which by sheer luck extracted the coal particle fully and without any side effects. The cornea did not show any damage, and I thanked Providence for helping me and the sailor. After that, the sailors declared that I was a *hevraman* ("good fellow"), a compliment which might determine to a great measure a physician's career in the Navy.

A more serious accident happened with a tall sergeant who was in charge of the provisions of the ship. He was not a nice person, too full of himself because he was a career sailor. One day, he went down in the belly of the ship on a very narrow ladder, carrying a lot of weight. He fell and got a luxation of his right knee. I was summoned and found him in agonizing pain. The diagnosis was obvious. Luckily, I'd brought some morphine, which relaxed him well. Knowing the orthopedic procedure, I replaced his knee beautifully. The problem, however, was how to extract this big man through the narrow ladder. The sailors were very resourceful and organized a system of ropes that brought him out in good shape and without any damage to his leg.

We were presented with a much more important and graver medical situation on our way to Toulon, France, for joint maneuvers with the French fleet in October 1957. Israel had the friendliest relationship with France at that time. Several of our high-ranking officers from Navy headquarters had joined us as our guests on the trip. The sleeping quarters on the ship were crammed. For two or three days we had nice sailing — until my medic reported a few cases of high fever. Upon examining the sick sailors, I noticed that they exhibited an unusual degree of lassitude, muscle pain, and coughing. I thought that we had a flu epidemic, and I reported the situation to the Chief Medical Officer of the Navy in Haifa. There was much concern on the ship because there had been an epidemic of Asian flu when we left the country. My medic and I worked day and night to help the sick men gain full recovery. We had up to one hundred sick men on board at one time. I had to ask the captain to return to Haifa to replenish our pharmacy supplies. When everyone had recovered, we proceeded to Toulon.

I remember our arrival in the Toulon harbor, and the twenty-one-gun salute of the French Navy. It was a great honor for the Israeli Navy, a very emotional moment for us, and overwhelming for me. Our destroyer, a fighting ship with a low physical profile, looked like a midget when moored between two giants, the aircraft carrier *L'Arromanches* and the battleship *Richelieu*. My captain received an invitation for lunch with the captain of *L'Arromanches*. He demurred, asking to be represented by the chief engineer, who was a Belgian, and me, as we were the only French-speaking officers. The lunch was superb. Dr. J. Gestat, one of the French doctors on *L'Arromanches*, invited me to go the next day with him and his wife to visit the medical school in Marseille, from which he had graduated. On the way, he showed me the Camargue, a bird sanctuary. In Marseille, we visited the basilica Notre Dame de la Garde (*La Bonne Mère,* as it is called by the locals), situated on a hill, the highest place in Marseille, with a superb view over the city and its harbor. It was built as a fort by Francis I and was the site of valiant battles at the end of World War II. We ate a fine and unforgettable bouillabaisse in the harbor, and my colleague showed me the town.

I very much wanted to visit Paris. The first thing I needed was my captain's permission, which he graciously granted to me for three days. I took a night train to Paris. I didn't realize that the next day, November 1st, was *Le jour des Toussaints* ("All Saints Day"), when all of France goes to Paris on pilgrimage. The captain asked the officers and the crew not to go in uniform but in civilian attire when we left the ship. We did not have passports; instead, we had documents stating that we were from the destroyer *Eilat* on an official visit to Toulon. The press published a good coverage of our visit to Toulon.

I got on the train to Paris in the evening. The train was full. Fortunately, a conductor discreetly led me to a sleeping compartment. It was dark and all I could see was that there were six beds, three on each side. I fell asleep right away. I woke up the next morning in the Gare St. Lazare. Much to my surprise, I realized that I had spent the night in the company of five ladies. Like a good gentleman, I turned my face to the wall and invited the ladies to take their time getting ready to leave the train. Then I left without further delay and looked for a hotel.

My mother's friend, Malvine Plopul, lived in Paris. She and her husband were co-owners of a 5-star hotel, Le Commodore, on the select Boulevard Haussmann. I did not want to call them until I had my own accommodations. Hence, I went to the first hotel I saw in front of the train station. They had a vacancy. When I showed my papers, the hotel receptionist balked. He did not understand English and could not read my Navy papers. He wanted to see my passport, which I did not have. Promptly, he took the telephone to call the police. In a flash, I could see myself spending the night in a police station. With a very dignified air, I told the receptionist: *Monsieur, vous devez savoir qu'il y a d'autres hôtels à Paris* ("Sir, you must know that there are other hotels in Paris"), and I left without delay. I did realize, however, that I would encounter the same scenario at other hotels, so I called the Plopuls, my parents' friends at the Le Commodore to get some advice. They insisted that I take the bus to their hotel right away. A beautiful dream followed: I was hosted in an elegant room, introduced to nice people, to their daughter, Yolande, and their son, Valentin. They had not seen me since 1940, when we had spent time together during our last visit to their villa on the shores of the Black Sea, near Constanța.

The Plopuls insisted that I take a tour of Paris. It started at the Basilica Sacre Coeur in Montmartre. I visited seriously, so seriously that I missed the call back to the tour autocar. There I was, alone in Paris. An interesting challenge. But it's always helpful to be young. I had my little map, I knew what I must see, and I walked and walked. I got back to the hotel late at night with only enough energy left to drop into my bed. The next two days, I wanted to be on my own. I started with historic Paris, the Notre Dame Cathedral, the Ste. Chapelle, Blvd. St. Michel, the Sorbonne University, the Panthéon, and the Quartier Latin. Next day, the Louvre and l'Orangerie, where the Impressionist paintings were exhibited. This was a dream come true. In Bucharest, I had studied the Impressionists and had memorized some of their paintings; to see those works of art in person was sheer happiness. It was a dream come true to see monumental Paris from the Louvre, through the Place de la Concorde, Champs Elysées, Arc de Triomphe, Eiffel Tower, les Invalides, le Trocadero, and Montmartre. I had learned in school about all these sites and monuments. I could not get enough of looking around and enjoying the classic European architecture and style. I had been raised with European values which were dear to me.

As a Lieutenant, Israeli Navy, 1957.

Yolande, Malvine's daughter, and her husband invited me to a show at the Crazy Horse, which was a strip-tease show. I had heard of this new vogue, but we surely did not have it in Israel. I also had the fun of seeing a show at the

Moulin Rouge to complete my "education." Other friends of the Plopuls took me to see theater, which I loved very much.

I returned to Toulon by TGV in time to participate in some exercises that had to do with the protocols of evacuation from burning ships, and all went well. After we finished the joint naval program, we left for Nice. Our unofficial visit to Nice was intended for fun and morale-building. We were invited by the Jewish community of Nice to a huge party in honor of our sailors, and they had a great time. It was indeed a memorable party. Our sailors were the focus of all the attention, and the officers enjoyed it as well. Young ladies courted our young sailors. The chief engineer and I were the ad hoc translators. The next day, the officers of the Israeli Navy headquarters, our guests on the ship, rented a car to visit the Côte d'Azur and invited me to join them. After I made sure that my services were not needed for the day, I left with them on the Moyenne Corniche and visited Le Bar, St. Paul de Grasse, Cannes, Villefranche, and Beaulieu on our drive to Menton at the border with Italy. Those entrancing views of the French Riviera must be seen. It was a splendid voyage.

On the way back to Israel, we threw anchor at Monte Carlo, a very elegant little town. I wanted to visit the casino. There was a problem, however. In my rush to leave on this trip, I hadn't had time to change into my civilian attire, and entrance to the casino is absolutely forbidden to military in uniform of any nation, a rule which I did not know. I got an idea: I gave the wardrobe person my jacket and took his, just for a short visit. The interior of the casino merits a visit; it is superbly decorated.

We were not going home yet. We stopped for a courtesy visit in Livorno (Leghorn), and I got permission to go to Pisa for the day. I marvelled at the Duomo, the Baptistry, and, of course, the famous tower. I was fascinated by the interior of the cathedral and of the Campo Santo. We stayed in Livorno another day, and it was the crowning day of my trip: I got permission to go to Florence, one hour by train. I fell in love with this most beautiful city. I knew quite a lot of its artistic history, but to see the Duomo, Giotto's Campanile, the marvelous Baptistery with the "Gates of Paradise" made by Lorenzo Ghiberti and Andrea Pisano, the Uffizi Gallery, the Bargello, the Accademia, and the Santa Croce was a great artistic, intellectual, and spiritual treat. There were no queues at the museums at that time, and I enjoyed my visit immensely.

◆

The visit to France and Italy stayed in everybody's memory. We were lucky. I was promoted to Medical Officer of Fleet No. 1, a fleet which was composed of the three destroyers: the *Jaffo*, the *Eilat*, and the *Haifa*. My work became more involved. I saw sick sailors on the three ships almost every day. A tugboat took me around while in the harbor of Haifa.

In February 1958, we made a short visit to Rhodes. The sailors and officers were enchanted. Our visit to the Crusaders Citadel and the ramparts was a trip into medieval history. We also visited the Acropolis of Lindos, where the view of the blue Mediterranean was inspirational. A small Jewish community of about three thousand people lived on the Island of Rhodes for centuries. All of them were killed by the Nazis. We placed a wreath on the monument in their memory.

INS Eilat Honor Guard at the Monument of the Jews of Rhodes who were killed by the Nazis.
February 1958

We had to perform a very difficult exercise between the *Jaffo* and the *Eilat*. The exercise involved transferring the medical officer from one ship to the other in case of an emergency at sea. The captain explained to me that I, as the medical officer of the ship, would be the subject of the exercise. The two ships were kept about two hundred feet apart because sailing closer to each other would have created a risk of collision. A system of transport cables was shot between ships and secured, leaving some slack. I was placed in a strong belt with an extension to my foot, which was held in a stirrup. I had to hold onto a handle above-my head, which was part of the harness into which I was placed. The whole thing rolled on a pulley on cables without much slack, which could have injured me. When they explained to me how the exercise worked,

I was not enthused, but I had complete confidence in the captain and the crew, who were responsible professionals. The turbulence of the sea between the ships was awesome. It was best to avoid looking down. It occurred to me that if any accident occurred, there would be no coming out alive. However, all went very well, and I arrived safely to the applause of the receiving crew. Then, however, came the second part of the exercise, which consisted of transferring a sailor on a stretcher from one ship to the other. The sailor had to be placed on a stretcher with raised sides that enclosed him and was attached by cables to two pulleys rolling on the cables between the ships. It became clear that for that exercise, I had to be the person on the stretcher, and I was returned safely to my ship. What an experience!

Hang on, Doc! I was hanging on. At sea. March 1958.

I was offered a contract as Navy physician. It included one year of specialization in marine medicine in Toulon, with a sub-specialization in undersea medicine, which was important for the care of our "frogmen." I searched my soul. I knew that, above all, I had to be true to myself. By temperament, I was a civilian who loved medicine as a profession. I loved medicine not only because of its science and its art, but also because of its liberal nature. I decided that I had to be free and in a position where I was not working under orders. I declined, thanked the admiral who had offered me the position, and went home to Tel Aviv.

Academic Pathologist

Discharged from the Navy in May 1958, I faced the problem of employment. The Navy had paid me a few lira while I was in service, too small an amount for saving. I sensed at that time that Mother and I had a different understanding of what I wanted to do. My dear mother would have liked me to get married, open an office, preferably in Tel Aviv, and have a family. Not a bad plan, but I wanted to practice medicine in a way that interested me, doing research in an area of expertise and teaching. I loved internal medicine, and considered a possible sub-specialization in endocrinology, which I had learned from Professor Parhon in Bucharest. Marriage did not interest me at that time. I thought of getting married only after I'd gotten my professional career under way. People around me talked about materially very convenient marriages, but I was not interested in settling my life in that way. I could not accept the thought of being obliged to another person's money to achieve social status.

There were no jobs available in hospitals or clinics. I knocked on many doors, but there were no positions available. Finally, I heard that Professor Toaff, an associate of the illustrious Professor Zondek of the Hebrew University-Hadassah Medical School, was coming to the Tel Aviv Maternity Hospital as the new Chief of Obstetrics and Gynecology. He wanted to establish a program in gynecologic endocrinology, a possible opportunity that seemed closest to my interests. Professor Zondek was of international fame; he had developed the first pregnancy test. Professor Toaff had a fine reputation in the field. I met with him, and I told him about my interest in endocrinology. He knew about the contributions of Professor Parhon to the field and thought that I would be able to learn gynecologic endocrinology on his service. Therefore, I applied for and obtained a position on his service at Tel Aviv Maternity.

I did recall obstetrics from my medical school years, but I was concerned when Dr. Farkash, my immediate chief, asked me to join him in a caesarian operation after only a few days on the service. I did well, with his help, and colleagues encouraged me, saying that I had talent. I learned to do the routine work, and I felt that there were no problems. I made rapid progress. One day, I was suturing an episiotomy, a cut made on one site of the vulva before a baby's delivery to prevent tears that might be caused by the passage of baby's head. The good Dr. Farkash came to see how I was doing. He quickly found that I hadn't done well: "The young mother may need her rectum," he said, with his humor. Whoops! I had caught the outer layer of the rectal wall in my suture. We undid what I hadn't done correctly, and I redid it well. Local anesthesia helped both the mother and me.

At night, after my days in the maternity hospital, I took calls at a private psychiatric hospital not far from Tel Aviv called *Neve Shalvah*. Some nights were quite busy, and I was chronically deprived of sleep. The money was good, however. I planned to do this only for a few months. My social life was reduced to nil, which was not very encouraging. New immigrants to Israel quickly learn the saying, "all beginnings are difficult," which is true in any part of the world. Life was difficult for me, but it was only a beginning, and I accepted it as an expected situation.

Tel Aviv Maternity was the place with the highest number of childbirths in Israel, up to twenty deliveries a day. In no time, I got to be quite proficient in normal obstetrics. However, it did not interest me as a long-term profession. We did not do much gynecology there, and there was not even a sign of gynecologic endocrinology. One day, I saw Dr. Toaff and asked him: "What happened with the plans you described to me at the time of my interview?" In his heavily Italian-accented Hebrew he answered: "Do you think that I came to Tel Aviv from Jerusalem to make science? One makes science in Jerusalem, not in Tel Aviv. I came to Tel Aviv to make money." It was a brutally truthful answer, and I felt very disappointed.

In my concern about what to do, I went to Jerusalem to consult with Dr. Necker, an older physician who had befriended me when I had met him in *Hanoar Hazioni*. He was now the chief medical officer of the Kupat Holim in Jerusalem, a very important position, and he also was a very wise man whom I respected, which was the reason I went to seek his advice. He was very impressed by my command of Hebrew, and, after listening to me, he said he thought that I should see Professor Ungar, of the Department of Pathology at the Hebrew University-Hadassah Medical School. I told him that I had never thought of becoming a pathologist, but he insisted that I should go and meet the professor just to get some advice.

Professor Ungar was the chairman of the highly esteemed Department of Pathology at the Hebrew University-Hadassah Medical School. At the interview, we developed a certain bond after I discovered that he had been very active in *Hanoar Hazioni* in Berlin. On the spot, he offered me a position as a junior assistant in his department. I told him: "Professor, I don't want to become a pathologist. I learned pathology in medical school, and it did not click with me as something I wanted to do as a lifelong medical practice. I was trained as a clinician, and my interest is in the diagnosis and treatment of sick people."

He answered: "Neither did I want to become a pathologist, but I got fascinated by this discipline and by the depth of medical knowledge it can offer. Try it for one or two years and then decide."

I could understand the rationale of studying pathology to deepen my medical knowledge, and I accepted the job.

As I wrote in the previous chapter, the Hadassah Medical Organization, a creation of the Women's Zionist Organization of America, had its original hospital on the campus of the Hebrew University on Mount Scopus. The various parts of the Hadassah Hospital were now scattered in various inadequate buildings in Jerusalem. The Institute of Pathology and the Medical School were housed in what had been a former maternity hospital under the British Mandate, an old building in the center of Jerusalem, an area called the City Hall Garden (*Gan hayriyah*). It was quite spacious. From the window of my lab, I had a good view of Old Jerusalem, which was in Jordan at that time. From the roof of the building one could see the Old Town, and on a clear day one could see the mountains of Moab, which were farther away in the East. We showed this view to visitors from abroad who were invariably very impressed. About three hundred feet down the street was the Jaffa gate, which was blocked. Soldiers of the Jordanian Legion held their post on top of the gate, looking down at our daily life, and we could see them very well. We refrained from communicating with them.

Hadassah gave me a room on the campus of one of its hospitals. It was a room for visiting doctors staying for short periods of time. It was a very monastic room, with a single bed, a table, two straight chairs, and a wardrobe. The showers were down the hall. It was simple, I did not pay any rent, and it was quite convenient because it was very close to the medical school, where the Institute of Pathology was located. One new and initially strange thing for me was hearing the church bells, which I had not heard since I left Romania. They were the bells of the neighboring Abyssinian church.

My first contact with anatomic pathology in Israel was not pleasant. I had never performed autopsies (post-mortem examinations) by myself in medical school; instead, a teacher had shown medical students the findings of autopsies. I had, however, taken a very good course in anatomic pathology. Now I worked very hard to relearn gross anatomic pathology and the microscopic examination of tissues. I remembered human anatomy very well, which helped me perform autopsies. Nobody took the time to teach me the technique of an autopsy, and I knew that without proper technique one could ruin the findings without the possibility of corrective action. Hence, I was quite concerned about making a mistake and, moreover, about missing findings. An autopsy provides enormous medical knowledge, an insight into the disease process, the course of a disease, its complications, and the cause of death. Besides this knowledge, the examination may give the examiner a feeling of professional humility when he or she finds how many findings are missed by clinical, radiological, and laboratory examinations. All the clinicians and their chiefs came to see the autopsy findings.

We faced difficulties in performing autopsies. The Jewish orthodox people of Jerusalem were adamantly opposed to postmortem examinations. Many times, we had to work while crowds were frantically banging on the outside doors. Much tension had been created by the way the physicians and the rabbis ignored each other. I saw that they had become entrenched in their opposed positions without ever trying to discuss openly and truthfully the imperative need to make progress through knowledge. Like in many other areas of life, the issue of the autopsy was dominated by uneducated emotions. To preserve life, a concept so valuable in Jewish philosophy, it was advantageous to understand the process of disease. In fact, the Talmud, the basic philosophical treatise of Judaism, emphasizes the importance of life — and doctors are servants and guardians of life. The rabbis did not see postmortem examinations in this light, although progress in medicine had been made through the medical examination of the dead. How could we otherwise know the course and complications of disease, the effect of our treatments, our failures, and the causes of death?

The academic staff of the Department of Pathology was excellent: Professor Ungar had a vast knowledge of pathology and an outstanding memory. He amazed all of us by remembering passages from the stellar pathology textbooks by Henke and Lubarsch and Rudolf Virchow. Professor Laufer was the authority on gynecologic and bone pathology. Professor Wollman was a pioneer in neurochemistry. Drs. Liban and Bechar were very knowledgeable in general pathology, great observers, but they lacked any immediate opportunity for academic futures at Hadassah. The country had less than two million people, and no new hospitals were being built. Hence, there were no new professional openings for scientists at their level.

The staff of the Institute of Pathology: Professors, lab technicians, and trainees. Jerusalem, 1959 (Front row, from left): Ruth Ungar, technician; Erika Litten, technician; Professor Moshe Wollman; Dr. Albert Bechar, lecturer; Dr. Eric Liban, lecturer; Professor Henry Ungar, Chair of the Department of Pathology; Professor Alexander Laufer; Ms. Laufer (visitor). (Back row, from left): A lab assistant; Armand Abramovici, student in charge of the museum; Hanna Silberstein, technician; Dr. J. Harris, trainee; the department secretary; Dr. Martin Eisner, trainee; Dr. Mario B, trainee; and Dr. Edgar Moran, trainee; technicians; Dr. Jack Plashkes, trainee; a technician; Ms. Hecht, secretary; Dr. Mario Ulmansky, trainee.

The study of anatomic pathology fascinated me in many ways. I became interested in the study as the basis of clinical medicine because it provided an understanding of the disease process. I became quite proficient in almost all aspects of the discipline, with a good command of the methods of analysis and histochemistry. My Hebrew was good, and I loved teaching medical students and lecturing.

After one year, I thought that it was time to move to a place of my own, and I found lodging with the Samet family in the center of Jerusalem, near the Zion Square. This was cozier, and I became friends with the Samet couple. They were very orthodox Jews and put only one formal condition on my having a room in their apartment: I was not allowed to bring in any non-kosher food. I did everything they requested to the letter because I respected other people's religion and customs. Yakov Samet had an impressive library of religious textbooks, and one day I asked him how long it would take to learn the Talmud. Looking straight into my eyes he replied, "A whole lifetime, a whole lifetime."

Professor Ungar asked me to join him in a study of experimental obstructive jaundice on rats. We were feeding them a toxic substance in oil, and the rats developed an inflammation of the bile ducts in the liver, which caused jaundice. We were able to examine the evolution and possible cure of this pathologic changes. I did all the work, starting with the care of the experimental animals, feeding the toxic substance, dissecting the livers, examining hundreds of slides of histologic preparations, writing up the results, and taking the microphotographs; after all that, I wrote up the results and new observations in a scientific paper. We published several scientific papers in leading American journals. The professor never thought of listing me as the senior (first) author, although I had done all the work. Later, a collaborator asked the professor why he had not listed my name as the senior author, and he corrected the situation. However, it was too late. By then I knew that under his pleasant façade as a senior cultured gentleman and man of science there was an egotistic and egocentric individual who could not conceive of the senior professional pride of raising new cadre of professionals. This explained very well why a good number of fine physicians had left the Institute of Pathology after several years of hard work.

We also had a major research project on atherosclerosis. We received a grant from the National Institute of Health (NIH) in the United States for the study of atherosclerosis and coronary heart disease. Israel was viewed by the NIH as a "natural laboratory of people," because Israel had people coming from all over the world, who lived on different diets. We studied genetic and ethnographic differences and the atherosclerotic lesions. For that project, I had to examine several hundred hearts and major vessels and code the lesions found. Not many publications came out from this very extensive and intensive research project. As I was always interested in clinical applications, I studied the radiological expression of the atherosclerotic aorta, and I published our observations in the *American Heart Journal*. We did not have CT scanners at that time, and radiologic examinations were the only indirect examinations providing insights on gross pathologic changes. The paper was very well received, but not by my boss.

♦

My social life was quite rich. Initially I was invited into the so-called "Romanian colony" by colleagues of Romanian background, but I did not like their interest in gossip. I made new friends. Armand Abramovici was a student in medical sciences who took care of our museum at the Institute of Pathology for a meager salary that the professor paid him. Armand was originally from Romania, well integrated in the Israeli life, a very jovial fellow. I usually worked late in my office, and I could hear Armand's steps in the corridor when he came to visit with me. He was full of good humor and recounted the day's gossip from the lives of the medical students. I explored all corners of Jerusalem with him. We had similar ideas about our sacred history and our pride in our national destiny. One day, we visited *Yad Vashem*, the Holocaust Memorial in Jerusalem containing the Holocaust History Museum. In an exhibit case we saw a leather jacket and some lamp shades: They were made from human skin of Jews killed in Auschwitz. At the request of the Rabbinate, these objects were removed shortly thereafter. As they were made of human skin, they were not allowed to be exhibited and had to be buried appropriately according to the Jewish religious laws.

The Navy called me the following year, in 1959, for the Officers Course. The course took forty days, the time we were obligated to give every year for military reserve duty. It was tough and fun. Our instructors wanted to show us the difficulties of being soldiers. We studied military theory and participated in exercises of all sorts. We had lots of interesting work, and we worked very hard. After my promotion from the officers' course, I created some advanced Navy plans, and I was promoted to the rank of Captain in the Navy.

◆

Our family became reunited when Jerome arrived in September 1959, almost one year after me. We were so happy! My brother had not gone through many difficulties in getting his exit permit. It so happened that the couple who lived in our apartment in Bucharest wanted to have our room. I've written that the man held a high position in the Communist Party, and his desire was an order. Jerome got his exit permit without moving a finger. Sheer luck. We were reunited in happiness. He learned Hebrew, served in the Army, and then found a position as a surgeon at a good hospital. He was a happy bachelor. I'll write more about him.

One day, I got a call from Dr. Marcel Iosefsohn, a very talented and knowledgeable surgeon. We knew each other from the medical school where he had been a lecturer. He had just arrived in Israel and had gotten a position at a clinic in Jerusalem. When he had difficult family problems, I spent each day with him, encouraging and supporting him. I knew from the Talmud that "not all days are gone in one day and not all years in one year," and I shared that with Marcel, who recovered well and became the same jovial person with whom I had been spending all my free time. He knew hundreds of jokes and became the center of the young society. Many evenings, he came to my lab and watched me studying and examining at the microscope. He was very convinced of my professional success.

◆

In 1960, after two years of work without vacation, I took a long trip using my two months of accumulated vacation time. A person could travel with an "open ticket" and check in at the airport whenever he desired to continue his trip. If there was no seat on a flight of the originator of the ticket, IATA convention provided that the passenger had to be accommodated on any available flight. I went to Spain and visited Barcelona, Madrid, Toledo, Seville, Cordoba, and Grenada. I did not know very much about the Spanish painters, and I learned about the mystique that surrounded their work. Then to Paris, London, Geneva, Chamonix, Zurich, Milan, Venice, Bologna, Rome, Pompeii, the Amalfi Coast, Capri-Anacapri, and Athens. I had learned history very well in school, and that knowledge helped me in my visits. I was able to experience the visual realization of much that I had learned.

On my return to Jerusalem, I was given a unique opportunity to visit the old Hebrew University-Hadassah Hospital on Mount Scopus. There were monthly exchanges of guards at this demilitarized enclave occupied by Israel. I was asked to go and inventory the Museum of Pathology, which contained rare specimens. After all the very complicated documents were completed, my colleagues and I met early in the morning at the Mandelbaum Gate, where United Nations personnel checked our papers. We had to go through Old Jerusalem in an armored military car without windows, under Jordanian guards. We were not allowed to talk in the car. The heat in the car was unbearable. Once into the Israel-held area, I felt alive again. The views from Mount Scopus were of an indescribable beauty. I felt transported into biblical times. For the first time in my life, I could see Old Jerusalem in much detail, with its quarters and gates. The hospital of the Hadassah Organization had been the most modern hospital in the area since 1939. It was closed after the War of Independence. Now, it was empty. Only the guards were living there. Visitors could stay a whole day on Mt. Scopus and return at 5:00 pm. I completed my task, and I came home loaded with an unforgettable experience.

Another escapade of great interest was when I climbed the Masada. There was no tourism in the area at that time. Yigal Yadin had his many volunteers helping him sort out the archeological remains. I volunteered to help during my vacation, and I climbed on the "snake path," as the difficult ascent on the eastern wall was called. I marveled at the findings on the plateau. To think that the artifacts found there had been used by our ancestors! There were many pottery and cooking objects, as well as personal items like sandals, belts, necklaces, and hair braids. I felt in my heart that "Masada shall never fall again." Those who don't know the history of the place and its people or don't understand the deep meaning of these few words do not understand the fine and intricate thread of the fabric of modern Israeli Jews.

◆

Back at the Institute, I got my certification in anatomic pathology, and I continued my research. In my seven years of service at the Hebrew University-Hadassah Medical School I published seventeen scholarly papers in American peer-reviewed journals. Most of the experimental work had a clinical impact. Case reports were not encouraged. The most popular weekly presentations were the clinical-pathological conferences (CPCs) held in our big auditorium.

All the academic staff attended these presentations and discussions. I focused my presentations on correlating pathologic findings with clinical events, at finding explanations for the changes in tissues and organs that occurred during disease, and aiming to explain the resulting clinical changes and the evolution of disease. This made my presentations very interesting to clinicians and valuable to our understanding of clinical events. I rose in the academic ranks to the equivalent of an assistant professor in the States and became a Staff Physician, which gave me the right to independently sign my pathology reports.

The School of Microbiology invited me to teach General Pathology and Henrietta Szold School of Nursing invited me to teach pathology to the student nurses. Colleagues and professors thought that I could become the future chair of the Institute of Pathology; however, I knew full well that in the local academic world, politics had more impact on the higher rank appointments than knowledge.

All these accolades were very nice, and they assured me of a permanent academic position, but I was a clinician at heart, and the need to see patients and to take care of living sick people prevailed in my sense of professional ideals. I became utterly preoccupied with my desire to practice clinical medicine, and I told this to Professor Ungar. He, however, was unable to understand me, although he'd had similar experiences with other young faculty members who'd left him. He displayed a certain degree of intellectual possessiveness. I thought of continuing at the Institute of Pathology if I could combine my knowledge of pathology with some activity in the diagnosis of clinical medicine. I thought of helping in the diagnosis of hematopathology problems, which is the study of the blood and of the blood-forming organs, which attracted me. Professor Ungar promised me that he would find a place for my sub-specialization in hematopathology and asked me to not make any arrangements by myself. I suggested to him to contact Dr. Henry Rappaport, who was a very well-known hematopathologist of international reputation. Professor Ungar went on a sabbatical to the United States and assured me that, he would find me a good place for one to two years of sub-specialization in hematopathology that I'll have upon his return,. I trusted him. Things developed differently, however, and he wrote me that "he could not find any place for me," which was untrue and shocking news. I understood then that I was left to take care of my own professional growth. My friends were outraged.

In 1963, I went on a long trip to European centers where I hoped to find a way to pursue my professional interests in further study and specialization in hematopathology. I went to Paris, Brussels, Amsterdam, Utrecht, London, and Milan. Although I was well received, I could not find an opening for my plan to go back to clinical medicine and specialize in hematopathology. Medical oncology was not even dreamed of as a medical subspecialty yet. I visited all the medical centers in Israel, and I had to accept that, for what I wanted to do, there was only one way: to go to the United States and specialize. But that meant that most probably I would not return because there was no place to practice and develop my career in Israel. I could not accept that. A couple of years of immense turmoil followed.

♦

I needed some downtime and moral uplifting. The only solace I experienced in 1963 was in my buying my first car, a Simca 1000, a small four-door sedan that had gotten the best reviews in its category at that time. It was a French Renault car with much Fiat input. I had saved money for about two years. However, every time I came close to having enough for the price of a new car, car prices jumped up to levels which were unattainable for me. The salaries of young physicians at Hadassah were modest, and buying a new car was a dream very difficult to realize. The car taxes in Israel were high and they increased each year; a person with my income could not buy a new car. With a small loan from my father, I got the car in April 1963, and I could finally start moving around. I knew the sites of the country from reading and teaching "Palestinography." Now, I could see for myself all that I had accumulated and stored in my mind, hundreds of saved images of our history and the beautiful landscape of our country. I traveled extensively with my good friend Marcel Iosefsohn. My father joined on some of our trips. This was an unforgettable time.

♦

I was accepted in the Freemasons Lodge *Haschahar* ("the dawn," in Hebrew) in Tel Aviv. I attended many interesting sessions. In 1964, in a very emotional meeting, I was raised to the rank of Master Mason. The night of my rise to Master Mason, I was asked to discuss the topic of "The significance of the letter G," a rather esoteric topic which I was able to discuss freely based on my general instruction on related topics. The Master Masons were genuinely pleased with my dissertation and asked me to write it down. Later in the year, my father wanted to join the Freemasons. This was quite a big event. He was known by some Master Masons as a member of a lodge in Bucharest during the time the Freemasonry was interdicted by King Carol II of Romania. King Carol wanted to become a Freemason, as some of his British royal cousins were. He was refused admission into this old fraternity. As a *de facto* dictator, he became furious and interdicted the Freemasonry in Romania. Father wanted to join the *Haschahar* Lodge, and I sponsored him. Usually this was done the other way around, the father sponsoring the son, but it did not matter. It was a beautiful event. I think that Father was a true Freemason because of his moral values, generosity, and altruism. He rose rapidly through the ranks and attained the thirty-second degree of the Scottish Rite.

◆

The decision to go or not go to America to learn hematopathology and, possibly, medical oncology, had been a most difficult one for me. It was indeed a complex decision. The experience I'd acquired as a pathologist made me think that there must be better medical care for cancer patients. From my observations, I came to think that we must observe more carefully and formulate our differential diagnoses based on very detailed evaluations of all clinical data with in-depth considerations of the known and allowances for the unknown to unravel. We needed to develop more empathy for our patients and take better medical histories. I did know what I wanted, but it was not yet available. Medical oncology as a subspecialty of internal medicine did not exist.

I did not have much information about medicine in the US or in Canada. All that I knew at the time was based on the stories colleagues and friends recounted upon their return from one- or two-year stays in the States, which were facilitated through arrangements made in advance by Hadassah. As a well-endowed American organization, Hadassah had clout in America, and it did not cost the hospitals to host visitors from Israel, who joined in hospital rounds, participated in seminars, and became involved in research projects with their American colleagues there if they so wanted. The residencies for specialization arranged through Hadassah were good for academic practice, but they did not open a new path for a person like me who was interested in changing my professional profile.

My plan was fraught with one overriding question: "What will I do if I fail?" In fact, my comfort zone at that point was anatomic pathology, and I did not have any assurance that my dream-plan of changing to clinical medicine would be successful. Deep in my mind and soul I knew that what I wanted was possible, but that it would be hard to achieve and probably would involve a long process. I should add that there were two totally different ways of approaching my professional goals. One, the simplest, was to be sent by the Hadassah Medical Organization to the US for one or two years and come back as a "fellow who had been in America." Hadassah would not have sent anybody to America without a plan for retaining that individual in Israel for future professional developments. Evidently, I did not get the support of my boss to be sponsored for such line of work. The other way was to go by myself and come back, an immense risk because it did not give me any assurance that I would be able to establish a medical practice in Israel based on what I'd learned in the US. Perhaps I could have been successful in such an enterprise, but I did not consider it viable at the time. Therefore, the more secure way of proceeding was the hard way, taking all the preparatory steps required from a young physician to get a license for the practice of medicine in America. That meant first to pass the ECFMG (Educational Commission for Foreign Medical Graduates) examination, then to take an internship and residency in medicine, and then a specialization through a fellowship. It would be a long and arduous route, but at its completion, I could either go back to my country or practice in America.

My first problem to surmount was getting an internship. The approved places for internship were assigned in the fall preceding the academic year. It was April 1965, and I did not get any reply to the many letters I wrote to hospitals in Canada and the US. I convinced myself to take the risk of going without a job offer, simply presenting myself. And so, I decided to leave my country with the goal of finding my way in the New World. My parents, my brother, and my intimate friends did not have any doubts about my success.

It was relatively easy to get an American tourist visa. For an immigration visa, however, there was a very long wait because for the purposes of immigration to the US, I belonged to the Romanian lot. I've always found the American immigration and nationalization rules quite strange. Suppose that one is taken out of one's country of birth as a baby and grows up in another country. That person is considered as a national of his/her country of birth.

This does not make any sense. I think it's more important to know where a person lived during his or her formative years. Many of the thorny issues we encounter in our immigration laws could be avoided. For a country formed through massive immigration, it is incomprehensible that the US's immigration laws have not been updated and made consistent with the avowed ideals and principles of the nation. The Canadian Consulate in Tel Aviv gave me an immigration visa without any problems.

Regarding life in the States, my readings about the US led me to believe that racism was an American reality with which I would not be comfortable. I'd suffered from intolerance and persecution all my life in Romania, and I had not forgotten their bitter taste. Therefore, I opted to go to Canada, thinking that it offered a quieter lifestyle and that its bilingual culture might suit me.

After a sabbatical spent on the internal medicine clinical service, I took a course in hematology at Hadassah, and it opened up a new perspective for me. Upon Professor Ungar's return from his sabbatical, I told him that I saw no possibility of accommodating my professional interests or ideals if I continued to work as a pathologist in his department. I talked with him very plainly and told him clearly that I had the right to pursue my professional goals. He was enraged.

Finally, my students told me that they (the *sabras*) would not hesitate to go away if they would face my professional challenges. This was the way the new generation of Israelis thought. My mother told me one day, "Life is too short to be spent in turmoil. It will be better for you to go to the New World. I know that whatever you will do, it will be very well done." This sealed my decision. I left for the New World on April 30, 1965. On the plane, an immense calm overcame my soul: I had just begun a new chapter in my life; I was on my way to my date with my destiny.

Part Two: Attaining My Aim

"Success is to be measured not so much by the position that one has reached in life as by the obstacles which one has to overcome while trying to succeed."

Booker T. Washington

And Now, to the New World

I left my home with the conviction that I was embarking on a very difficult professional path towards an ideal that would be attainable only through great effort. It was essential to do it right because my profession played a major role in my life, and what I did for a living was cardinal to my psychological and philosophical balance. I was moved by a passionate desire to be a clinician again. Perhaps my desire was so intense because my basic attraction to medicine was the significance of its clinical practice: interaction with sick people, whom I wanted to help. I felt that I had made the correct decision.

I was now on my way to realize my dream with all the trepidations that accompany major changes in life. I thought a lot about myself in my new place in the world, and I analyzed myself as critically and as objectively as possible. Who was I? What value did I present to society? With complete candor, I told myself that I had some value: I was a thirty-seven-year-old man who had regained dignity and self respect as a citizen of his own country, Israel. I was very proud of having served my military duty in the Israel Defense Forces, for which I had an immense respect and admiration. I was a captain in the Israeli Navy Reserve. I was honest and fair to people. I valued friendship and candid relationships. I was a bachelor because I had not wanted to engage any woman in the path of life I had chosen, which was fraught with material, moral, and spiritual difficulties. I was proud of my moral values. I wanted to help people unconditionally in any way I could. I was not religious. Religions have caused more death and war than salvation and succor. The most imposing and obvious conclusion was that only political and religious tolerance could bring respite and peace to humanity. I believed in mutual help. There were so many resources in the world that could be shared if properly and honestly exploited. My purpose in life was to serve others.

I was a physician who had acquired invaluable basic knowledge on the pathology of diseases, on the mechanism of the disease process, as well as on the process of healing. I had seen the gamut of human diseases, some with strange presentations and complications that were sometimes difficult to diagnose. I had a good grasp of diagnostic methodology and its role in the timeliness and cost of medical practice. I felt the humility of the profession; I realized the limitations in our knowledge of all that happens inside the intricate evolution from the balance of health to the disease state, the subtle changes in our cells, tissues, and organs that occur before the manifestation of a disease, when signs and symptoms may make themselves known to the attentive eye of a careful physician. I had seen many clinical presentations that had passed unnoticed by clinicians. I had learned that every sign of disease should be recorded, even if not fully explained, because it might contribute to the understanding of the clinical presentation. I was convinced that I could become a good clinician simply because I had solid experience in anatomic pathology. I thought, and I still do, that clinicians should spend one- or two-years studying pathology, which is the basis of medicine. It was necessary to take the right steps to achieve my goals.

◆

The first day in Manhattan, I was overwhelmed by a heat wave and high humidity, exactly like in Tel Aviv, with the difference that, in Israel, people walked around outside dressed very informally. In New York, I was advised to dress well, to wear a tie, and to appear "presentable." I walked a lot, trying to learn as much as possible about New York City, impressed by its gigantic dimensions, its skyscrapers, and its monuments. I did not like the brown houses, and I could never understand why people chose brown bricks for their buildings. I did not like the entries of apartment buildings up on a few steps, a typical old British style, and I assumed that that style had been adopted many years ago, when the British way of life was still dominant here. I did notice, however, that many new apartment buildings were built of white stone, and they appeared quite modern.

I learned the city plan quite fast because it was simple. I also learned the subway plan. I liked the Rockefeller Center, the Radio City Music Hall, the Empire State Building, Fifth Avenue, the Avenue of Americas, the Central Park, and downtown. The Statue of Liberty fascinated me, of course, as did Wall Street and Trinity Church. I was certainly quite vigorous, able to walk hundreds of blocks and defy my tiredness. I was poor, but it did not bother me.

One memorable experience was a visit to Harlem during one of my first few days in New York. I had read quite a bit about Harlem, but I didn't understand the situation of a white person walking through its streets. While walking through Harlem, I did sense that locals sitting on the steps of their entrances were looking at me with curiosity but not saying anything. Here was this young white man, relatively well-dressed, with a camera around his neck, walking through the streets and bidding them hello. In the evening, when I told friends about my outing in Harlem, they thought that I was out of my mind. Perhaps, but since I had left Romania, I had never feared people.

I had purchased a "99 days for 99 dollars" Greyhound ticket, and I went to Boston to see my friend Victor Loran, a learned microbiologist who was a professor of microbiology at Tufts University. He was happy to see me in the States, as he was among those who felt that my academic future was in America. He insisted on going with me to visit Professor Stanley Robbins, the editor of a well-known pathology textbook. Dr. Robbins had recently visited Jerusalem and lectured at Hadassah Hospital. At that time, I had been asked to present my experimental work on thyroid cancer, which I'd done with Professor A. Hochman, the director of the Radiation Therapy Institute of Hadassah. Dr. Robbins liked my presentation, and he showered me with compliments on the elegance of our study. He remembered me well when I visited him at the Mallory Institute of Pathology in Boston. He listened to my plans for a change in my career but insisted on advising me that my professional place was in pathology, the discipline in which I had been so productive.

My experience with Dr. Robbins prepared me for a visit with Dr. Hans Popper, the authority on the pathology of liver diseases, who chaired the Department of Pathology at the Mount Sinai Medical Center in New York City. Dr. Popper too had visited the Institute of Pathology at the Hebrew University-Hadassah Medical School and was very aware of our work on cholangitis and intrahepatic obstructive jaundice, which was frequently cited in the specialty literature of that time. In New York, Dr. Popper was charming, though he advised me that I was on the brink of committing myself to a great mistake by leaving pathology and said that he could not help me change my professional specialty. After that visit, I concluded that those who knew my work in pathology would not understand my desire for a new professional orientation because it was so unusual and so unconventional.

I had three letters of introduction written by professors on the faculty of the Hebrew University-Hadassah Medical School. These gentlemen had open minds regarding my professional wishes and plans. One of the letters was addressed to Dr. Sydney Farber at the Dana-Farber Cancer Institute in Boston. He was out of town. Another letter, from Prof. A. Hochman, was addressed to Prof. Henry Kaplan at Stanford University in Palo Alto. I wanted to go to California, but I realized that, travelling on my Greyhound ticket, I'd need a minimum of three days of travel, and I did not have money for airfare. The third letter was from Professor Nathan Saltz, professor and chair of one of the two departments of surgery at Hadassah, who recommended me in warm terms for training in internal medicine. In Jerusalem, he had listened to me and understood me well. He had assuaged any doubts that were lingering in my mind concerning the unknown, and particularly the unknown of a new life in America. He told me, quietly and emphatically, "Moran, you know what you want. Don't listen to those who tell you what to do. Listen to yourself and do it." His letter introduced me to Professor Alfred Gellhorn at Columbia University. Professor Gellhorn was one of the three full professors of medicine at Columbia at that time and chaired the Department of Medicine at Francis Delafield Hospital (FDH). "We are internists with an interest in cancer care," he said to me when I visited. Those were the words I'd hoped to hear, and it was the first place where I could see that what I wanted to do was also central to the interest of other academic physicians. He told me that he had started his career as a pharmacologist and had become interested in carcinogenesis and the study of new cancer drugs. There were only a few cancer drugs available at that time, and his service, funded by the city of New York, was known for its interest in cancer. Patients with cancer were referred there. The medical wards at the Presbyterian Hospital, the main teaching hospital of Columbia University, tried to avoid admitting cancer patients at that time because the hospital physicians were not interested in cancer medicine.

The staff at FDH included very good internists who were studying various aspects of cancer. Dr. Elliot Osserman was an authority on plasma cell dyscrasias. Dr. John Ultmann was interested in Hodgkin's disease and lymphomas. He thought that I was "crazy" leaving pathology because pathologists were making "a lot of money in US." Dr. George Hyman was known for his work on chronic lymphatic leukemia and blood banks.

I was told that the service was offering a two-year residency in internal medicine to individuals who already had some postgraduate experience in preclinical studies. They did not accept candidates who came straight from an internship. My study of anatomic pathology was very appropriate to their interests. Dr. Gellhorn offered me a two-year residency in internal medicine after I took an internship in an approved program and passed the ECFMG examination. This was the first glimmer of hope for me.

Memorial Day came, and friends suggested that we go together to Washington, D.C., for the long weekend. I was certainly curious about the Capital and eager to visit it. Using my Greyhound ticket, I made the trip to Washington. I was impressed by the European plan of the city and said: "The city plan of Washington looks like a European city." "It was planned by Pierre L'Enfant," responded the friends who later invited me to go together with them to listen to Adlai Stevenson reading from Abe Lincoln's writings on the lawn of the Mall. It was a memorable experience.

During my few days in Washington, I visited the White House, the chambers of the House of Representatives and of the Senate, the National Archives, the Lincoln and the Jefferson Memorials, the National Gallery of Art, the Smithsonian Institution and its attached museums, the FBI, and the Treasury. It helped me understand the history of the country and its ideals. The last day, I went to Mount Vernon to visit George Washington's house and to Alexandria, VA, to pay my respects at the Freemason Lodge where Washington had served as its Worshipful Master. I was thoroughly impressed by all that I saw.

◆

I arrived in Montreal on June 11, 1965. At Dorval airport I got the address of a guest house in Montreal. At the College of Physicians and Surgeons of the Province of Quebec, I was indoctrinated into the medical licensure in Canada. The medical licensure was under the jurisdiction of the provincial government, like in the States. In Quebec, foreign graduates had to serve a year of internship. The license was given only to Canadian citizens. Therefore, immigrants could get licensed to practice medicine only four years after immigrating into Canada during which time they could serve as residents in hospitals with modest compensation. Not a very nice welcome to Canada.

Without delay, I looked for an internship position at the Royal Victoria Hospital of McGill University, at the Hôtel Dieu of the Université de Montreal, at Notre Dame Hospital, and at the Montreal Jewish Hospital. There were none. However, I was well received, and I had the feeling that, although the directors of the residency programs thought that my intentions and plans were unusual, the problem was that it was much too late to find a position on the internship roster for the academic year 1965-1966. I visited with Professor Robert More, chair of the Department of Pathology at Queens University in Kingston, Ontario, who was very interested in the findings of our ethnographic research on atherosclerosis. He offered me a position as an assistant professor in his pathology department with a salary of twelve thousand dollars per annum. I got a similar offer from the Department of Pathology at Dalhousie University in Halifax, Nova Scotia. Friends told me that such salaries would have placed me in a comfortable position, but the jobs were not on the professional line I was interested in.

A new regulation of medical licensure came to my attention: The State of New Brunswick would give a license to practice medicine to foreign graduates if they worked in a department of pathology for at least two years. I encountered a new experience in learning how the business of medicine was done at that time. A pathologist in Fredericton, New Brunswick, to whom I had been recommended, invited me for a visit. He offered me a full-time position in his department, with a generous salary. My pathology reports would have to be countersigned by him. The fact that I was not allowed to write a prescription because I did not have a medical license did not interest him. To check on the legal aspect of his offer, I went to the Provincial Board in St. John, NB, and they confirmed to me that, indeed, after two years of pathology practice under the conditions offered to me, I would be eligible for an unrestricted license to practice medicine in the province of New Brunswick.

After my visit to the State Board, I went to see the "Reverse Falls," a known phenomenon of the ocean tides, which was quite interesting. Then, with time until my evening's train back to Montreal, and my interest in maritime stations, I took a walk in the harbor, which is one of the largest Canadian maritime stations on the Atlantic shore. At a certain moment, I felt that a man was following me. I knew the feeling of being followed in the street from my experiences in Romania. I found this to be quite strange, but it was obvious. At a certain moment, I lost my patience with this person walking on my footsteps; I turned around, and politely but firmly I said: "You have followed me for the last two hours. May I know why you do this?" The man, a bit surprised and embarrassed, as he did not expect my irritated stance, replied: "I am with the Royal Canadian Mounted Police-Security Branch. You do not look like one of us, and I am to report any unusual activity in the harbor." I identified myself. The man changed his facial expression and became relatively friendly upon seeing that he was on the wrong track. After some words of apology from him, we parted. After midnight, I was back in my room in Montreal.

During the long train voyage from Fredericton back to Montreal, I thought a lot about my experiences in Canada up until then, and I had to realize that my Canadian experiences had not opened a way towards what I wanted to do with my professional life. In fact, it appeared that, most likely, I would have to waste at least one year before I'd be able to get an internship and initiate my plan.

It happens to many of us that in moments of hopelessness, an unexpected ray of light occurs and shows us the way to follow. I had such an experience the next morning, when I got a call from Dr. L. Cohen, the medical director of the Montreal Jewish Hospital. He recalled my visit with him about two weeks earlier. He did not have any place for me, but he had just received a call from Dr. François Larramée, the medical director of the Hôtel Dieu: A young physician had gotten sick and could not take his internship position: "Would I still be interested in such position?" "Most certainly," I replied. Right away, I went to see Dr. Larramée, and I signed the papers to start my rotating internship the following month, on July 1st, 1965. It was more than I could have hoped for. Right at the time when I could not see what more I could do to attain my goals, an opening was offered to me: A ray of light!

In Montreal

I found a one-room studio in the King Arthur Apartments, a modern building on St. Urbain Blvd., right across the street from Hôtel Dieu. This was in the central-east part of Montreal, close to the area where immigrant people lived. At that time, most immigrants came from Portugal and Greece, and, accordingly, there were many interesting ethnic stores catering to their needs. The hospital had a long and distinguished tradition: It was the first hospital in North America and the first in Montreal, built in 1645. Burned down and rebuilt several times, it housed several pavilions and a total of about five hundred beds. It was the hospital of the Université de Montreal, the French language university. Since 1657, the nursing at the hospital had been performed by the *Réligieuses Hospitalières de Saint-Joseph* ("Religious Hospitallers of St. Joseph"), an order of nuns founded by Jerome Le Royer in 1636. Several major surgical operations had been performed for the first time at Hôtel Dieu. Members of the attending staff were experienced physicians and surgeons who were highly regarded in Montreal.

On July 1, 1965, I presented myself for service, and I received my instructions from the good nurses of the St. Joseph's Order, who were still administering the hospital. I had a monthly salary of two hundred and four dollars, and my rent was one hundred and thirty-five. One could not live on only sixty-nine dollars a month, but I had a personal reserve of about two thousand dollars in a bank account, which was the money from selling my car before leaving Israel.

In the first weeks, I could not understand much of what the clerks and nurses chattered about, as their pronunciation was different than classic French. I could understand the doctors well, even though they too had a different French accent. I learned that people without a higher education often spoke in a dialect called *joual* in Montreal. I also learned that the dialect was different from place to place in Quebec. Soon I heard that I was thought to be *un belge* (a Belgian) because my French was good. Colleagues immediately reassured me that this designation was in my favor because French people were not particularly well loved in French Canada. Country folks called them *les maudits français* (the damn French) because of their lack of support in the 1759 battle with the English, the loss of which resulted in Canada becoming an English dominion. French-speaking Quebecois had a major problem with this.

My first rotation was on surgery, and I was assigned to Dr. Jean Fauteux, a talented surgeon. My job consisted of taking the medical history of the newly admitted patients on his service, writing it in the medical record, following the patients in post-op, and attending to their medical needs while duly reporting everything to the boss (*le patron,* in French). Fortunately, I wrote French well, and this gave me a good name among the staff. The patients were either private or regular. Private patients were admitted to the elegant pavilion called Le Royer. They were accommodated as if they were in a five-star hotel; the interns were at their back and call in their flower-bedecked private rooms. Non-private patients were admitted to and cared for on the wards by the house staff (interns and residents) under the supervision of an attending physician.

On the private surgical services, interns were not allowed to make major decisions except in case of an emergency. During surgical operations, the interns held the retractors. The hours of holding the retractors were killing me. One day, toward the end of an operation, the surgeon told me: *Vous pouvez allez luncher* ("You could go to…")… I could not understand the last word, and I continued holding the retractors. He repeated his statement, I still did not understand what he was telling me, and the situation became a bit embarrassing. I think I appeared to be a bit obtuse until it became clear to the boss that I was not familiar with the practice of "Frenching" English words. In this way, I learned that in Montreal many English words were pronounced in a French way, and that he wanted to tell me that I could go and have my lunch. With time, I became more sophisticated in this usage of English words with a French polish. Besides work and trying to understand how things worked in this new environment, there was not very much in my life at that time. There was not much camaraderie among the interns. Some of them were from Quebec and many were from all four corners of the world.

◆

Soon after I started my internship, while I was still on my surgical rotation, I got a telephone call from home. My brother, Jerome, had problems in his work at a government hospital in Israel. As happens in many places, when a physician is talented, he might be taken advantage of. Jerome had had enough of the professional abuse perpetrated by a chronically absent chief. He worked hard all day without appropriate recognition. However, when I told him that my internship was tough, he could not believe it. He remarked, "If Edgar finds it tough, it must be terrible." After a few more telephone conversations, he decided that he must take his chances, that he wanted to make a change in his professional life. Thus, our poor parents were left alone again after nine years of happy family life in Israel. I recall this with much regret, but I also recall with admiration that our parents always encouraged us to follow our own paths in life. Jerome and I were very different personalities in many respects, in our lifestyles and philosophies. We had, however, a very strong family bond and a shared sense of humor that enlivened our daily life. We'd had our different opinions on practical matters, but we felt that we were brothers and were always helpful to each other.

Jerome was a very talented surgeon. His nickname in the hospital was "the bloodless surgeon." He had acquired excellent surgical technique while working at the Caritas Hospital in Bucharest, where he'd had very good mentors. He was endowed with a rarely seen perfect surgical technique. I found a position for Jerome as a resident in surgery at a community hospital in Montreal, and I exchanged my studio for a one-bedroom apartment in the same building. On October 1st, 1965, I waited for my brother at Dorval airport, and I smiled upon seeing that, again, he had it so easy while in similar situations I'd had to fight my way through. Jerome started his work at St. Jeanne d'Arc Hospital in Montreal the day after his arrival.

♦

One day, I got a phone call from Dr. Thomas C. Hall, Professor of Medicine at Harvard University and co-director of the Dana-Farber Cancer Institute in Boston. He said that he was replying to a letter written on my behalf to Dr. Sydney Farber, the director of the institute at that time. Dr. Farber was sick and had asked Dr. Hall to reply in his place. Dr. Hall said that he appreciated my background in anatomic pathology and suggested that I come for a visit to Boston so that he could discuss with me my best choices. I felt that he would be an excellent person to advise me on my path from pathology to clinical medicine and cancer. It was very difficult to get a day free from my surgical rotation, but I got it, and I flew to Boston.

I will never forget my meeting with Dr. Hall. He appeared to be impressed with my work as a pathologist and assured me that it would open many research opportunities in the future. He could understand my professional plans. He stated that there were only three other places in United States where cancer was studied and practiced extensively. They were: The Memorial Hospital and Sloan-Kettering Institute in New York, the M.D. Anderson Institute in Houston, Texas, and Stanford University in Palo Alto, California. He felt that for serious professional development in the States, I should take a two-year residency in internal medicine, followed by a fellowship in medical oncology. He offered me such a fellowship at the Dana-Farber Cancer Institute upon completion of residency training in internal medicine at Francis Delafield Hospital in New York. It was a confirmation that I was on the correct track for what I wanted to achieve at a time when medical oncology was not yet recognized as a medical subspecialty.

♦

After the three-month surgical rotation, I took my internal medicine rotation. This was my lucky time. I was placed on one of the wards with a resident, Dr. Gilles Dagenais. He was coming from a year spent in research at McGill University's Royal Victoria Hospital, and in all respects, he was different from the other medical residents. He was knowledgeable, well-spoken, and intelligent. He knew how to intelligently formulate and discuss his working diagnoses and how to proceed logically with his diagnostic workups. In our discussions, he gave me the impression that he appreciated my background in pathology and my general medical knowledge. It was fun working with Gilles. Above all, he was a good colleague, and I valued him as a man.

I felt that I was doing well in my daily work, and I think that my several months of experience on the medical service of Hadassah before leaving Jerusalem had helped me regain my clinical acumen. At Hôtel Dieu, the house staff took care of the non-private patients and worked under the supervision of an attending physician. On the attending rounds held almost daily, the patients were presented in detail to the attending on call, and many interesting discussions ensued. The chair of the department of medicine was Dr. Jacques Genest, an internist and researcher of great reputation for his work on arterial hypertension.

One day, Gilles came with cigars which he offered to his colleagues. I learned that this was an American custom when one has a new son. He had two new twin boys, François and Marc. Most unusual for my new colleagues, one day Gilles invited me for dinner to his house, and I met his wife, Roxane, a charming young lady. It was a very pleasant evening. We soon became friends, and I am happy that we have continued our friendship throughout the years.

There were scientific sessions in cardiology and cardiovascular research. Gilles had already decided that he would specialize in cardiology. He invited me to go with him to one of these scientific sessions. The discussion centered on the early changes in the heart muscle during coronary insufficiency and the effects of tissue anoxia (lack of oxygen). Before I'd left the department of pathology in Jerusalem, we'd been involved in new research on the activity of the enzyme alkaline phosphatase in the cells of the blood capillaries in the heart muscle. We demonstrated that this activity was lost in the very early stage of an acute lack of blood, as happens in an infarct. I got up, introduced myself, and recounted our experience. The audience was a bit perplexed, seeing me talk about such sophisticated stuff while I was in the uniform of an intern. I still remember their puzzled faces.

We had the right to one month of elective service. As I was very familiar with the cytology and histopathology of the blood and bone marrow, I asked for an elective in hematology. The service was rated as one of the best under the chairship of Dr. Léopold Long, a well-regarded senior hematologist. One of the other senior hematologists was Dr. Gilles Gosselin, a very experienced and astute hematologist, and a very pleasant human being. There was also a senior medical resident, Dr. Huguette Léger, who wanted to specialize in hematology. She was a third-year resident, very well regarded by her colleagues as well as by the attending staff. In addition, she was attractive, serious, and energetic. I'd already noticed her at our weekly noon conferences. She was quiet, and our colleagues held her in high esteem for her knowledge.

The attendings did not pay attention to the members of the house staff. Although we respectfully saluted them on the corridors, they barely noticed us. One day, I overheard a corridor conversation between attending physicians, Dr. Antoine Gattereau and Dr. Gilles Gosselin, about the newly described lymphoma known as Burkitt's lymphoma. I had quite a bit of experience with that type of cancer. While in Jerusalem and interested in hematopathology, I'd had the opportunity to serve as a consultant to the Makerere University School of Medicine of Uganda, which sent us many cases of this lymphoma for diagnosis. Everything was new about this disease at that time and the fact that it appeared to be transmitted by a mosquito indicated a possible viral transmission. I knew the literature published on the topic, and I dared to drop a word or two into the attendings' corridor conversation. As in my previous story, they were mighty surprised that an intern would know the literature on such an important topic of the day, and they asked me how I knew it. In simple terms, I told them. Without hesitation, Dr. Gosselin asked me whether I would give a lecture on this topic at the weekly noon conference of the Department of Medicine. This was certainly a great honor for me. He announced the lecture on big posters throughout the hospital. My problem was that I had to give the lecture in French, and although I could converse freely in French, I was not comfortable lecturing to an audience of French-speaking physicians. I asked Huguette to help me with the lecture, but she did not have time. I worked hard and gave a very successful lecture. From then on, the bosses knew me and responded to my bidding them "good morning."

I worked quite closely with Huguette on the hematology service, and I liked her very much. The more I talked with her, the more I liked her. I became enamored. When I told this to Jerome, he was very amused because it was so unusual; during my life, I had not often been love-stricken. I invited Huguette to the opera and to some concerts, and she told me that she was busy preparing her examination for the college certification in medicine. It was only normal for me to think that she might have another soulmate — or that I was not her type. As simple as that.

As part of our hematologic investigations, we had to do bone marrow examinations in some cases. Under good local anesthesia, a small area of the hip bone is anesthetized. Then, a needle is inserted in the hip bone cavity and few drops of bone marrow are extracted; this is smeared on glass slides, stained, and examined under the microscope. This type of microscopic examination is essential in the diagnosis of leukemia. However, if cancer invades the bone marrow, the bone tap may become "dry," which gives a very worrisome signal to the clinician; namely, it can be evidence that the bone marrow has been replaced by cancer. However, it is also possible that a "dry tap" results from a faulty technique. One day, I went with Huguette and a technician to examine a patient, and the bone tap was dry. I knew that my technique was good, and I was concerned only about the condition of the patient's bone marrow. To my surprise, when I returned to the lab, I was confronted by many unpleasantly questioning looks because either the technician or Huguette had told them that I hadn't been able to extract any bone marrow, insinuating that my technique was faulty. I was a bit surprised that word had spread so quickly and incorrectly. On further examination, it became evident that indeed the patient did have cancer that spread into the marrow, which explained the dry tap.

My next rotating assignment was obstetrics, which we took at Miséricorde Hospital. It was an old hospital in Old Montreal. Private patients were attended only by their private doctors. I was shocked when I learned that unmarried mothers were called *filles mères* ("girls-mothers"), and that they were attended by the house staff under the supervision of attendings and not by the attendings themselves. I recalled obstetrics from my experience in Tel Aviv, and I felt quite comfortable with our daily work. An attending was always available to advise us on the best management of a pregnancy and on the delivery of babies.

Next was my last internship rotation in pediatrics; it was at the big hospital, St. Justine. It was a renowned medical center for pediatrics, with about three hundred beds. We worked under the supervision of a chief resident and were instructed by Dr. Le Royer, a former colonel in the Canadian military, a dry, severe, and remote person. I learned something from him, but in general, the days passed very slowly. During my last night on call, after working non-stop in the emergency room, I told the student who worked with me that I wished to take a shower and shave and I'll return quickly. When I came back, the student showed me a ten-year-old boy with high fever who had been brought in by his father, a taxi driver. The boy's name was Zeev Carmely. The student could not take his medical history because neither the child nor his father could speak French; the student thought that they were Portuguese; however, I knew that the name was a typical Hebrew name. I approached the boy, and, in clear Hebrew, I asked him to open his mouth, which he did without hesitation, and I heard the gasping voice of his father saying in Hebrew over my shoulder: "All honor to you." He was surprised that a Canadian physician could speak Hebrew. This was the last event of my internship, and I went home with a good feeling.

Jerome and I bought a new Dodge Coronet, a four-door sedan which was a great addition to our otherwise Spartan life. We used money from our reserves. The following day, our parents arrived for a visit, and it is difficult to describe our joy. We had two weeks of a happy vacation; the four members of our small family reunited. I offered my parents the idea that we go and visit places in upstate New York, New York City, and Washington, D.C. Jerome could not join us. It was one of the most beautiful trips I'd ever taken. I showed them Ausable Chasm Canyon, the Adirondacks, the beautiful places around Hudson River, Hyde Park, Sterling Forest Garden, New York City, and finally, Washington, D.C. On the return trip to Montreal, we visited Vermont and crossed Lake Champlain. It was a memorable trip for the three of us. Then we returned to Montreal and waited for my US visa.

In New York City

I got my US visa, packed my belongings in my car trunk, and, on August 11, 1966, I left Montreal for the USA, where I would continue my training in internal medicine at Francis Delafield Hospital at Columbia University in New York City. I crossed the border at Champlain, New York. It was a very rainy day. I recall the massive sheets of water falling as I drove through upstate New York. I had never seen such a downpour, which caused all cars to stop on the freeway in the Adirondacks. The air was hot and humid. I got to New York quite late in the evening and started moving my belongings from the car to the apartment I had rented a month before.

It was late at night when I finished carrying up my books from my car, and I was soaked in sweat and wanted to rest a bit in the car. A man appeared from nowhere and wanted to break into my car. I was startled. Instinctively, I blew my horn loud and long. Much to my surprise, and with a pounding heart, I saw the man being frightened and ran away. This was an unfamiliar experience.

♦

The medical practice at Francis Delafield Hospital (FDH) was a totally different system compared with the one in Montreal. At FDH, we were effectively in charge of our patients. Each resident had about ten to twelve patients and was responsible for their diagnostic workups and treatments. We had daily rounds with an attending physician. Some attendings were nice; the younger attendings had well-deserved reputations for being a bit arrogant. I attributed this to their inexperience. The attendings went with us on the biweekly radiology rounds, which were very instructive. We loved Dr. Bachman, Chief of Radiology, a very knowledgeable diagnostic radiologist with whom I took one month of elective study and learned things that were not mentioned in the textbooks.

There were no CT or MRI scanners at that time, and clinical medicine, laboratory examinations, radiology, ultrasound, ECG, and the pulmonary functions laboratory were the principal tools for diagnosis. Clinical-pathological conferences (CPCs) were highly respected reviews and exercises in diagnosis and were attended by the entire staff — medical, surgical, and radiological. I recall one CPC early in my first year. It was on a case of systemic lupus erythematosus in a patient under my care. I didn't know how much I was expected to discuss of the case, and I presented my diagnostic work-up and clinical course with diagrams I had prepared for the conference. I was very thorough, and the attending staff let me talk. Dr. Gellhorn asked the chief resident to instruct me on my role, which was that of a presenting resident rather than of discussing the case. I took my lesson well. A similar thing happened to me while I was presenting cases to my attendings on rounds. They let me talk until I learned to be succinct and to the point. I had been accustomed to having the last word as a pathologist, but now I had a new role, that of a postgraduate student. All my new experience was captivating to me. I read a lot, and I listened carefully to my colleagues and to my attendings.

It was the early stage of a new medical revolution in cancer care. Many of our patients had cancer, but at least thirty percent of them had a variety of internal medical disorders. Dr. Alfred Gellhorn was the chairman of the Department of Medicine and director of the Institute of Cancer Research at the College of Physicians and Surgeons at Columbia University. He was beloved and respected for his excellent clinical acumen and his ability to sort out the salient features of a case presented to him to devise an effective plan of diagnostic work-up and treatment. The most important thing about Dr. Gellhorn was his original, unconventional thinking He inspired me and convinced me that all my efforts towards retraining in clinical medicine and medical oncology were well founded. In one of his lectures, and in an article published in the medical journal *Cancer Research* in 1963, he concluded by saying: "The fruits of our efforts in cancer research, when successful, will not be the prevention of death, but enrichment of life." His was the most positive thinking of the times.

I liked one attending physician, Dr. John Ultmann, a fine clinician who befriended me when I spent an elective month in his laboratory. As a teacher, he inspired me with his ability to summarize difficult problems in a tight, organized, and complete manner. He was a hematologist, and he had a good reputation for his study of Hodgkin's disease and lymphomas. In retrospect, I think that we knew very little about those diseases at that time.

Dr. Bernard Weinstein was a medical geneticist, a developing subspecialty. He was a pioneer in the field of the genetics of cancer, which is now in the avant-garde of cancer research. I wrote earlier, about Dr. Elliot Osserman, a well-known specialist on plasma cell dyscrasias. I did not work with him on the clinical service, but we admired his thinking. Dr. O. Heinemann was a fine internist and a much-appreciated attending physician. He oversaw the ECG and pulmonary functions laboratory. He was very knowledgeable, inquisitive, and logical. I did take a rotation in his lab. Dr. George Hyman was a senior hematologist, an expert in the field of blood banking and malignant hematologic diseases. Dr. Manuel Ochoa was one of the first dedicated medical oncologists. Intelligent, tough, not very friendly, he was a role model to many of us. Dr. Frederick Klipstein was an authority on folate metabolism and tropical sprue. Dr. Robert DeBellis was a hematologist and pioneer in the field of molecular biology of the red cells. Dr. Rivlin was a specialist in thyroid diseases. Dr. Franco Muggia was at the beginning of his career in medical oncology. He was a fine internist and very easy to work with. He became one of the best-known American medical oncologists.

There were also several research associates and research fellows. We had two chief residents, Dr. Frederic Flatow, a research fellow, and Dr. Flora Barlotta, a fourth-year resident in medicine. Both had a solid knowledge and experience in internal medicine, and I learned many practical things from them. I became good friends with Flora. I was indeed very lucky to have gotten a post that introduced me to the vast arena of medical research in the United States in the 1960s.

I learned clinical medicine with much devotion. All the residents actively participated in the clinical research of the department. This was carried out in the recently established Institute of Cancer Research, which was being built in a new wing of the FDH. Our research involvement was focused on the clinical pharmacology of investigational antineoplastic medications such as vincristine (Oncovin), vinblastine (Velban), and procarbazine (Matulane), as well as on the effects of new combination chemotherapy modalities on lymphoma, Hodgkin's disease, lung cancer, and on cancer chemotherapy in general. We worked very hard, developing charts and flow sheets, a simple sort of record-keeping which I learned to use as our first clinical investigational tool. We discussed our results and our personal observations among ourselves and with staff attendings. Our efforts were well recognized in the Annual Scientific Reports of the Institute of Cancer Research.

The Staff of the Department of Medicine, Francis Delafield Hospital, New York City, May 15, 1968. Front row, from left to right: Dr. Dan Benvenisti, senior resident in medicine; Dr. Fred Flatow, senior chief resident; Dr. Alfred Gellhorn, Professor of Medicine, Chair of the Department of Medicine and Director of the Cancer Institute; Dr. Flora Barlotta, chief resident; me. Second row: A student; Dr. Raphael Belanger, resident; Dr. David Kiang, resident; Dr. John Ultmann, attending; and Dr. Robert DeBellis, attending. Third row: Dr. Frederick Klipstein, attending; Dr. Franco Muggia, junior attending, a research fellow; Dr. George Hyman; a visitor; Dr. Bernard Weinstein; and a visitor.

I had some success in diagnosis, a fact which was very encouraging to me. I developed a sense for good medical care, and I gave my patients the best I knew. I believe that the most important thing for us at that time was the respect with which were treated as junior colleagues and the consideration we were given in support of the development of our professional futures. I had my first Thanksgiving dinner at Dr. Gellhorn's house. He and Ms. Gellhorn had a tradition of inviting all the residents and staff. It was a moving experience, learning about the beautiful Thanksgiving tradition, and we all enjoyed the evening.

The nurses at FDH were remote, even careless. I was perturbed by their insensitivity to the needs of our patients. The hospital belonged to the City of New York, and the nursing and ancillary personnel were city employees. There were some whose work ethic and attitudes did not bring honor to the place. We held afternoon clinics in which we assumed complete responsibility for the diagnosis and progress of our patients. We did have the opportunity to consult with attendings, but our workload required us to act independently and move fast and effectively.

I soon learned more about the work of Dr. Cushman Haagensen in the department of surgery, where he was the star. He impressed me with his minute evaluations of the operability of breast cancer. He would begin a breast cancer operation by searching to see if the case were clinically eligible for a curative radical mastectomy: He examined the internal mammary lymph nodes in the second and third intercostal spaces. Only if these were negative for cancer involvement did he proceed with the mastectomy. He frequently said: "The surgery of cancer must be the minute surgery of the satellite lymph nodes." This, probably, was one reason for his high cure rates. I learned from him the clinical application of our knowledge of the territorial distribution of lymph nodes potentially involved in breast cancer. I gradually developed the idea that the question to ask in breast cancer care — and in cancer care in general — should not only be why we might have had a therapeutic success, but more importantly, what were the causes of the failures of our diagnoses and treatments.

◆

In June 1967, The Six Day War started after a time of tensions in the Middle East. I saw on the hospital TV screen how Soviet destroyers were passing through the Bosporus and the Dardanelles straits for the first time in centuries. They were supposed to be helping the Syrians. The situation was critical. I went to the Israeli Consulate in New York and told them that I wanted to go back and serve in the armed forces, as I was in the reserves of the Israel Defense Force. They told me and other colleagues who had the same intention that our returning home was not necessary at that time.

The second year of my residency at FDH was very rewarding. By that time, I had acquired the independence that I was looking for as a clinician, and I became able to act very well by myself in my clinical work. I managed well interesting cases of cancer and benign internal medicine diseases. Life became enchanting for me.

We were a small group of young men on the house staff. Most of us took this training program as training in Internal Medicine. Four of us: David Kiang, Raphael Belanger, Dan Benvenisti, and I were determined to work on cancer. David was a good colleague and friend. I admired his fund of knowledge, superb organization, and effectiveness. He went to University of Minneapolis, dedicated himself to cancer research and made major contributions in breast cancer research, which established his scientific reputation. Raphael was my colleague during the internship in Montreal. He had a beautiful scientific career in Montreal where he conducted the Medical Oncology program at the Notre Dame hospital of the Universite de Montreal. Dan had been my student at the Hebrew University-Hadassah Medical School in Jerusalem. He was mighty surprised when he saw me as his colleague at FDH, but I think that he admired my determination in becoming a cancer specialist. I last saw them at Dr. Gellhorn party in our honor at his summer house in New Jersey. We got many compliments and nice presents. I received a silver tiepin with the name of Francis Delafield Hospital nicely engraved, which I have as a dear memento.

◆

In the fall of 1967, my friend Gilles Dagenais told me that Huguette Léger had become a fellow in medical genetics with Dr. Victor McKusick, the "father of medical genetics" at Johns Hopkins Hospital in Baltimore, MD. I went to visit her and continued to do so every time I had a free weekend. Many times, I stayed for the famous Grand Rounds in Medicine at Johns Hopkins on Saturday mornings. From my place on Haven Ave. in Uptown Manhattan to her place in Baltimore, it was a trip of two hundred and four miles one way, which did not appear to me to be too long, as I was in love. We had a very nice time of courtship and learning about each other.

Huguette was born in Bouctouche, NB, Canada, on the Northumberland Bay. Her father, Gerard C. Léger, was a family doctor in Moncton, NB. Huguette had received her college education at the Collège Notre Dame d'Acadie in Moncton, NB. Her family was Acadian, descendants of the French Canadians who had landed on the shores of eastern Canada in the seventeenth century and settled in Nova Scotia and New Brunswick. They fought the English until they were overwhelmed. I went to the Columbia University library and learned this sad chapter of history. I learned about the odious deportation of French Canadians by the British from their homelands in Nova Scotia and New Brunswick, how they were then dropped along the eastern American shores, akin to what the Soviets did with millions from the Baltic countries, Poland, and Romania, in World War II. I learned Longfellow's poem "Evangeline," a heart-breaking story. Huguette went to medical school at Laval University in Quebec. She graduated in 1955, interned in Toronto, and then decided to go to India with the Canadian University Service Overseas (CUSO). She served as a physician for one year in Orissa, one of the most impoverished regions of eastern India. Back to Canada, she took her residency in medicine at Hôtel Dieu de Montreal, where she was the star resident. I've written that I met her there when she was in her last year of internal medicine residency. She passed the examinations of the Royal College of Physicians and Surgeons of Canada, and Dr. Léopold Long, the chief of hematology at Hôtel Dieu, offered her a position on his staff if she would study medical genetics at Johns Hopkins. With her credentials in internal medicine, it was easy for her to obtain a position there.

Before Christmas, I met her parents, Annette and Gerard Léger, in Baltimore. They lived in Moncton, New Brunswick, in Canada, where her father had a good medical practice. She had a sister, Marie-Marthe, who lived with her family in Quebec City, and a younger brother, Jean-Marie, who lived with his family near Vancouver, B.C. I was very much inclined to think that her parents would be opposed to our union because of our different religious backgrounds. They were strict Catholics, but Huguette did not practice any religion. I recall that Annette liked me, whereas Gerard was a bit circumspect, though I had many interesting conversations with him, talking about Catholicism as part of the Judeo-Christian heritage and way of life. In the spring, we decided to get married. Jerome was delighted. I wrote to my parents about our plan, and they asked me in the typical way that Israelis ask about the status of other people who are supposedly immigrants: "Where are they from and when did they go to Canada?" I responded that Huguette's family had come from France in 1665. This was a witty reply that my parents liked very much.

◆

In spring of 1968, the American nation was shocked by the assassinations of Dr. Martin Luther King Jr. and Robert F. Kennedy, and the cities were burning. It was a terribly sad and tense situation. At the same time, the students became discontented on many campuses throughout the United States, and they staged a sit-in at Columbia University in New York, which disrupted the regular academic activities for quite a while. The year of 1968 brought to real life all that had been covered up for many years not only in the US, but also throughout the world. It was the year that shook the world. The war in Vietnam and the Tet Offensive prompted student rebellions in many US cities, and that spirit of rebellion spread worldwide, with students demanding long-due reforms and the modernization of university policies. There was the feminist movement, urban riots, Black militancy, and political assassinations.

♦

Huguette and I had to find work placements for the following academic year. Huguette got a position as a research fellow in medical genetics at Albert Einstein College of Medicine in the Bronx, New York. With Dr. Gellhorn's warm recommendation, I got a fellowship in hematology at Mount Sinai Medical Center in Manhattan. The chief, Dr. Louis Wasserman, was a hematologist highly regarded for his work on polycythemia rubra vera and chronic myeloproliferative disorders.

We decided to get married at the end of my medical residency. We looked for an apartment, and, after some searching, we found a very nice two-bedroom apartment in mid-Manhattan on Park Ave. It was in a modern building located on the northeast corner of Park Ave. and 96th Street. I could walk to Mount Sinai. Huguette had a very nice new Plymouth Barracuda, which she planned to use to get to the Bronx.

We had our civil ceremony at the Baltimore City Hall on June 11, 1968. Jerome came from Montreal to be my witness. We had only a few friends with us, and everything was perfect. Helen Herr, Huguette's best friend from Johns Hopkins, organized a little reception at her home, inviting a few colleagues.

Huguette's mother was not happy with our civil marriage and without a religious ceremony. She told Huguette that we would be living "in sin." We did not care about that, but Huguette did not wish to offend her parents.

However, a formal wedding in Moncton, the residence of her parents, would have presented some logistical problems for my parents. They surely wanted to attend our wedding, but, as we planned on leaving on our honeymoon right after the wedding, what would they do without knowing a soul in Canada? Jerome was there, but as a chief resident in surgery in Montreal, he could not have offered them much companionship.

After much thought and consultations, we decided to have the religious wedding desired by Huguette's parents in Paris, where each of us could have an appropriate travel plan. My parents had very good friends there with whom they could have a very nice time, and the Légers could also have a lot of fun in Paris. Without hesitation, I called the office of the Notre Dame Cathedral in Paris and asked whether we could get married in that august place. There were no problems if we had a marriage certificate, which we did possess. I then proceeded with hotel reservations and chose Hôtel d'Angleterre, which was recommended to me by friends in the hotel business. The small hotel, on the Left Bank in St. Germain-des-Prés, had a beautiful history. Everything was well planned and organized, but the student revolution and the barricades in Paris in the spring of 1968 made us rethink our plan, particularly when good friends called me to say that visiting Paris in June was not recommended. I had to cancel all the reservations and thought that Switzerland might offer a more peaceful location. I called the St. François de Sales church in Geneva, where they were only happy to accommodate our wedding on June 21, 1968. I then made reservations at the nearby Hôtel d'Allèves. To avoid leaving our families immediately after our wedding, we made reservations for a one-week tour of Switzerland for all of us, starting the day after the wedding. We were a party of seven: Huguette, me, her parents, my parents, and Jerome. After all the plans had been organized, we left for Geneva. My parents, Huguette's parents, and Jerome arrived in Geneva two days before the wedding. Huguette's sister could not come as she had very young children, and her brother and sister-in-law were expecting a second baby on the day of our wedding. The seven of us took a nice boat tour on Lake Léman in anticipation of the big event.

We had a modest ceremony in the church, which was bedecked with flowers that Huguette and I had brought that same morning. The priest, l'Abbé Jean Claude Murith, gave a nice simple sermon, and everybody was happy. Huguette's father invited the group to a superb dinner at the Restaurant des Eaux Vives in Geneva, a restaurant that is still very well regarded. At the restaurant, everybody wrote words of good wishes for us. Jerome wrote in French: *J'epère que c'est pas contagieux* ("I hope it is not contagious"), meaning the wedding. However, he got married one year later.

Wedding Day. St. François Church, Geneva. June 21, 1968

The next morning, we left on our tour of Switzerland with the Danzas travel agency. It was a seven-day tour on which we had much fun. My parents and Huguette's parents liked each other. Her parents also liked Jerome. We visited interesting places, first going north to Bern, Lucerne, Zurich, Zug, and Schwyz, then east to Einsiedeln, Vaduz (Liechtenstein), Chur, St. Moritz, then south to Lugano, Ticino Valley, St. Gothard Pass, the Rhone Glacier, Interlaken, Lausanne, and then back to Geneva. We got a good view of the Swiss way of life and of the beautiful country. We had much time to visit and be together. Everybody was happy.

Our tour guide was a very nice lady, Mathilde (Tilly) Herzog, a native Swiss-German young woman from Lucerne. She was very presentable, and during the tour I noticed that Jerome paid quite a bit of attention to her. On the day of our return to Geneva, Jerome went out dancing with Tilly on a boat on Lake Léman. They continued their idyll, and in December, Tilly went to

Moncton, where Jerome had taken a job at the local hospital. She wanted to see how the Canadian winter was, and she experienced plenty of cold weather. This did not affect her too badly, however, and they decided to get married in Quebec at the end of June 1969. So, it seemed that matrimonial events may indeed become "contagious" in some cases...

Our honeymoon was a superb voyage for a full month in a small rented car. My father gave us four thousand dollars for our honeymoon, and we used the money very wisely. We left Geneva the morning after our return from the tour. We drove through Evian-les-Bains, Sion, St. Nicolas, and Zermatt, and we entered Italy through Domodossola. We visited Stresa, Isola Bella and Isola Madre, and then Milan, Cremona, Mantova, Lago di Garda, Sirmione, Verona, Venice, Padova, Ferrara, Bologna, Florence, Fiesole, Sienna, Rome, and the Vatican. We climbed the Vesuvius, visited Pompei, and then Positano, Amalfi, Sorento, and we spent one week on Isola Ischia, a place which was very much in vogue. One day, we visited Capri and Anacapri. In every place we visited we had time to enjoy and love each other. After the last week of bliss, we returned to New York with only a few dollars in our pockets. I'd sold my Dodge Coronet, and we started our married life with two thousand dollars, the money I got for the car.

The very next day we went to our respective places of work. Huguette to her research fellowship in the Department of Genetics at Albert Einstein College of Medicine in Bronx, and I started my training in hematology at Mount Sinai Hospital and Medical School. Our social life in New York was quite pleasant. We had a few friends, and our apartment was nice and very well located.

Postgraduate Training in Hematology

On our return home from our splendid honeymoon, we had very little time to adjust to our new life. We enjoyed being in love, but we were also busy assuming our respective new responsibilities. At Mount Sinai Medical Center, we were nine fellows in hematology and three senior residents on elective rotations. The Department of Hematology was one of the best in the States for training in hematology at that time. It was a free-standing department rather than a section in the Department of Medicine, as was the case at most medical schools and hospitals. It accommodated many patients who had a diverse array of diseases. It was a referral center for hemophilia, an active participant in the Cooperative Acute Leukemia Group "B," and it was the center of the National Polycythemia Rubra Vera Study Group under the leadership of Dr. Louis R. Wasserman, the department chairman. In addition, Dr. Victor Herbert conducted original studies on vitamin B_{12} metabolism, and Drs. William Dameshek and Arnold Rubin worked on lymphocyte abnormalities and immunosuppression, which was a novel study. Coagulation disorders were also studied intensively. The amount of work was almost overwhelming for the fellows; we had to actively participate in all the studies.

Examining and interpreting the morphologic findings of blood and bone marrow was very easy for me because I had previous experience in hematopathology. I had learned the morphology of blood with excellent hematologists in Israel. I helped many of my colleagues with the interpretation of blood and bone marrow smears, which we examined under the microscope and on which we wrote our reports. All our work had to be checked by an attending with whom we had good discussions on our regular rounds. We were a group of mature young men and women, very united in our protests about not being well treated, but that was the chronic state of mind of the young doctors-in-training at that time. The working conditions and the salaries of physicians-in-training became a national issue that received much attention in the press. It was a few months after we started out that the salary structure of postgraduate doctors (interns, residents, and fellows) was corrected, thanks to the active fight of the American Medical Students' Association. We also received back pay, which made our daily lives a bit easier.

The most demanding service was the acute leukemia service conducted by Dr. Janet Cuttner. She was very experienced in the diagnosis and treatment of leukemias, and she was a much-appreciated principal investigator of Mount Sinai's participation in the Acute Leukemia Group "B." Energetic and insightful, she had a great deal of experience, and she was a very good teacher whom we loved. We had great respect for all our attendings.

We had weekly morning rounds with Dr. William Dameshek, who was one of the founders of American hematology. He was not nice to us; he picked on us and criticized our incorrect statements. We hesitated to speak up during our rounds with him. It was, however, fascinating to listen to him. He knew everything that was known in hematology at that time. He introduced new concepts and terms into the mindset and vocabulary of the specialty. One did not dare to contradict Dr. Dameshek or to state anything that was not well documented. We expressed our thoughts carefully, and that was very good for physicians-in-training. Our meetings with him were intellectually stimulating.

We also had to cover Dr. Dameshek's service. He had patients flown in from all over the world, particularly from South America, where Dr. Dameshek had the reputation of being "the best physician in the world." I recall admitting a patient with a variant of a collagen-vascular disease who came from Argentina. In my broken Spanish, I took a good medical history, and in the middle of the night, I wrote up a good discussion of the case with a plan for a diagnostic work-up. In the morning, Dr. Dameskek wanted to see me, and he congratulated me. A more difficult interaction with Dr. Dameshek occurred a few weeks later. One late afternoon, I had to admit one of his patients who had been diagnosed with aplastic anemia. The patient was scheduled for a splenectomy (surgical removal of the spleen) the next morning. Aplastic anemia is a disease in which most of the cellular elements of the bone marrow are wiped out. A splenectomy may be useful, considering the role of the spleen in destroying the cells still generated. I examined the patient that afternoon, a nice middle-aged gentleman, and I performed a bone marrow examination. Much to my surprise, I found many promyelocytes (progenitors of the white cells) in the bone marrow, but there were also more mature white cells, which made me exclude the diagnosis of leukemia. In this case, the findings could have represented a spontaneous regeneration of the bone marrow or, worse but not likely, the evolution of his bone marrow disease into a promyelocytic leukemia, a very grave disease. Clearly, there was no indication for a splenectomy at that time. What was I to do? I had learned that, in medicine, one must proceed based on facts and only on facts. I knew that Dr. Dameshek thought that way too. I had to call Dr. Dameshek and inform him about my findings. I consulted with his assistant, Dr. Arnold Rubin, who, surprised by my audacity, said: "You aren't thinking of calling Dr. Dameshek at this time of the day?" I had only one clear way to act, and that was to cancel the surgery, which I did. I wrote a very good note, thinking that if I was wrong, Dr. Dameshek might ask to reschedule the operation. The next morning everybody in the department was talking about my "foolish audacity." However, Dr. Dameshek agreed with my decision, and this made the rounds of the hospital. The patient's marrow was indeed recovering. I was asked to present the case at Grand Rounds in Hematology, which was attended by most hematologists in New York. I prepared my illustrations of the case and a good discussion, and I presented my findings and thoughts to the audience. Dr. Dameshek concluded with words that I still remember: "Thank you for saving this patient from what could have been a sordid situation." He was a scholar and a gentleman.

I believe that Dr. Wasserman and Dr. Cuttner did not like my asking questions that did not have ready answers when we discussed lymphomas. As a former pathologist who had encountered many undetected or clinically undetectable abnormal findings, I was concerned about the way in which clinical and radiographic assumptions were made based on the disease's involvement of the abdominal lymph nodes. They were based on the findings of bipedal lymphangiography, which I learned to perform. I realized that this diagnostic imaging study, although it opened new vistas, was not very reliable because of the structure of the lymph nodes as visualized by the injection of a radio-opaque dye. I knew that many non-neoplastic (benign) conditions might create radiographic images that resemble those of lymphomatous involvement. Consequently, in a scientific session with Drs. Cuttner and Wasserman, I had the courage to state quite firmly that lymphangiography was not a reliable diagnostic technique, that we might err in our interpretations, and that basing our treatments on its findings might have bad results. I recall that they chastised me, saying: "Would you then like to open the abdomen and check these lymph nodes?" I replied: "It's exactly what I think we should do if we want to develop a rational treatment of lymphomas and Hodgkin's disease, based on facts." "You are a fool," they said, and we left it at that. I knew that I should not pursue the conversation. One year later, the practice of staging laparotomy with an examination of abdominal lymph nodes became routine at Stanford, at the National Cancer Institute, and at the University of Chicago.

Huguette was quite happy at Albert Einstein in the Bronx. She worked on a research project with her boss that followed a different line than what she had done at Johns Hopkins. We had a few friends in New York during our year together in the Big Apple, and a few friends and visitors from Canada and from Israel. Otherwise, the intensity of the learning experience at Mount Sinai did not leave much time for social engagements, but we saw theater, opera, some concerts, and visited museums. Whenever possible we traveled outside town.

◆

The year 1968 saw major changes in American society. As I described in the previous chapter, the year started with student marches and demonstrations motivated by the Vietnam war and by racial and social inequities. My colleagues at Mount Sinai introduced me to American politics and controversies. I followed closely the pre-election campaign, although I was not yet allowed to vote. I got the permission to have a few days off for Christmas, and we traveled to Moncton, NB, to spend the holidays with Huguette's parents. The carols and the culinary festivities were new to me and enlivened my memories of the early years of my life.

The New Year 1969 brought us the news that Huguette was pregnant, and we were overjoyed. We were not sure where we would settle. Huguette could have continued for another year at Albert Einstein, and I could have taken another year in a senior fellowship in hematology at Mount Sinai. Medical oncology still did not exist as an established internal medicine subspecialty.

In February, Dr. John Ultmann came to New York to give a lecture. He had left Francis Delafield Hospital and taken the position of director of the new medical oncology program at the University of Chicago. He offered me a position as a senior fellow in the hematology section of the Department of Internal Medicine at the University of Chicago, with a junior academic rank as Instructor in Medicine at the Pritzker School of Medicine. My responsibilities were to help him develop the program in medical oncology, which was a vast enterprise. I told him that I wanted to develop an expertise in the field of neoplastic diseases of the blood and blood-forming organs, which I wanted to pursue later in my academic career. John proposed that I work on lymphocytes of lymphoma tissue and study their ability to transform when subjected to antigenic stimulation.

John also thought that Dr. Albert Dorfman, the chair of the Department of Pediatrics at the University of Chicago, would be interested in developing a program in medical genetics for which Huguette could assume the responsibility after the delivery of our baby. Huguette agreed to this plan. In February 1969, I was invited to Chicago for a visit and interviews. I met all the faculty in hematology, and I discussed the possibilities for laboratory research and clinical research development. I was offered a position as a Senior Fellow and Instructor in Medicine, which I accepted.

Much to my surprise, Dr. Wasserman offered me a junior staff position in his department at Mount Sinai. He did not like my intention of going to University of Chicago and tried to dissuade me from going to work with Dr. Ultmann. However, I could not revoke my promise to John.

◆

In June 1969, we went to Moncton, NB, where Jerome married Tilly Herzog. I've written about how they met, and they had developed a nice loving relationship. Huguette was in the last trimester of her pregnancy and stayed with her parents in Moncton until our place in Chicago got organized. Ruth Ultmann, John's wife, was very nice to us and rented for us a two-bedroom apartment in Hyde Park, quite close to the hospital.

Mother came to Moncton for Jerome's wedding. Father could not come. I happily attended Jerome's wedding, but stayed in Moncton only for the weekend and returned to New York to finish my fellowship and pack our belongings. After the movers loaded all our stuff, I left Manhattan by car on a two-day trip to Chicago on the evening of July 1st. It was a hot summer day, and traveling was quite unpleasant.

◆

I arrived in Chicago on July 3, 1969. Our new apartment was located on the ninth floor of a modern building called the University Apartments, which was in Hyde Park, then a quiet area in the south part of Chicago near the University of Chicago campus. The apartment was nice, with two bedrooms facing west, a very large living room facing south, and a dining room at its end. The movers came in time and I worked fast to prepare our place for the arrival of my little spouse. On July 6th, I waited for my little *chérie* ("darling") at O'Hare airport, and we started our life in Chicago. A few days later, Mother came from Moncton. She wanted to be with us for the birth of our first child.

◆

I knew that the University of Chicago, with its Pritzker School of Medicine, was one of the ten best universities in the States. The university had a fine reputation for the Nobel Prize laureates on its faculty and the large number of graduates who had gone on from the university to distinguished academic positions. There had been some problems with the student body; discontented students had entered the provost's office in the previous year, but by that time peace had been restored to the campus.

Regarding the discipline of hematology, I knew about the work of Leon Jacobson and of Janet Rowley on the chromosome translocations associated with clonal malignancy in what was at that time called "preleukemia." I also knew the work of Dr. Charles Higgins, director of the Ben May Laboratory for Cancer Research at the University of Chicago. In 1966, he received the Nobel Prize for his monumental work on the hormonal dependence of cancer cells and the effective treatment of hormone-dependent prostate cancer.

The campus of the university's hospitals and clinics was in the heart of Hyde Park, in the southern part of metropolitan Chicago. The main hospital, Albert Merritt Billings Hospital, was large, with beautiful rooms of one to four beds, and the clinics had ample waiting areas for patients and well-appointed examining rooms. The wing along Ellis Avenue was the Argonne Cancer Research Hospital, which was operated by the University of Chicago for the United States Atomic Energy Commission. The hematology section's offices and inpatient ward were in this wing. Most of the faculty lived in Hyde Park in old houses, some of them of the Chapman style, and they walked or rode bicycles to the hospital. There was an active community life, with lectures and local festivals that we liked very much.

All departments of the medical center were staffed by highly recognized academic physicians. One very unusual feature was that all the physicians were full-time faculty members, and they did not have any privilege of private practice. This meant that patients, staff, and students had access to the physicians at any time. I very much liked this system. I was impressed by the reputation of the academic staff, and I felt honored to be a junior faculty member. Still, there was no medical oncology service. In fact, there was not yet medical oncology anywhere in the United States. I was able and enthused to help Dr. Ultmann develop the program in medical oncology.

The fellowship program in hematology had a good reputation, but it was without expertise in any particular field of research. Fellows learned from experience, and all attendings were very much involved in the teaching program while also conducting their own experimental work (in which they might or might not involve the fellows). The Chief of Hematology was Dr. Stanley Yachnin, who was well regarded for his work on lymphocyte function. He was a fine hematologist, and a very fair and pleasant person. The section had a thirty-bed ward, with only few beds occupied. The outpatient clinics were well furnished, and I was surprised to see that on the clinic roster, under the name of each doctor, there was a note stating: "No more than five." The clinic clerks told me that this meant not to give more than five clinic appointments on any day to any doctor. I thought this was unusual.

I started my lab work with the help of a technician. We began an approved research study on the function of lymphoma cells. Were these cells responding to antigenic stimulants, as did normal lymphocytes? This was the essence of my research. I had to introduce myself to the patients and asked for their permission to have part of their removed tissues saved for my research. This was quite simple, because patients coming to the University of Chicago knew and respected the university's interest in research. I needed fresh and untouched small specimens of lymph nodes and spleen from which I would obtain the lymphatic cells. This was a bit difficult. First, I had to know the exact time a patient was scheduled for a lymph node or spleen removal in the operating room. Then I had to introduce myself to the surgeon and get permission to be present in the operating room to obtain a specimen from the removed organ/s in a sterile way before it was sent to surgical pathology. The pathologists were not always keen to let me take some tissue before sending the specimens. We dissociated the tissues to obtain cell suspension, and the cells were cultured with and without phytohemagglutinin (PHA), a substance (mitogen) that triggers the "activation" of the lymphocytes. I had to be available any time, twenty-hour hours a day, seven days a week. We worked hard, and we got some data.

◆

My personal life was blissful with Huguette, who was then at an advanced stage of her pregnancy. We saw Dr. Luis Cibils, Professor of Obstetrics and Gynecology at the University of Chicago's Lying-In Hospital. He was a highly regarded specialist who agreed to take care of Huguette's prenatal care and delivery. Things evolved normally, and on September 8, 1969, we knew that we had to go for Huguette's delivery. For a first pregnancy, all went well until the actual delivery, when she started showing signs of uterine fatigue. Dr. Cybils said, "Edgar, help her!" and showed me what to do. I put my right arm around the top of her abdomen and pressed on the fundus of her womb to help her during the uterine contractions. In no time, Daniel appeared, safe and in good shape. I was so moved that I did not look at his gender. I was simply so happy with him being born as a normal, active, and vitally crying baby, and that my dear wife was OK. We spoke French at home and had a family joke between ourselves, calling each other "little cat" (*chaton*, in French). When Huguette asked me "Qu'est ce qu'il est?" ("What is he?") I replied: *Un petit chaton* ("a little kitten"), a funny answer that remained in the annals of the family jokes. There was an uproar of laughter in the delivery room, breaking the tension that had permeated the place during the actual delivery. We were enchanted. Huguette was a bit tired, but she had always been a valiant and strong lady, and she recovered in no time after she had gotten a bit of rest in her room. It was only then that I left her and went to see my mother and share with her my happiness at the birth of our first baby. On my way to my little office, I met Dr. Yachnin, who, after congratulating me, felt that it was important for me to go to the personnel office and announce the arrival of my new family member because I was now entitled to an addition of five hundred dollars to my modest yearly salary. I thanked him and sped off. Mother spent the day with Nana, Ruth Ultmann's mother, a fine German-speaking lady. I was so excited that I was not able to speak coherently and was barely able to recount the event. I was so truly happy! One of the happiest days of my life!

We lived modestly at that time; we were happy with just loving each other. Huguette taught me a French saying: *Les gens heureux n'ont pas d'histoire.* ("Happy people don't have stories" (in the sense of problems).

♦

Soon after I started the lab work, I read a paper from the Yale University School of Medicine. The investigator did the same work we were doing and had published an abstract on their findings. I showed this to John, and he said that if we could not be original in our work, I should drop that line of research and find something new. This came as a bitter surprise to me because I'd come to Chicago to have a role model, and I felt being let down by him.

I thought deeply about what I could do. In the past, when I'd faced insurmountable problems, ideas that I'd kept in the back of my mind surfaced to life and altered my course. What was on my mind at that time had to do with the difference between the findings of our clinical and radiological examinations and those revealed by the pathologic examination. The evaluation and treatment of lymphomas were based on superficial and frequently incorrect diagnostic methods and were often made without any validation. In addition, all lymphomas were thought of as being one disease, despite their different histologic (microscopic) pictures, and I knew that they had quite different clinical presentations and course if carefully analyzed. Moreover, they had different patterns of progress and response or resistance to treatment.

The tissue diagnosis of lymphoma in patients was always correct because it was based on a biopsy which was then expertly interpreted. The stages of the disease and the disease's spread, however, were based on clinical and radiographic impressions, not on facts, and the clinical course of the disease was often poorly or not at all understood. I did not feel comfortable with the way the clinical diagnosis and staging of the disease were made, and it was the staging (the extent) of the disease that determined the type of treatment at the time. Lessons taken from autopsy studies taught me that clinical investigations cannot always be correct in assessing the spread of cancer. I had some disagreements with my teachers at Mount Sinai, but I had to refrain from expressing my opinions too vocally because that would be contrary to the accepted norms of behavior in a trainee. But I strongly felt that, as cancer is a pathologic diagnosis, it must be treated based on pathologic, rather than clinical, staging, because treatment was different for each of the stages of the disease at the time. There were quite a few aspects of the diseases that were not well studied or documented at that time and errors abounded.

I was given the permission to develop protocols for the diagnosis and treatment of lymphomas, of Hodgkin's disease, and of acute myeloid leukemia. In a few months, I wrote ten new research protocols that were approved by the Institutional Review Board. By examining tissues in the abdominal cavity, we attempted to validate the information obtained from clinical, radiological, and nuclear-medical diagnostic studies.

There was no unified concept on how to treat lymphoma and Hodgkin's disease. Regarding Hodgkin's disease, we had seen many patients at Francis Delafield Hospital in New York who had been treated with "postage stamp" radiation therapy, which consisted of treating only the site of apparent involvement, but the disease had then relapsed in areas adjacent to the treated "involved field." It meant that, as Dr. Elisheva Goldsmith, the chief of the Radiation Therapy Service at FDH, had emphasized, the disease needed the treatment of an extended field, larger than the group of lymph nodes that appeared to be involved, because the neoplastic process spreads from one area to an adjacent area, and that spread was not evident clinically or radiographically.

Acute leukemia was treated by an old method at the University of Chicago. I had an excellent experience at Mount Sinai in New York using cytosine arabinoside, a new investigational medication for acute myeloid leukemia. At University of Chicago, based on the protocols I wrote, I had my first success in treating a man with acute myeloid leukemia who obtained a complete remission. I believed at that time that the concept of the synchronization and recruitment of the leukemic cells into the actively dividing pool of cells was instrumental in the evolution of the disease. I made a good Grand Rounds presentation, which was the way to introduce a new concept into practice. We started to see leukemic patients referred to us, patients who had never been treated and those who had been treated unsuccessfully. Bone marrow transplantation was not yet introduced into the medical practice. Patients with lymphoma came from far away. Word spreads fast when there is something new on the therapeutic horizon. The staff was excited. The faculty started talking in positive terms about the management of lymphoproliferative diseases.

Without doubt, we had a great advantage in having Dr. Henry Rappaport's group with us, so that we could be certain about diagnoses. Henry was also the Chair of the National Institute of Health's Repository Center and of the Pathology Panel for Lymphoma Clinical Studies, which brought an enormous amount of interesting and difficult pathology material to the University of Chicago. He was indeed a highly talented, knowledgeable, and insightful pathologist, world-famous for his studies on lymphomas. I became friends with Henry, and we developed a long scientific collaboration.

With the Institutional Review Board's approval of our studies, hard work became the routine of my daily life. I had to see every patient who might be a candidate for our research protocol studies. It was only normal to explain to patients and their families the nature of their disease, what we thought about its extent, how much we might err, and that our success or failure in controlling the disease depended on our having the correct knowledge about its extent. Above all, I assured the patients, that I will be with them at each step of the diagnostic and treatment process. I think that our patients felt reassured by my promise.

We had a relatively large number of patients with mycosis fungoides, a rare cutaneous lymphoma, which has an initial indolent phase when it involves only the skin, and that phase can go on for many years. Eventually, however, the disease involves the internal organs, starting with the lymph nodes. Patients with mycosis fungoides were seen in the dermatology clinic. Many skin biopsies were taken, and sometimes the biopsies failed to show the correct findings for a diagnosis of mycosis fungoides. In fact, in many patients, the skin appearance was characteristic for the disease, while the biopsies failed to confirm the clinical impression. Dr. Allan Lorincz, an eminent dermatologist, was the chief of the dermatology service. We agreed to see the patients with suspicion of mycosis fungoides in a special clinic and to join with pathologists and radiation therapists in a cooperative effort. Our clinic acquired a fine reputation, and we became a referral center for the disease. There were differences of opinion among us because, for many years, dermatologists did not recognize the malignant nature of the disease and the possibility of its involvement of internal organs; they thought that mycosis fungoides was a disease limited to the skin. Consequently, the dermatologists used lotions and sometimes superficial electron beam radiation to treat it. However, pathologists and medical oncologists identified the need for systemic treatment at a certain stage of the disease, and, in some cases, there were serious disputes among us. We developed protocols for the treatment of each stage of the disease.

In January 1970, after I passed the Federation Licensing Examination (FLEX) for my licensure, I started my service as a junior attending physician on the hematology ward. The clinical team included a fellow in hematology, residents in medicine, interns, and medical students. It was a pleasure and a challenge working with them. I knew well most of our patients because they were included in our research protocols. I tried to serve as a role model to our younger colleagues, interns, and residents. I was committed to passing on to younger physicians whatever experience and knowledge I had, and I believed that those who were genuinely intent on learning knew to use this to their advantage. All that we learn and know must be shared with others, otherwise it does not have true value.

I was asked to teach Physical Diagnosis to the third-year medical students, and I loved it. I'd had excellent teachers in medical school, and their teaching had helped me greatly. I always felt that one cannot learn the art and science of history-taking and physical diagnosis only from books. One needs a good teacher, preferably a role model. The problem in most medical schools is that talented, knowledgeable teachers are not rewarded academically. I did not see any academic promotion based on excellent teaching. It was grants and publications that resulted in promotions. But it was almost magical to see third-year medical students, those who had been initially uncomfortable about facing a patient — not knowing how to start a medical interview, not knowing how to proceed with the physical examination — become relaxed, poised, and confident, even good teachers at their turn.

◆

In the summer of 1970, Daniel had become a very nice little boy. We travelled with him, and people made many nice comments about him. We decided to take a long car trip from Chicago to Quebec and then to Shediac, in New Brunswick, over two thousand miles. My parents came for a visit from Israel, and we met them in Quebec City, where my brother Jerome and his wife were living. My father had not seen his first grandson yet, and I will never forget the moment of presenting Daniel to him at the entrance of Jerome's apartment. It was highly emotional. We spent the summer with my parents and Huguette's parents, who had a nice summer house in Shediac, on the cliff above Northumberland Bay. We had a very pleasant vacation, and Jerome and Tilly were able to spend some time with us.

◆

At the beginning of the new academic year (1970-1971), I was asked to lecture to the students on infectious mononucleosis and on acute leukemia in adults. The students said that they liked my lectures, and this made a good beginning for me as a lecturer at the University of Chicago. Soon I was asked to lecture on leukemia and lymphoma at South Chicago Hospital, a large community hospital. I developed a good friendship with the hospital's director, Dr. Bernard Lieb, and we agreed to establish a full course on medical oncology, starting with some basic lectures on cancer and environmental carcinogenesis and then reviewing all major clinical topics in medical oncology. In addition, the Cook County Hospital in Chicago asked me to lecture on hematology and on the topic of "Cancer for Physicians," a well-attended course which prepared the doctors for the American Board of Internal Medicine examination. The course received many favorable comments, and I gave it yearly. All these lectures were given without any honorarium.

Christmas 1970 was very nice. Huguette's parents came to visit. Daniel started walking, and he was very amusing with his looks and gestures that charmed all of us.

At the University of Chicago

In early 1971, I received a letter from the university provost informing me that I had been appointed Assistant Professor of Medicine. I was not familiar with the system of appointments and promotions at the University of Chicago, as each university has its own criteria, philosophy, and preferences. Dr. Alvin Tarlov, Professor and Chairman of the Department of Medicine was the first to explain me how the University of Chicago's academic appointments were made. He was encouraging in his review of my work, referring to the impact of the clinical programs I had initiated, and my teaching. I appreciated his candor. He said that it was for me to show how much I would be able to publish. Alvin Tarlov was supportive, and every year he sent me a little handwritten letter acknowledging my contributions and increasing my annual salary.

In November 1971, students on my service talked with me about the Chicago Housing Authority's Robert R. Taylor Homes, an apartment complex, mainly populated by low-income African Americans, on 4700 S. State Street in Chicago, where there was a medical clinic without a physician. The students were interested in doing volunteer work there and asked me to supervise and teach them in evening clinics three times a week. I talked with Huguette, and we thought that I could help. I went there, and I was shocked to see the degree of neglect and the lack of elementary medical services. Adults and children came to the clinic after 6:00 pm. They paid one dollar to be seen by a nurse. Nurses administered the clinic. There was only basic elementary equipment available. No medication was provided. The patients had to buy their medications at a discount pharmacy. If hospitalization was necessary, we sent the patients to Michael Reese Hospital, which was not too far away and very responsive. I had never seen so many women with pelvic inflammatory disease, often in an advanced stage. Children with upper respiratory and ear infections came in on every clinic day, and it was difficult to take good care of them. Their home situations were not conducive to good nutritional and health care. There were men and women with chronically infected wounds, chronic skin ulcers frequently infected and draining pus, bone fractures that had not healed properly, elderly smokers with chronic obstructive lung disease, and many alcoholics. It was a huge real-life Charles Dickens story. I came home late at night thoroughly disheartened. So much human misery! It was a great lesson in social injustice. The only good thing was that we could provide some health care to the local people, and my students had the opportunity to learn extraordinary lessons, particularly in diagnosis. Our work was appreciated by those who needed our care. Soon after we started our work, the ladies in charge of the clinic appointed me Medical Director of the Robert Taylor Homes Clinic (without salary, of course). The university heard about my work there and asked whether I was being remunerated. As this was not the case, the university made sure that I was not seen as doing the work as an employee of the University and declined any responsibility. From a purely legal point of view, this was normal, logical, and well understood. I served the Robert Taylor Homes Clinic for four years, until 1975.

◆

On December 21, 1971, André, our second son, was born. He was delivered without difficulties, a charming baby. Daniel received André with love. We had two little cribs in our study and moved our desks into our bedroom. It was great fun having our boys. Huguette took such intuitively good care of their physical needs and development. At that time, I was working at the hospital many hours a day and was unable to hear the baby cry during the night. I recalled an old Jewish saying: "God could not be everywhere, and therefore He created mothers."

Huguette decided to stay home for another year to take care of the boys. Dr. Albert Dorfman, the Chairman of Pediatrics at the University of Chicago agreed to hold the job for her with the plan of developing a cytogenetics laboratory when she could start working. She joined his department in 1972 and established a fine cytogenetics laboratory where she studied the karyotypes of patients seen in Dr. Dorfman's mental retardation program. She also attended the Mental Development Clinic. Our social life was pleasant as we developed new friendships with colleagues, fellows, house staff, and students, mostly in Hyde Park. At Christmastime, Huguette's parents came from Moncton to spend time with us. It was a great holiday, our two little boys amusing the family. Daniel had started to "discover life," and André (Andy for us at that time) was a fine baby.

◆

We had many patients with sickle cell disease, and I had acquired some reputation for having saved the life of a thirty-four-year-old African American woman who had been admitted on my service in sickle cell crisis. She was in terrible pain and thirty-four weeks pregnant. We had controlled her pain when, on a Sunday morning, she started having contractions and appeared to be in a state of imminent delivery. I was making my rounds when our nurses called me to her bed. I asked for the obstetrics fellow on call, but time was of the essence, and I helped deliver her baby in good condition. The event stirred some echo throughout the hospital. I had some experience with sickle cell disease, having taken care of many patients at both Francis Delafield and Harlem Hospital, as well as at Mount Sinai in New York, and I had become interested in this terrible genetic blood disease.

In mid-1972, Dr. Frederick Zuspan, the Joseph Bolivar DeLee Chairman of the Department of Obstetrics and Gynecology at the Chicago Lying-In Hospital of the University of Chicago, asked me to mentor his fellow, Dr. E. Fiakpui, on a study on sickle cell disease and pregnancy. We worked hard, reviewing the world literature and local experiences, and we wrote a paper: "Pregnancy in Sickle Hemoglobinopathies." Dr. Zuspan and the staff liked it very much, and it was published in the *Journal of Reproductive Medicine* in 1973. The importance of this paper was our documentation of a high rate of intrauterine growth retardation (or "small for date" babies) in gravidas with sickle cell disease or sickle cell-thalassemia, most likely because of the general state of hypoxemia (low blood oxygen) and placental infarctions. My take from our work was that, logically, we should give transfusions of normal blood to pregnant women with these genetic blood abnormalities to lower the amount of red blood cells with the sickle cell and keep their blood with normal levels of oxygen-carrying capacity. It also appeared to me that a most radical therapeutic attitude would be to improve the bone marrow, where the red blood cells are formed. That meant giving a bone marrow transplantation to pregnant women with sickle cell disease, but this was too early yet in the research phase to become an accepted practice.

Of both historical and medical interest is that soon thereafter, in 1972, Dr. James Bowman, director of the blood bank and of the Comprehensive Sickle Cell Center, initiated a major proposal for the funding of the Sickle Cell Center at the University of Chicago, and he asked me to contribute a hematology study on "Sickle Cell Disease in Pregnancy." Based on what I had learned and experienced, I introduced in my part of the proposal the introduction of blood transfusions as a method to maintain a normal hemoglobin level in the blood during pregnancy. The site reviewers asked me if I thought that that would be effective. I stated that the real effective treatment — and possible cure — of the disease was bone marrow transplantation, which could repopulate the bone marrow with red blood cells with normal hemoglobin. The reviewers appeared shocked by my ideas and audacity. They asked me if I realized the cost of such a program, and I replied that I was surely cognizant of the financial implications of my ideas, but human life could not be judged in terms of money. Later, I heard that, unofficially, one of the reviewers made some not-very-nice comments on my thoughts, and the University of Chicago Sickle Cell Center was not approved for NIH funding. However, now, after many years, the approach to the disease, alongside supportive treatments, and chemotherapy, has come to include stem cell transplantation, which is considered a cure in many medical centers in the United States. Many colleagues have said that I was ahead of the times.

I've narrated these three episodes in my work on sickle cell disease because I think that they show an interesting connection. One: I helped a woman deliver her baby while in sickle cell crisis. Two: I participated in a study and help write a paper in which I was able to identify the problems of the babies of sickle cell mothers; as a result I learned what might help other pregnant woman with sickle cell disease. Three: In 1972, the NIH reviewers of the University of Chicago's application for a funded Sickle Cell Center did not think that I could be correct. And yet: the modern treatment of sickle cell disease includes what I recommended at that time.

♦

I became a citizen of the United States in spring of 1972. Soon thereafter, I received a letter from the Citizenship Council of Metropolitan Chicago asking me for details about my life and my work. Then I was informed that I had been chosen from among fifteen thousand new citizens to be awarded the distinction of "Outstanding New Citizen of the Year." I was awarded a citation as "An outstanding new citizen of the year, having demonstrated an appreciation of American Citizenship, provided a contribution to the advancement of knowledge, and given good service to the community." It was a very pleasant surprise. The citations were to be given at a ceremony in downtown Chicago on Citizenship Day, September 18, 1972, during Constitution Week. Much to our surprise, Ms. Patricia Nixon, the First Lady of the United Sates, came to honor the new outstanding citizens, and she gave us the citation. My wife and my parents were very proud when they received the picture below.

"Outstanding New Citizen of the year." Honored by Ms. Patricia Nixon. Citizenship Day, Constitution Week, September 18, 1972.

My clinical work intensified by the day. Whether I was the attending physician on service or not, I had to see in detail every patient admitted on our research protocols, and this was extremely time consuming. I personally had to review, collect, and enter all the voluminous data. I was in charge of the inpatient service three to four months a year. I was also the consultant on medical oncology eleven months a year. (John Ultmann could not do more than one month of consulting service per year because he was immensely occupied with hospital politics.) It was known that I was the person to call in consultation for the management of a new cancer patient. I took good care in writing my consultations, giving appropriate references and objective opinions on the best possible evaluations and treatments. Despite the prevailing views on cancer treatment at that time, which were not encouraging, my consultations were very well received. I heard faculty saying that they liked the honesty of my formulations.

My daily work entailed much direct contact with our patients, new or in follow-up. I felt for them; I was elated when we obtained a remission of a patient's disease, or even an improvement in a symptom. I died a little with every patient we lost. An adage from the Talmud came often to my mind: "One who saves a soul is deemed to have saved the entire world." I was working at least twelve hours a day, and when I came home in the evening, I played a little with my boys if they were awake, and then I worked at my desk, entering data on large flowsheets. Many nights I had to work all night to complete my daily research tasks.

In 1972, Dr. Leon Jacobson, the beloved Dean of the Pritzker School of Medicine, asked me to be the principal investigator of the University Breast Cancer Program. The University and the Medical School intended to apply to the National Cancer Institute (NCI) for recognition as a comprehensive cancer center under the leadership of John Ultmann. The NCI had let it be known that, without a breast cancer program in place, there was no chance of being recognized as a cancer center. I wondered, "Why me?" and "Why should I be the leader of such a vast program?" I had a great interest in breast cancer, I had given a very good lecture reviewing state-of-the-art breast cancer research that possibly made the faculty think that I was knowledgeable on the topic, but to lead such a huge program was not what I'd expected.

I was interested in the subject of breast cancer because of the newly discovered hormonal receptors in breast cancer which were at that time a topic of potentially vast importance. I could see their applications not only for the future treatment of breast cancer, but also for their importance in our understanding of the biology of cellular receptors in general. I accepted the position of co-investigator with Dr. Elwood Jensen, a professor of biophysics and theoretical biology and the director of the Ben May Laboratory for Cancer Research, who had discovered the estrogen receptors and demonstrated their importance in breast cancer.

We started developing the program under high pressure because of time limitations. I thought that we had an opportunity to develop a multidisciplinary study of breast cancer ranging from its tissue biology to its treatment, applying the novel knowledge on hormonal receptors. I thought that we had a unique chance to scientifically approach this most important aspects of the disease. The emphasis was on the correlative clinical and laboratory findings with the hormonal receptors in the tumor tissue. I did not like the surgical approach, which was very old and unimaginative, but there were political pressures. My choice was either to abandon the program or to accept the pressure of the surgical staff to keep the program viable. John insisted that I keep leading the program. I was motivated by my desire to see the University's Cancer Center successfully approved by the NCI and the hope that I could learn more about what preoccupied me intensively in treating any cancer: What were the reasons for our treatment failures in some patients when the same treatment was effective for other patients? We developed ten projects in the Breast Cancer Program. It took a lot of time and persuasive effort to bring investigators onto the same page. I found out that many of my coworkers had never written a research project, and I had to write theirs. Furthermore, I also had to prepare their budgets, and I learned from administrators how this was done. I think I learned it well, and the program looked well put together; all the scientific and administrative features were written well, and most of them were quite interesting. I presented the program to the NCI reviewers. They said that they were impressed by the design of our studies and by my passion. The following year, the University of Chicago's Comprehensive Cancer Center was approved by the National Cancer Institute, and we started working on our projects. There was great excitement among the faculty, trainees, and students. The nursing staff and the technologists were all equally proud of our new center of excellence.

We soon started to see many patients, referred by their doctors or self-referred to our program. At the beginning, they were mostly women with advanced breast cancer who had suffered mutilating mastectomies. Our body image is an eternally central feature of our senses of self-worth, and doctors should understand and respect it. It was heartbreaking to see these women, and I admired their courage. I had to muster my equanimity and faith, but I do remember that I often came home disheartened. Yet, I was able to encourage my patients and treat them compassionately. As it was, we could not study the hormonal profile and receptors in each patient. The correlation with the hormonal receptors was possible only in the minority of them.

◆

We communicated the first results of our research on lymphomas at the annual meeting of the American College of Physicians in Chicago in April

1973. Based on the findings of staged laparotomies, I was able to demonstrate the gross inaccuracy of the tests commonly used to diagnose the extent (staging) of lymphoma. Nobody had ever approached the issue in our particularly systematic and well-organized way. Our findings challenged the sensitivity and the specificity of clinical examinations, as well as of radiographic and nuclear imaging, and they confirmed the correctness of the concept that had led me to initiate these studies — that is, the unreliability of the available diagnostic techniques. It was the first public presentation of my research findings, and I was overwhelmed by the enthused response of the audience.

◆

Dr. Hava Neumann, a researcher from the Weizmann Institute of Science in Rechovot, Israel, was a visiting professor in the Gastroenterology Section. She proposed to investigate an abnormal alkaline phosphatase activity in the serum of patients with lymphoproliferative diseases (the growth of lymphatic tissue). I surmised that the activity of this enzyme might be related to the proliferation of lymphatic tissue, and if we could document that, it might serve as a valuable marker of the disease. Hava was the guest of Dr. Irwin Rosenberg, Chief of the Gastroenterology Section, and known investigator of folate absorption and metabolism. He and Hava asked me to actively participate in their research. I proposed to investigate the enzyme activity in patients with infectious mononucleosis, a very active but self-limited benign lymphoproliferative process, and in patients with chronic indolent lymphoproliferative diseases such as chronic lymphatic leukemia, as well as in those with various lymphomas. Our results were stunning, showing a sharp rise in the enzyme activity in the serum of patients with infectious mononucleosis, which declined and disappeared with the resolution of the disease, but did not decline in the cases of malignant disorders. We published the paper in the journal *Science* in 1974. It stirred a remarkable national and international interest.

◆

I was invited to teach on the "Diagnostic Staging of Lymphomas" and the "Chemotherapy of Hodgkin's disease and Lymphomas" at the International School on Medical Oncology held at the National Cancer Institute in Milan, Italy, in 1973. I was a member of the American delegation of teachers led by

Dr. Henry Kaplan of the Stanford University School of Medicine. I think that my membership in the delegation contributed to my being seen as an authority in lymphomas.

♦

We were approached to buy a four-bedroom house in Hyde Park, near the University of Chicago campus. We did not have the necessary funds. I had calculated that, because mortgage interest payments were tax deductible, the real monthly cost of a mortgage would be less expensive than our rent, which was quite substantial. The problem was that we did not have any savings. I sought counsel about my professional future from my department chair, Dr. Alvin Tarlov. He assured me that I was viewed as a valuable member of the department and that he saw me as having a professional future in the Department of Medicine at the University of Chicago. That same year, he had raised my salary substantially in recognition of my scientific contributions. He promised to ask a bank with which the University had ties to give us a loan for the earnest money; we were also approved for a low-interest mortgage. And so, we became the owners of a very nice four-bedroom house. We were very happy, and our move was very smooth. We even had a room for a study. The children were thrilled. They now had their own rooms and a big family room with a TV set, which they watched with fascination. I very much enjoyed watching *Mr. Rogers Neighborhood* and *Sesame Street* with our boys, and we had plenty of room to play with the train that I gave them at Christmas.

♦

Later in the year, Henry Rappaport asked me to review the clinical features of some cases diagnosed as having lymphoma on which he had noted some unusual pathologic findings: The patients were elderly, had severe acute constitutional symptoms (fever in most cases), and generalized enlargement of the lymph nodes, spleen and liver. In addition, they had an elevated levels of an abnormal polyclonal gammaglobulin. Most of them had been treated with chemotherapy, none had benefitted from it, and most of them died of severe infections. He assigned one of his fellows, Dr. Glauco Frizzera, an Italian fellow-in-training, to help me. Henry left for Paris, where he was a visiting Pathologist-in-Residence at the Institute of Cancer and Immunogenetics in Villejuif, near Paris.

I studied the cases extensively and methodically, and I received the cooperation of the clinicians who took care of the patients and of the pathologists who had sent pathology material for consultation to Henry. Only a few patients had been treated at the University of Chicago. There was a characteristic histologic (microscopic) picture in the lymph nodes, spleen, liver, bone marrow, and skin, which we described in detail. We found that most patients treated with chemotherapy for lymphoma died of sepsis, but a few survived after treatment with steroids. We formulated the opinion that the microscopic findings could not support a diagnosis of malignancy but were rather similar to those seen in graft-versus-host disease. We could not exclude the possibility of a malignant transformation in the future. Clearly, intensive chemotherapy of the type used in treating lymphomas and Hodgkin's disease was not to be employed. We recommended not using chemotherapy; instead, we recommended supporting symptomatic treatment with small doses of steroids, and careful long-term follow-up. We wrote our report, sent it to Henry for his review and approval, and, without any objections from him, we mailed the paper to the British journal *Lancet*. We thought that we had described a novel disease, which I called "Angio-immunoblastic lymphadenopathy with dysproteinemia" (abbreviated "AILD") because I thought that the name should state the pathologic process. In one week, I received an airmail letter from the Editor-in-Chief of *Lancet* informing me that our paper had been accepted for publication and would go to press immediately. Such a rapid response from the editor of a leading bio-medical scientific journal had rarely been seen.

♦

In the summer of 1974, I was invited to participate in the eleventh International Cancer Congress, in Florence, Italy. I presented some papers and had much fun visiting the museums with Huguette. At the end of the Congress, we rented a car and visited the Ligurian Coast, the French Riviera, the French Provence cities, and the Costa Brava of Spain. Then we flew to Madrid, where we witnessed one of Franco's fascist regime's infamous police roundups, where all suspected or undesirable people were arrested and the outcomes of those arrests never published. It was in the evening when we were returning to our centrally located hotel, where we saw the police cars and the rounded-up people many in tears and scared. I knew what all the commotion was, because I have lived through similar episodes during the Nazi, but Huguette was in awe.

♦

In retrospect, the years 1973-1975 were very productive for me scientifically. Our team published a good number of papers reporting on our original research. These were seminal observations on the natural history and diagnosis of Hodgkin's disease and lymphomas, with an emphasis on the diversity of the diseases included under the latter name. We wrote about the limitations of the accepted diagnostic studies, the importance of bone marrow evaluation in lymphomas, their responses to treatment, the natural history of mycosis fungoides, and a novel design of radiotherapy in Hodgkin's disease. The publication of the AILD paper in *Lancet* had attracted many invitations to lecture about our discovery, diagnosis, and treatment of this newly described disease.

In 1975, Dr. Thomas C. Hall, the director of a new cancer center at the University of British Columbia in Vancouver, BC, invited me to consider a position with them in medical oncology. I liked the idea of working with Tom and of moving to Vancouver, which I found to be a most beautiful city, but the political situation of the new cancer center had many problems. I sensed internal opposition from the old-timers who disliked Tom Hall's new and integrative approach. I shared my reservations with Tom. It soon became evident that my intuition was correct.

At my microscope, University of Chicago, 1974.

I was also invited to visit the Department of Medicine at the University of Texas School of Medicine in San Antonio with the idea of potentially establishing a section of medical oncology there. It was obvious that the hematologists, who were well respected old-timers, did not favor a new medical oncology program, but Bill McGuire, a fine endocrinologist who had described the progesterone receptors in breast cancer cells, wanted to have it. Radiation therapy took place in a private setting, and that service had a less than amicable relationship with the medical school. After three visits and a good many personal interactions with both Bill McGuire and Dr. Lawrence Earley, the Chair of Medicine, it became clear that San Antonio had too many infights and political problems, and it was not the place for us. The situation taught me a lesson about the difficulties associated with starting a new program. Huguette and I decided not to pursue that path for the time being, though later I did not heed the lesson that led us to that decision.

In March 1975, I received the appointment of Associate Professor of Medicine at the University of Chicago. I felt very honored to have received this appointment after only four years as an assistant professor. In most universities, the appointment of associate professor is the most important achievement in the academic recognition. At the time, I felt that I had to follow what I thought of as the right path for me, namely, an academic position that would allow me to develop my own program. My work at the University of Chicago had undoubtedly fostered my development as a clinician, as a researcher, and as an educator. Those were also the years in which I learned how to be a loving father to my two boys.

◆

In September 1975, Jerome was fifty years old, and Tilly's family celebrated his birthday in Lucerne, Switzerland. We wanted to be with him and got on an Iceland Airways flight over the North Pole to Luxemburg, where we rented a car and drove to Lucerne, Switzerland. My parents came from Israel, and we had a very enjoyable time together. After celebrating Jerome's event, we drove through Switzerland and spent an unforgettable vacation in Lermoos, Kitzbuhel, and Reith in Tirol. We then visited Innsbruck, Salzburg, and Lienz. At the end of our vacation, we started on our return through northern Italy: Cortina d'Ampezzo, Merano, and Bolzano and then St. Gallen in Switzerland. We arrived at the Zurich airport just in time for my parents' return flight to Israel. This was our last European vacation with my parents. They were then in their early eighties, and our separation had become painful. We hoped that they would come to the realization that they needed to live close to us.

◆

When I received a call from Dr. Melville Jacobs, Associate Director of City of Hope (COH) in Duarte, California, who wanted to visit with us in Chicago, we invited him for dinner. He told me that he had been charged by the director of COH, Dr. Rachmiel Levine, to convince me to accept the position of Director of Medical Oncology within their internal medicine department. I asked him why his medical center did not have a separate medical oncology service. His reply was that they did not yet have the right person to provide leadership, which I took as a reply intended to flatter me. He asked me to come for a visit.

I went to Duarte, California, for an interview. City of Hope was a very unusual institution, treating only patients with a select number of illnesses which were studied by doctors on the Staff. It was not a general hospital. Many services were missing. The existing services were built around the special scientific interests of notable investigators. Hematology was very strong under the chiefship of Dr. Ernest Beutler, who was also Director of the Department of Internal Medicine. He was interested in Gaucher's disease, in the enzymatic functions of the red blood cells, and in developing a service for bone marrow transplantation. I asked him why he did not develop a medical oncology service, and his reply was convoluted and evasive. I had been candid with all the interviewers, describing what I had done at the University of Chicago and what I could do at COH, if offered a position. I wanted them to understand exactly what my abilities and values were.

I was invited to present the idea of a medical oncology service to City of Hope's board of directors. I stated my views on how medical oncology works and its relationship with other departments and programs. Specifically, I described the role medical oncology would play in the creation of a cancer center. I was told the next day that I had "conquered their minds and souls." The board members were delighted with the idea that a medical oncology service was finally going to be established at their medical center in Duarte. COH's publicity material mentioned cancer care and research as one of its primary focuses. Ben Horowitz, the CEO of COH, and the most valued leader of the organization for many years, became a very good friend of mine. He explained to me that it was an old rule of the COH that gave the Board the key to the kitty that funded the Medical Center. The same rule also denied the Board the power to make decisions on the Center's internal organization and policies. It seemed awkward. The doctors were allowed total independence of thought and action. Patients were admitted only if there was an interest in their medical problems, and, if accepted, they were treated optimally. On their discharge from the hospital, they received a paper that indicated the cost of their care along with a statement that said: "Thank you for allowing us to take care of your needs. The Friends of City of Hope." No charges were made to the patients or their families.

The City of Hope did not have any academic affiliation. Each researcher received or could receive academic recognition for his own scientific accomplishments. Some were professors at the California Institute of Technology or at the University of Southern California. Ernie Beutler had been elected to the United States National Academy of Sciences, a high scientific recognition for his work on the physiology of red blood cells. There were no residents-in-training, which I did not like because it meant not being able to enjoy the stimulation and pleasure of teaching. In March 1976, I was offered the position of Director of Medical Oncology, with two staff physicians' positions, and a resident in medicine. I accepted the position with the understanding that I would have the opportunity to establish a new medical oncology service with all the functions I had proposed to the medical center Staff as well as to the Board of Directors. I promised to develop associations with other cancer centers in Southern California that could enrich the clinical work, the research, and the teaching at COH. Based on the formal agreements, I saw the move to COH as a fine possibility for the fulfillment of my professional ambitions and desires. I also had some reservations about my functioning well in an organizations like COH, but I was determined to work hard with my new colleagues.

Huguette did not want to look for a position for herself, thinking that it would be better for her to focus first on organizing our new life in California. Because I was involved in my work of attending on service at that time at University of Chicago, I could not make additional trips to look for housing. Huguette went to Duarte, California to look for a house and found one in Sierra Madre, a small town adjacent to the wealthy Arcadia, in the foothills of the San Gabriel mountain range. She took some photos of the house she liked — which I also liked very much. It was something totally new for us. The town was in the Arcadia School District, which was one of the best in Los Angeles County. Daniel was almost seven years old and had finished his first two grades at the University of Chicago's Laboratory School. André was four and a half years old and ready to go to kindergarten.

On July 16, 1976, we left Chicago for California.

At the City of Hope Medical Center in California

I was confident that my family would enjoy life in California, though the boys were not very happy because they had to leave their friends in Chicago. We could only reassure them that they would make new friends in Sierra Madre. Driving through Iowa was not very pleasant in the summer heat. The corn was tall and loaded, and the landscape was quite monotonous. We started to enjoy our trip only after getting to South Dakota. The Badlands were strange and interesting, and we marveled at Gutzon Borglum's majestic Mount Rushmore statues of the US Presidents. From there through Wyoming, we enjoyed every stop of our journey and spent four unforgettable days in Yellowstone National Park. One afternoon we rested in Bryce Canyon National Park, where we admired the rocky formations in the golden light of the sunset: A rare geological creation that moved us very much. The ranger advised us to stay overnight at a motel near the entrance gate so that we could see the canyon in the early morning light. This was one of the greatest experiences we had on our trip southwest. The canyon appears totally different in the early morning when the brilliant white color gives an eerie sparkle.

We arrived in Las Vegas in the afternoon and checked into a motel close to the freeway. We were advised to leave in the early hours of the morning to avoid the high heat of the Mojave Desert. We arrived safely in Sierra Madre and inspected our new house, which was situated at an altitude of about three hundred feet with a view over the foothills. It had five bedrooms, three and a half bathrooms, a beautiful verandah, a front lawn, and a large garden in the backyard with a nice swimming pool. This was a totally new ecosystem. There were flowers and more than twenty pots of plants, which we later discovered to be splendid cymbidium orchids, about which we knew nothing. The previous owners had not been able to take them because they'd moved to another state and were not allowed to bring plants from California. There was a large red hibiscus and a banana tree. We were very happy in the new surroundings. Daniel started third grade at Highland Oaks, a very good school in the Arcadia School District, and André started kindergarten. Huguette interviewed for a position in medical genetics but there were only few posts in research, all of them funded through research grants, and she did not want to dedicate herself to lab research. She was more interested in the clinical applications of genetics like she'd worked with in the mental health clinic at the University of Chicago. On January 1, 1977, she took a position as an internist with Kaiser Permanente Medical Group, which she enjoyed until her retirement twenty-two years later. We explored with great interest the towns of Arcadia and Pasadena, and we enjoyed our new life. Los Angeles offered so many places to visit. Henry and Dina Rappaport had left Chicago a year earlier and were living in Arcadia, a five-minute ride from us. We frequently visited with them.

I had some reservations about my appointment at COH because of the lack of an academic environment, the lack of house staff, and the absence of interaction with the cancer centers of the local universities. Moreover, I had a big concern about COH's failure to establish a medical oncology program while it had heavily advertised its dedication to cancer research. I set aside those thoughts, and I focused on my work with a keen desire to deliver what I had promised and to establish the missing medical oncology program. The administrative staff were marvelous. Bob Sloane and Sally Martin, old timers at COH, were instrumental in helping me develop the new section. Effective and resourceful, they advised me on every step, and I was able to deliver my charges with responsibility and accountability, two basic principles that I had always respected.

The laboratory personnel were highly qualified and experienced. Henry Rappaport was the chairman of the Department of Anatomic Pathology and had great authority. I conducted a research project with him and his associates. It was encouraging to work with excellent and friendly pharmacists. They were very much interested in the acquisition of investigational drugs from the NCI, but that possibility was restricted to institutions with NCI-recognized cancer centers, which was not the case with COH. The radiologists were good but not daring about using or implementing new diagnostic methods. Computer scans were being introduced in many hospitals, but COH did not have them yet. Radiation therapy was under Dr. Melville Jacobs, who was also associate director of the medical center. The service was old-fashioned and quite resistant to new ideas. The leadership convinced Dr. Jacobs to recruit a new radiation oncologist. The hematology section was very active, with about fifteen beds. There were three hematologists, very knowledgeable, and much effort was made to develop a bone marrow transplantation service. Other sections with beds in internal medicine included cardiology and pulmonary (chest) diseases. There was an intensive care unit under the care of cardiologists and a consultation service in Gastroenterology. Consultations in other subspecialties like infectious diseases could be obtained from outside COH but had to be approved by Dr. Beutler. The surgical service under Dr. Ralph Byron was good, but there were no surgical oncologists, there was resistance to adopting the modern concepts of cancer surgery, and the surgeons used cancer chemotherapy without any training.

The nursing staff was very cooperative and highly qualified. They wanted to be trained in all aspects of medical oncology, and I started by training them in the use of intravenous infusion pumps, which had been only recently introduced into practice. I also held in-house courses on the uses and side effects of cancer drugs and the preparatory steps for the nurses' certification in the administration of cancer chemotherapy, a new sort of certification at that time. I had two very talented nurses who assisted me in the outpatient clinics. I developed a very effective check-out list for outpatient visits that summarized the medical care given, the diagnosis, the procedures performed, the time spent, the complexity of the visit, and the type of follow-up needed. It provided necessary information to the administration. There were small bungalows very close to the hospital where patients and their families could be accommodated — a great and thoughtful system that has since been adopted by other hospitals.

I was given four beds, and they were immediately occupied by referred patients from many chapters of the "Friends of City of Hope." Shortly thereafter, I was given eight beds, and those were filled too. There were short stays, and the hospital administrators were pleased with the turnout. I noticed that Dr. Beutler was intrigued by this rapid development, and he must have realized that it was good for the medical center. Most of our patients came to COH after having been treated ineffectively or unsuccessfully; they were in clinical relapse, or in need of a hospital stay in order to explore the possibility of improving their care. In a short span of time, I was given twelve beds, which was quite a large assignment compared to other sections in the hospital.

I received an appointment as Clinical Professor of Medicine at University of Southern California (USC). A medical resident from USC elected to have a one-month rotation with me. She worked diligently and told her colleagues that it was her best clinical rotation. Encouraged by her reports, two more medical residents took their month of clinical training in internal medicine with me. There were no more trainees after that. Dr. Levine was unclear about this, and Dr. Beutler thought that there had been a mix-up in the Department of Medicine's office at USC, but that was very unlikely. I told them that I wanted to pursue the plan of establishing a training program in hematology-oncology as a joint fellowship program with University of California, Irvine (UCI). This idea had no precedent but could not be opposed because it had scholarly advantages. I fulfilled all the necessary formalities, and we established this postgraduate association that was agreed on and signed by Dr. Levine and Dr. Daniel Aldrich, the UCI chancellor.

Soon, I learned that Hsiao-Lin Chang, a technician who had worked with me at the University of Chicago on the serum alkaline phosphatase research, had moved to California and was interested in working with me. This was good news, and I asked for the lab space which had been granted to me at the time of my recruitment. Some construction work was necessary. After a while and much to my surprise, that work stopped without explanation. This was a bad signal.

My most intense work was on establishing research cooperation with the local major universities. With few exceptions, research studies needed many untreated patients, and at that time COH had mostly patients who had been treated extensively and were in relapse and/or in an advanced stage of the disease. With the approval of the directorship, I explored the possibility of COH's participation in the clinical efforts on cancer with the director of the University of California-Los Angeles Comprehensive Cancer Center and with the director of the recently NCI-approved University of Southern California Comprehensive Cancer Center. They and their respective chairs of medical oncology were very pleased by the prospect of COH joining their research efforts. I was shocked when I heard that this did not please certain individuals at COH Medical Center. I had to realize that, contrary to what I was told at the time of my recruitment, COH leaders did not want any cooperation with established cancer centers — and that it was unwilling to open a venue for productive research for the benefit of our cancer patients: This represented a major blockage on the path toward my plans for a new medical oncology program at COH.

◆

My parents came to California from Israel at the end of December 1976, with the intention of moving to the States, and we received them with love. My brother and Tilly came from Canada, and we enjoyed a very nice family reunion. We traveled around the area and marveled at the nice weather after all those years of Chicago winters. Soon, however, we learned that the beautiful weather meant drought, which was of great concern to all in Southern California.

I thought that my parents would enjoy their new family life. They were very well accommodated in our house, but life in Sierra Madre was strange for them. They could not see anybody outside because neither of them drove, and during the day, when we were not home, they were unable to meet anybody with whom they could talk. Suddenly, they found themselves isolated. For individuals accustomed to the very active social life they had had in Tel Aviv, this was very difficult to support. Mother did not feel well physically. After much thought and discussion, they decided to return to Tel Aviv, and they left at the end of February 1977. After all my hopes for a restoration of a full family life, I felt that I had failed in this dream.

♦

I gradually learned more about the understandings and agreements between the City of Hope Medical Center and its Board of Directors. It all seemed unusual to me. The Board could not make internal decisions on the healthcare organization and its scope. The Board could express its desires, but only the director and the chiefs of service decided if new programs were to be established and which patients would be admitted. It became evident that for many years the Board had wanted to establish medical oncology as a service in the Department of Medicine, but this development was resisted by some fearing competition with the hematology service, where lymphoma and leukemia were treated in an obsolete way. Dr. Beutler had agreed to a medical oncology service with me as its director, but he wanted to keep it small and under his control. The surgical service used chemotherapy after surgical procedures on cancer, most of the time without correct medical indications and with a poor understanding of side effects. My surgical colleagues were resistant to any cooperative studies.

I discussed with the COH leadership the possibility of joining the research efforts of the large cancer centers, in compliance with our pre-employment agreements. As I've mentioned, clinical research needs many untreated patients, which COH did not have at that time. We did not have the necessary infrastructure and medical staff to ensure productivity in clinical research. The recruiting for the physicians promised to me was not initiated. Without the necessary research cooperation, we could not have access to investigational drugs. The work on my lab was interrupted without any notification. Management did not make any effort to modernize the heavy radiology equipment such as buying a CT scanner. To clarify the situation, I asked for a meeting with Drs. Levine, Beutler, and Jacobs, and we reviewed all the agreements made at the time of my initial visits. It was clear that I had fulfilled our pre-employment agreements, but the medical center had not done its part. I could not accept this situation, and I had to remove myself from this inequity.

Huguette and I agreed that it did not make sense to continue my work at COH under the existing conditions. I knew that I could never sacrifice my integrity if I wanted to preserve my wholeness. Henry Rappaport said that he felt guilty about not having anticipated this outcome. Dr. Levine was utterly surprised when I gave him my written notice of resignation, effective December 31, 1977. I stated that my resignation was caused by the medical center's breach of promise. He could not comprehend that I'd leave without having another position. I told him that I had my principles and that my independence was dear to me. He knew full well that I had come to COH to start a new venture with confidence. I was not ready to lower my professional principles and standards.

Dr. Levine did not hold back his words of appreciation for my work in founding medical oncology at City of Hope, and he felt genuine regret over my leaving. He thought that I was on my way to winning my battle with the local opposition to the future in cancer care. He lauded my work and said: "You showed your strength when you had to cope with adversity."

I talked with Ben Horowitz, the CEO of COH, about my COH experience, and I suggested to him and the COH Board of Directors that they seek an objective review of the cancer care situation at COH through a consultation with an outside group. Ben discussed all that I'd related to him with his colleagues on the Board of Directors; he felt bad about the situation that caused my decision to leave.

The COH Board was instrumental in making the most decisive action regarding the future of medical oncology and the development of a cancer center at COH. In 1977, the Board invited CDP Associates from La Jolla, California, a business advisory and consultation service, to study the possibility of developing a cancer center at COH. Almost all the physicians and scientists on Staff were interviewed, and their opinions were included in a detailed two-volume report. I had been interviewed on all aspects of this initiative. In December, I received my copy of the CDP reports. It stated plainly the problem of internal opposition to the development of a medical oncology service and the emergence of a cancer center at COH. Some of the opinions of the staff were quite interesting:

"City of Hope is already a cancer center and we must let everyone know." (Totally incorrect.)

"City of Hope has a comprehensive cancer center similar to USC and UCLA." (Totally incorrect.)

"Why have a cancer center if there is already one at USC, UCLA and a strong program at Cedars-Sinai?"

"City of Hope cannot be classified as a major cancer center because of lack of information on protocols, lack of (several) clinical services." (Quite correct.)

"(A cancer center) is badly needed at present. It should have been established years ago. It will require a singleness of purpose. Cancer is and should be the major interest of City of Hope." (Very correct.)

The findings and opinions of the massive CDP report were the same problems that had caused me to leave the place. It was a wake-up call for COH. It moved the institution towards understanding cancer care with an open view toward the future. The CDP staff felt that I was a catalyst who had uncovered the well-hidden causes of inactivity in cancer care at COH. They felt that I had caused the institution to deal openly with its stated commitment to progress in cancer research. Ben Horowitz called me and wrote me, thanking me for what I did, and telling me that he regretted the outcome. However, he understood very well my position, and he agreed with my decision.

It took about two years until another medical oncologist came to serve. For obscure reasons, he too left after a short time. More years of inactivity, a change in directorship, and probably a better and more effective balance in the structure of the relationship of the Board of Directors with the COH management had to occur before the institution could become a highly respected cancer center.

At the University of California, Irvine

The word of my resignation apparently spread out, and I got a call from Dr. Jeremiah (Jerry) Tilles, Chair of the Department of Internal Medicine at University of California, Irvine (UCI). Jerry was a very good virologist with a fine reputation. He offered me the position of Professor of Medicine at UCI with the major responsibility of establishing an academic program in hematology and medical oncology at the Long Beach Veterans Administration Medical Center (LBVAMC). He told me that the affiliation of LBVAMC with UCI was rather tenuous because of a long history of personal dislikes, mutual distrust, and disrespect. The staff of the hematology-oncology services at the two hospitals were not on speaking terms. The poor affiliation had historic reasons: Part of it was simple professional jealousy, and it is true that there were some better-equipped and better-staffed services at LBVAMC than at UCI. The teaching was superior at LBVAMC, chiefly because all the attending physicians were full-time employees, whereas at UCI the physicians had private practices and were too busy to dedicate much time to teaching the house staff and the students.

The main problem with the troubled UCI-LBVAMC affiliation was that no dean had ever addressed it in a global way. For example, in San Diego, all the physicians were part-time faculty at the University of California San Diego School of Medicine and part-time at the VA. This worked out very well. They gave very good service and were also productive in research and in teaching. At the West Los Angeles VAMC, most of the faculty had responsibilities at the University of California at Los Angeles (UCLA), and were very much involved in teaching and research. While at City of Hope, I had been invited to make teaching rounds with the fellows in hematology-oncology and with medical residents-in-training at the West Los Angeles VAMC, which was affiliated with UCLA. I found there that an academic affiliation with shared responsibilities could be very productive. I never understood the reasons why this had not been introduced at UCI, and I foresaw problems. Friends told me to beware: "You will have to fight from within." I did not have any idea about the Veterans Administration's medical system because I hadn't received any part of my training through the VA. Neither Columbia University nor Mount Sinai Medical Center in New York or the University of Chicago had affiliations with the VA.

The history of our national obligation to veterans goes back to the early seventeenth century, when the first colonists of America warred with the local Native Americans. Over the years and in various ways, the American government has taken care of those who served honorably in defending the nation. In 1930, after several administrative changes had occurred, the Veterans Administration federal agency was created, and in 1988 President Reagan elevated the agency to a cabinet-level department. The basic philosophy of the VA was first expressed by Abraham Lincoln: "To care for him who shall have borne the battle, and for his widow, and his orphan." I liked this idea, and I loved very much the VA dictum: "All gave some, some gave all."

I respected and I loved the VA's philosophy. I also liked a system of healthcare which employed physicians full-time (as long as the care given was optimal) with an emphasis on research and teaching. In the history of modern medicine, it has been amply shown that research enhances teaching — and teaching improves the quality of healthcare. I did not have any information on the intensity or quality of the postgraduate teaching in the VA, though I knew that research was a well-developed program in the VA, and that there had been Nobel Prize laureates who'd worked full-time for the VA. I also did not know the internal affairs of the medical center, the bureaucracy, the interpersonal relationships, and, most importantly, the dominating "institutional culture." I viewed the veterans as well-deserving citizens who should get the best medical care. Without any doubt, I agree that veterans are entitled to the free care they have been promised by the government.

I hesitated to accept a job in a system which I did not know from personal experience. Jerry Tilles, whom I knew and respected as a fair and trustworthy person, assured me that I would do well. I was to report to him directly on all academic matters. He told me that there were many problems because the program had been "let down." He promised me his full support.

I asked to visit all the chiefs of medical and surgical services, and I openly stated that my main reason for meeting with them was that I wanted to gain a better understanding of the system. I knew that at such interviews, most interviewers (as well as interviewees) don't say all that they could and should. I had my own bitter experience with pre-employment interviews and promises. I've always thought that so many misunderstandings, so much wasted time and energy, might be avoided by candid conversation and agreements. I met all the chiefs of services, and I felt good about my conversations with them. Some of them were physicians with many accomplishments who had come to serve the VA for reasons very similar to my own. I liked meeting with Dr. Justin Stein, a radiation oncologist who had been on the UCLA faculty and had served as the president of the American Cancer Society, California Chapter.

The Chief of Medicine had been Jesse Steinfeld, one of the first medical oncologists who served as Surgeon General of the US. He introduced the lung cancer warning on cigarette packages. I have met Jesse, and I liked him very much, but he accepted a position as Dean of the University of Maryland School of Medicine. The acting Chief of Medicine was a relatively young physician, Dr. Fred Wyle, a specialist in infectious diseases and a friend of Dr. Tilles. He had a strong personality, was devoted to the scope of the VA, and was ambitious in his goal of achieving an academic program in internal medicine and its subspecialties. His actions had ruffled some feathers; there were some physicians who'd demonstrated a lackadaisical attitude in the discharge of their duties, and Fred did not tolerate this. He wanted the chiefs of sections to be full-time employees, and he'd asked the chief of hematology-oncology to change from seven-eighths-time to full-time. He declined, and Fred offered me a full-time position as Chief of Hematology-Oncology, plus positions for two full-time physicians (one of which had to be recruited), two fellows, one resident, two interns, and students. My appointment was as Chief, grade ten, which was the highest grade for practicing physicians in the Civil Service. I agreed to start full-time after the New Year holiday, 1978.

I was interested in the organizational structure of the place I would be associated with, but I could not get complete answers to all my questions. In 1978, the Veterans Administration was an agency of the United States government. The VA Healthcare Administration (VHA) was the major component of the VA, and it decided on everything, from personnel to standards of care to equipment and construction. The edicts of its Central Office (VACO) were quite dictatorial, without a chance of discussion or recourse. All the VACO orders had to be followed; it was reminiscent of a military organization. The Chief Medical Director in the Central Office was the supreme commander of the VHA. Each of the 172 hospitals and several hundred clinics (the "field stations," in the institutional vernacular) had its own local medical director, a person with full and absolute power. That person was appointed by the VACO and was rarely a physician. The Medical Director was typically a person with many years of service in the administration who knew the right people and who had performed and behaved well in his or her bureaucratic service. The Medical Director's knowledge of how medical care is or should be delivered was variable, creating better or worse times in the local practice of medicine. Criticism could be made only after fulfilling a dictate and was rarely effective. I did not like this aspect of the system because it reminded me of a military regime or a dictatorship — something I hated passionately. However, I knew that there were many VA hospitals with fine reputations earned for excellence in clinical care, teaching, and research. I figured out that this was possible mostly because of the vision and practices of their respective managements, and on their good work with medical staff to help our veterans.

The VA Long Beach was in the south part of Long Beach, less than a mile from the seashore: a very fine location. It had about sixteen hundred active beds and over two thousand employees. It was probably the largest or among the largest VA hospitals in the nation.

The Long Beach VA Medical Center, 1980.

The LBVAMC was one of the few VA medical centers with a very well-equipped research building that accommodated a good number of independent investigators. Doctors who had research projects could have space and access to the equipment as well as to the animal facility in the spacious research building. There also was a program devoted to Spinal Cord Injuries and a functional 180-bed nursing home.

In my thirty-five years of service, I had to interact with several medical directors and their associates. I learned to build positive professional relationships with most of them, and I heard that they respected me for what I brought to the medical center, although their learning curves were not always smooth. It often happened that by the time we had developed a personal and functional relationship, they moved on to other positions in the VA, and I had to restart my educational efforts on the practice of modern cancer care.

The Chief of Staff (COS) was also a VACO appointee and had the authority on all medical services, diagnostic and therapeutic, and on the nursing service. I could never understand why the COS was not a clinician. Two of the chiefs of staff I worked with had been research pathologists. It appeared to us, the clinicians, that the Central Office was perhaps fearful of appointing clinicians to the COS position, something which was very much needed. The wisdom of the VACO's decisions was frequently but not openly questioned.

The Medical Center's Director, Associate Director, and COS formed a triad referred to as "the Management." There were several medical center committees, the most powerful among them being the Clinical Executive Board (CEB), which advised the management on all problems, appointments, and new policies, which were written as medical center memorandums and professional service memorandums, rigorously recorded, enforced, and renewed yearly. The CEB advised, and the director had the latitude to agree or not. This was a mini-dictatorial regime of sorts. The Resource Committee was another important committee which advised on the funding of research projects. Many jealousies and hidden intrigues operated within these committees. The Position Management Committee functioned for a while when many personnel cuts had to be implemented. There were many other committees, strictly professional, such as the Pharmacy and Therapeutics Committee, the Transfusion Committee, the Education Committee, the Residency Review Committee, etc. The medical center's budget was huge. Each service had its own budget that had to be respected to the letter. The federal government's rules were very strict. The exact use of funds for the budget-specified items was mandatory. The Chief Financial Officer had unusually important power, although he was not trusted by most of the clinical service chiefs.

The Medical Service (Internal Medicine) had several hundred inpatient beds for general internal medicine and for all medical subspecialties. The Hematology-Oncology section (Hem/Onc) was located on the eighth floor of the Tower building, facing south, with a splendid view on the ocean. It had thirty beds with about fifty percent bed-occupancy. The first day there, I found a dirty office with an empty file cabinet. The nurses told me that the previous chief had taken all the section files, correspondence, written regulations, and fellows' applications for training. This was not the usual or professionally accepted practice. My secretary was officially listed as the secretary of a defunct tumor registry, which I agreed to revive and lead. When I asked her to call somebody to clean an empty file cabinet, she told me that it would require a typed memo. "This is how the VA works," she said. I recalled my friends' admonition: "You will have to fight from within." An alarm rang in my ears. My usual demeanor was that of a polite, quiet, and not self-assuming individual. I suddenly realized that I could not survive in such environment if I didn't change my way of relating to work issues. And I did change my demeanor and tactics quite abruptly. No wonder I got the reputation of being a "tough man," a reputation which helped me on many occasions when I had to face old-fashioned work attitudes that opposed progress.

The real single thing that helped me overcome my first reaction of promptly leaving the place was the nursing staff. The nurses were knowledgeable, attentive, and they showed a keen interest in the patients' well-being. Most of them were Filipino and had been trained in the Philippines. They had a superbly humane attitude. I've always thought that the most essential part of a medical service — for inpatients as well as for outpatient clinics — is the nursing staff. It is the heartbeat of any hospital and clinic. I started reorganizing the nurses as part of my new service. It was imperative to introduce the use of pumps for the intravenous administration of fluids, blood, and medications. The pumps rendered the fluids administration more easily and precisely than the outdated gravity intravenous equipment. The pumps had been used in medical practice for several years and were costly. I thought that it would be simply a matter of buying them with funds available. However, things were much more complicated than that. The pumps had to be bought by the Nursing Service from its own budget, not by the Medical Service. To be approved for purchase, it required the consent of the chief nurse, at that time a close-to-retirement nurse, who would not hear about such purchase. Without even studying the items to be ordered, she declared that they might be "dangerous to the patients" if they were not properly set. I stated, however, that I would train the nurses in the use of the pumps or that they could also get such instruction at another place of their choice. I argued strongly that the pumps had already been in use for a long time and that they were safe. We had to go to the COS for a decision. An additional surprise awaited me there. It was a second lesson in how things worked at the LBVAMC, though not at other VA centers, I must add. I learned at that time the unwritten politics of the place: The COS was reluctant to displease the chief nurse, as she was very well placed politically. It took about one year to introduce the pumps — when that chief nurse retired. My nurses appreciated the new equipment.

There were no daily rounds on the inpatients on the Hem/Onc service or on the other services when I arrived. No formal teaching or discussion of the diagnoses, treatments, and complications was done. I asked the physicians to see and examine the inpatients daily, including on weekends. I made my reputation by saying that "sick people are sick every day, including the weekends." I also introduced weekly chief rounds with my physicians. I wanted to hear a succinct presentation of each patient at his or her bedside, a discussion of the diagnosis, problems, complications, treatment, and plan of rehabilitation. This was normal in a teaching program. One of the staff physicians saw this as an attempt to exert a sort of control on what he was doing, and he told the fellows not to favor my weekly rounds because it placed them on the spot, although I'd showed them that we were to work as a team, and that we could learn from each other. In my philosophy of medical practice, the attendings could be challenged by the younger physicians, the fellows could obtain more experience (and get other opinions too), and the residents and interns would be able to see that one could welcome an honest critique and that one must think outside the box. I also taught them a thing or two, and gradually everybody was happy. The patients liked these rounds because they could see that we were acting as a team and that we indeed cared about delivering the best possible care.

There were two fellows-in-training in the hematology-oncology section, one in her second year and one in the middle of his first year, who had not read up on their patients' diseases and problems. One day, they asked me if they should read about the mechanisms of the action of the usual chemotherapy drugs. I was astounded upon hearing such an elementary and self-evident question, and I gave them articles to read. I had a complete set of articles and good reference material on practically every topic in hematology and medical oncology and this helped me in my teaching. There was not yet information "online," and we did not have personal computers. The medical library subscribed to only a single cancer-related journal. That was another little battle, arguing for the expansion the library's collection of medical journals so that we could keep up with new thoughts, findings, and discoveries.

I reviewed every new case with the fellows and residents, discussing the patients' problems. I wanted them to develop critical thinking, to resist blindly accepting what another physician, including myself, said or did. At that time, most of our patients were referred by private physicians, usually after the patients had exhausted their commercial insurance benefits and personal financial resources. Experience taught me that we had to review objectively every step we made in their care, including the initial pathological diagnosis and the medical care given by other physicians. Many outside physicians felt that we were obligated to accept patients without reviewing the initial tissue examination on which the diagnosis of cancer had been made. Many outside doctors had an arrogant attitude, to which I had to resist in a polite and firm way. We were medical oncologists and had an obligation to thoroughly review each case referred to us so that we could devise a correct treatment plan to the extent possible. We had all the diagnostic and treatment modalities. My fellows started to realize the value of our case reviews, a point that I preached to them because we had many cases in which, based on our review of the patient's medical history, diagnosis, and clinical findings, we had to change the whole treatment plan. My training and experience in diagnostic pathology helped me consistently throughout my many years of practice. Gradually we began to see more self-referred patients and more patients recently diagnosed and not yet treated.

A young medical oncologist from Melbourne, Australia, Dr. Ivon Burns, had visited with me at City of Hope and wanted additional training with me in the management of lymphomas and in our recently described AILD. He was supposed to return to the US to start his fellowship at COH, and I had to write him that I'd moved to LBVAMC. He came to Long Beach, and he was the first fellow whom I appointed to the joint UCI-LBVAMC Medical Oncology

Program. He was quite advanced in his studies and abilities, but he said that he wanted to learn from me how to establish and conduct a new oncology program because he expected to be appointed chief of such a program at the University of Melbourne Hospital upon his return to Australia. I thought that this was an excellent opportunity for him to see me in action fighting for everything deemed necessary in establishing a Hem/Onc training program.

I wanted to give the Hem/Onc consultations at a high professional level, with good discussions of the case, detailed differential diagnoses where appropriate, and suggestions for additional work-ups and treatment. Our notes had to be well written, intelligible, and without any bias whatsoever. Yes, my standards were quite high, and colleagues noted this with the surprise of seeing a newcomer breaking the local established norms. I asked my fellows to write the consultations with me because I wanted to improve their writing style. I was totally opposed to them writing in pencil, which was illegal in any institution.

I asked patients to allow me to physically examine them, and they almost always resisted this, saying that they had never been asked to undress. Quite a strange way of practicing medicine, I thought. I patiently explained that to help them get better, we must be allowed to examine them. I also told them and their families that if they preferred to see other doctors at other VA hospitals, I could refer them to the doctors of their choice. No one left. Gradually I began to hear them commenting very positively on our medical attitude. As it is widely known, trusting our doctors is essential and critical for good healthcare, and we had a good number of accurate diagnoses and successful treatments.

We saw around thirty to forty patients in each afternoon clinic, and about ten of them received chemotherapy. A nurse prepared the medication solutions in syringes, which were labelled with the names of the medications and their dosages. Fellows picked up those syringes and administered the chemotherapy to the patients based on the instructions of the only staff physician available before my arrival. Nobody examined the patients. This had to change.

All new patients had to be reviewed with an attending physician. I asked for complete physical examinations of all new patients and a summary examination on the follow-up visits. This had never been done before. I wrote and distributed to the team all the chemotherapy regimens, the way to calculate the doses, the necessary modifications, and the expected toxicities. I also introduced an elementary oncology tool, the flow sheet: a written tabulation of the disease parameters, doses of chemotherapy, and changes in the disease parameters as objectively measured. This gave the staff all the necessary treatment-related data at a glance. To my astonishment, the clinic clerks removed the flow sheets from the medical records. They argued that the flow sheets were not "VA-approved documents," though they did not inform me of that at the time, and surreptitiously removed the sheets from the medical records. When I found this out, I exploded in anger over their incompetence and their disregard of the professional staff. The flow sheets were our work product and had to be respected by the institution. If our flow sheets did not fit the administration's protocol, then there needed to be a careful process of deliberation with the practitioners before any of our work was altered or removed. It took a lot of work with the medical administration service to make them understand the value of the flow sheets in our practice. It became obvious that the medical administration as well as other so-called support services were not accustomed to the idea that the physicians might be interested in and devoted to their patients, whom they wanted to treat with dedication. Doctors need some tools of their own in their practice of medicine. However, for many in the hospital's medical administration, doctors were supposed to be unheard and unseen. This had resulted in a good many physicians losing interest in the medical practice at the VA.

We had a major problem and many difficulties in the clinics because medical records were not always available to the doctors or were incomplete because medical reports were not posted regularly. In 1978, we did not yet have computers; we were working with paper medical records, and they were often incomplete or unavailable. It is very difficult to make correct evaluations of a patient's medical problems without past notes and pertaining documents. Most of my colleagues and the clinic clerks simply said: "This is the VA," and took no action. I took a different path, asking the clerks in the medical administration service: "Would you like your father to be taken care in this way?" I spent an inordinate number of hours in the medical administration offices with too many individuals who lacked professionalism. I never could understand how it was possible to keep on staff such uncaring persons. It seemed that these clerks felt pleasure in seeing the doctors beg for their cooperation with the medical records, cooperation which in fact was the clerks' duty. Based on this experience and on similar events related to the quality, recruitment, and performance of various personnel, I came to the incontrovertible conclusion that it was the Personnel Service (Human Resources) and its rules that were responsible for the recruitment and promotion of many incompetent individuals in the service of the delivery of medical care to our veterans. I found this most detestable and irresponsible.

The general attitude about cancer was very parochial. It was dominated by a strong negativism that permeated the whole practice of medicine at the LBVAMC. I sensed it also in discussions of various related topics with the Chief of Medicine. I give him credit for listening and for keeping an open mind, for realizing that a new page was about to be written — and that he himself might well become an active participant in that endeavor. He acted swiftly in my favor when we discussed who would take care of cancer patients. It was obvious to us that if the Gastroenterology Service took care of the patients with cancers of the esophagus, stomach, liver, pancreas, colon and rectum; the Pulmonary Service took care of the patients with lung cancer; and the Urology Service took care of the patients with cancers of the kidney, bladder, and prostate; the Hem/Onc Service would be left to deal with only cancers of the blood and lymph nodes and only a small group of solid tumors, not enough for a Service with its own postgraduate training program. We agreed, therefore, that all cancer patients will be taken care of by the Hem/Onc staff. This required a long and persistent battle of wits and arguments.

As soon as possible, I started the process of recruiting a staff physician. The VA made the announcement in medical journals, and we received many applications. The Southern California locale was very attractive to the applicants, but the lack of a firm affiliation between LBVAMC and UCI acted as an important negative. I learned this in a most inconvenient way. I've already described the historical reasons for the poor affiliation. I wanted to attract good physicians. I had promised the UCI Department of Medicine that I would recruit only good clinicians who were dedicated to academic medicine. Having had my own bitter personal experience with clinical obligations and a lack of time for study and research, I wanted to assure that the physicians I recruited would be treated fairly and well. I shared the service responsibilities with the new physicians, and I was able to guarantee at least fifty percent time off for study and research. This was a good opportunity for any young hematologist-oncologist. The program could give a young doctor an excellent professional opportunity to develop his or her clinical research. An academic appointment was available and was based on the individual's merits. I received many applications for positions on staff. Some of them were from physicians who thought that the VA might give them a place to do some clinical medicine without teaching and without any research interest. However, I was committed to recruiting academic physicians, and I persevered in searching for such candidates. Young medical oncologists joined and contributed their share. I learned that, at that time, the VA did not attract young physicians with academic interests, although the salary structure was very good. Those talented in research wanted a university staff position, and the VA did not attract them. It seems they knew more about the VA than I did, because they'd had part of their training in the VA, and in general they did not have very good memories or opinions of it. The challenge that had led me to accept my position did not appeal to younger doctors. Without exception, however, all the young physicians whom we were able to attract, including our fellows-in-training, learned a lot and developed their own successful careers.

A group of researchers from the Mayo Clinic's Department of Ear, Nose, and Throat asked for my participation in a research study of the Epstein-Barr virus markers in the diagnosis and prognosis of nasopharyngeal carcinoma. This is a relatively rare cancer in the States. My program was selected as co-investigator, and we contributed to the joint effort, which resulted in an interesting paper published in the *Cancer* journal. Later, when I learned about the NCI-sponsored study on the "Effect of Total Parenteral Nutrition on the Chemotherapy of Small Cell Anaplastic Carcinoma of the Lung," I wrote a good application that was approved and funded by the NCI. Only ten programs were selected nationally, and we did our very best despite many technical difficulties with the local medical administration, difficulties that impeded any clinical research effort, though by ignorance and not by intent. Later, we developed research projects on the treatment of refractory anemia in the elderly, on prostate cancer, on male breast cancer, and on colon cancer. We presented our results at national and international scientific meetings and published in peer-reviewed journals.

♦

Huguette and I decided to continue living in our house in Sierra Madre and see how things would work out in Long Beach. I drove thirty-seven miles one way twice a day. Huguette worked in a Kaiser Permanente clinic in East Los Angeles, and she liked her work. For her, driving to work would have been about the same whether from Sierra Madre or from a southern location in Long Beach. However, we started looking for houses on weekends, and I remember that the boys did not like those outings. Meanwhile, we lived our little happy life in Sierra Madre and discovered many places of interest in Los Angeles — small theaters in West LA, opera at the Dorothy Chandler Pavilion — and we attended concerts at the Occidental College Auditorium in Pasadena. The Norton Simon Museum in Pasadena was our most-visited museum.

On February 19, 1978, a sunny Sunday, we drove from the neighboring town of Azusa into the San Gabriel Canyon and stopped on the road to enjoy the view. I crossed the two-way road with our son Daniel (eight and a half years old at the time). I was holding his hand. Suddenly he pulled his little hand out of mine, as boys often do, and ran across the highway. In that fraction of a second, a car came on at high speed, and I saw my little son thrown up in the air — and then falling unconscious to the ground. I was shocked. I felt that my life had ended. Huguette was down the road with André, and they came close. Police and a rescue helicopter arrived on the scene with amazing speed. The paramedics took Daniel and Huguette in the helicopter to the closest hospital, the Methodist Hospital of Arcadia. I drove with André, imagining all the bad outcomes a doctor-father might think up in such circumstances. Fortunately, by the time we arrived at the hospital, Daniel had recovered well from his shock. He had a leg fracture and was transferred to the Kaiser hospital in Los Angeles. He made a speedy and complete recovery and went on to continue his good performance in school. The accident, though — the image of my child thrown up in the air — has haunted me all my life. It remains one of two mental pictures of shocking events that come to my mind now and then. It took me some time to recover from the experience.

◆

Daily clinical practice showed me that, despite the renaissance of interest in the diagnosis and treatment of cancer in American medicine at that time, most of our attending physicians, their fellows-in-training, and our medical residents maintained an entrenched negative and hopeless attitude of neglect toward cancer. Therefore, it was essential to educate, to make possible a better and perhaps more accurate understanding of the disease. I began a series of twelve-monthly lectures on all aspects of cancer which I updated and presented every year. Gradually, students, residents, and even attendings started to come to my noon lectures and learn. It was one of my greatest satisfactions.

The most frequently diagnosed cancer at our institution was prostate cancer, as was to be expected in a mostly elderly male population. I was interested in the hormonal intervention used in controlling advanced prostate cancer, and soon after my arrival a new pharmaceutical preparation (the LHRH agonist) was introduced into practice. It was easily administered and tolerated by patients, and it showed good clinical effect. I could not believe that my colleagues in the Urology service refused to use this medication. One of the senior urologists emphatically stated that all his patients with advanced or inoperable prostate cancer would be treated with bilateral orchiectomy (removal of the testicles). It was the old treatment, and it made a very negative effect on patients' body image. We had innumerable meetings, discussions, and many times quite unpleasant protestations. One of my new colleagues, well trained and interested in developing new modalities of treatment, became disillusioned upon realizing the extent of the opposition we continued to encounter from our colleagues in Urology. What made the situation much worse was the fact there was no recourse. The Urology Service, like any other service in the medical center, had the liberty to practice as they preferred. There was no oversight.

Lung cancer was also a major type of cancer in our veterans. They were seen in the "Chest Diseases 'A' Section" and occasionally in "Section 'B.'" Section 'A' was a very large section with many beds under the care of a pulmonologist interested in lung cancer who had made some original contributions on chemotherapy-sensitive small cell lung cancer, a type of lung cancer. The 'B' section, in competition with section 'A,' displayed a totally negative attitude to cancer and oncology in general. During one of my interviews, I asked to see how the Chest Diseases Clinic functioned, and I visited it. In my presence, the doctors told a veteran that he had cancer of the lung, that there was no treatment for him, and that he was discharged from their care. They told him to go home and say his prayers. This was very disappointing; I could sense that I'd have to fight for correct cancer care.

The Ear, Nose, and Throat service had a very large number of patients with head and neck cancer who were operated on with a total disregard for their functional recovery and quality of life. I asked the chief of the service to accept a weekly case review in a cancer conference (tumor board), and he was vehemently opposed. The prevailing attitude of the old-timers was that of resistance to new ideas for the treatment of their patients. I exerted all my persuasive ability, telling them that we wanted to learn from them and explore together new ways of treatment that might improve the end results. New treatment modalities and joint conferences were adopted only when a new chief came.

Many of our patients acted as their own enemies. One day, I met a veteran on the main corridor of the hospital who shocked me: He was in a wheelchair, had signs of the removal of his voice box (most likely because of cancer) and smoked a cigarette through his tracheostomy (an orifice in the trachea). I felt that I had to talk with him to help him change his attitude. He covered his tracheostomy and, in loud sounds, insulted me for daring to talk with him. Smoking any place — in the patients' rooms, on the corridors, and in the elevators — was permitted. I dared to ask a smoking patient to extinguish his cigarette in the elevator and he insulted me until several people were able to calm him down. I could understand the frustration of the many unfortunate patients, but we just wanted to help them. The VA was dedicated to giving them the best treatment possible, and it never held back on funds for the most expensive new medications.

With the help of Dr. I. Rheingold, Chief of the Laboratory service, we started weekly meetings to review the histopathologic material of our new patients and many times we found that the outside diagnoses were incorrect. I was well versed in the histopathology of the lymphatic organs, and when I had doubts, I asked to send the necessary material for consultation to Henry Rappaport's group. Henry made a point of never charging for services performed for the veterans.

After Dr. Rheingold's demise, we had problems with most of the pathologists. One day, I saw a secretary from the Laboratory service (which included Pathology), remove a typed pathology report from a medical record and replace it with another report. It seemed strange, and I asked her what was going on. She said that she had been asked by her chief to replace the old report with the new one in the medical record. On close examination, I found that the two reports dealt with different interpretations of a lymph node biopsy. The first report stated that it was benign, while the second report indicated lymphoma (cancer of the lymph nodes). This was illegal. A change in a diagnosis must be written as an addendum to the original report and immediately reported directly to the treating physicians. Subsequently, I found more of similar changes to pathological diagnoses, changes which called for changes in treatment. There had also been several instances in which there was disagreement on a diagnosis and the pathologists resisted my pleas to send the material for consultation to Dr. Rappaport, who was an international and national consultative authority.

I spent a great deal of time on the microscopic examination of blood and bone marrow findings. I noticed that this interested very much my fellows- and residents-in-training because it was for them a new learning experience, and they became quite able to make good diagnoses.

There were also many political plays made for personal interest and in disregard of patient care. I was just only a few weeks on staff when the COS told me about a problem with the Transfusion Committee chaired by a senior pathologist who was chief of the blood bank. She had not held any committee meetings because she did not "have a secretary to type the minutes." As a result, the activity of the blood bank suffered, and surgeons would not operate without enough blood in the blood bank. The COS asked me if I would I assume the role of Chair of the Transfusion Committee. I accepted without hesitation because I thought it unconscionable to jeopardize the supply of blood because of not having a secretary to type up the committee's minutes. In no time, I reactivated the work of the committee, and the supply of blood and blood products resumed.

I encountered my most acute difficulties with the Human Resources (HR) Service. These occurred very soon after my arrival when I wanted to start the tumor registry. There were no positions for tumor registrars in the master plan of the medical center. I had to explain to the COS and to the chief of the HR that a tumor registry needs professional registrars who are specifically trained in cancer epidemiology, its environmental causes, symptoms, diagnosis, treatment, and outcome — in addition to providing lifelong follow-up services. Trained registrars are the most essential part of a tumor (cancer) registry. To get them, I had to write the position descriptions (PDs) without which no position may be classified and added to the staff of a government institution. To my horror, the person in charge of "classification" in the personnel service thought that a tumor registrar should be recruited on a GS-4 grade, which was close to the lowest grade of clerical personnel. Any new hire from that grade would be horribly underqualified for the position. This made clear the classifying personnel's inability to understand what a tumor registrar should know and do, as well as the complexities of the job. We had big fights, but eventually we became friends, and my PDs were accepted. In this way, we reestablished the tumor registry.

The tumor registry functioned with difficulty because of the problem of retaining good registrars at the approved salary. We provided intense and good training to the registrars. I was available daily for questions on diagnosis and cancer staging. However, as soon as the registrars learned the basics of their work, they were able to find better-paid jobs outside. In fact, we developed quite a good reputation in the community for the quality of training our registrars had; we trained more than twenty registrars. One day, the chief of Personnel explained to me the situation in the VA — what he cynically considered to be the VA's actual role: "To train well, pay little, and have the employees leave for better-paid positions." I thought that this was irresponsible personnel management. It would have been more efficient to train and retain employees to better serve the veterans. It was a long and intense battle, but in the end, I got my registrars' positions upgraded.

I knew from my work at the University of Chicago that a tumor registry must be computerized, and I started working with the computer room to develop a dedicated computer software. I achieved this after a long period of intense work with the help of a computer specialist with whom I developed the software for the tumor registry. I think it was the first such software in the VA.

One day, the COS invited me to his office and gave me a shoebox with some papers inside. He said that it was the only record left from the hospital's defunct cancer program, which had not been re-approved by the Commission on Cancer (CoC) at its last review in 1975. One of the papers was the official CoC letter from 1975 describing the reasons the cancer program had been disapproved: Inactive tumor registry, no tumor boards, absent multidisciplinary clinical cancer conferences, absent education efforts, reporting, etc. A small memo showed how the chiefs of service had passed the buck among themselves, asking each other what to do about the CoC disapproval. They did nothing. It clearly showed the collective state of mind of the chiefs of service. If I had seen this information before accepting my position, I would not have taken the job. The COS asked me to revive the program. I told him that I could do it, but that it would require some staff resource allocation. He promised cooperation. When the plan for reestablishing the cancer program under my leadership sought the approval for well-justified resources from the Resource Committee, two chiefs of service told me: "Edgar, the resources you need and ask for will be taken from our hides." It was not the most elegant way of expressing themselves, but I got the flavor of their views.

A cancer program required a cancer committee, a functional tumor registry, cancer conferences, and educational and analytical work on cancer care. Our tumor registry finally worked satisfactorily, and we had modestly printed our first biennial report. The report was very well received by the CoC and was given as a model of graphic presentation to other tumor registries. It was indeed important to write such reports to communicate with other registries.

I invited some colleagues to serve on the Cancer Program Committee. I could sense their lack of interest, but I did not show that I noticed it, and I kept them involved in the reorganization of the cancer program. It was obvious that almost none of the physicians understood the role of a cancer program, and I explained it to them again and again, starting with the management. We had to place the institution on the correct track. I frequently thought that no hospital in United States would be certified for the practice of medicine if it practiced the cancer care in the manner of LBVAMC. I was very vocal about its low standards.

There were huge problems in every aspect of cancer screening, timely diagnosis, and correct treatment. It was very tough work, very time-consuming. Many asked me why I did it, and my answer was that "it had to be done." Every time I thought of using my time more proficiently in another institution, but I reset such thoughts because I felt passionately about improving the cancer care of veterans. In addition, I had a young family, I could not move with ease, and Huguette had a good professional position. In addition to my active clinical work, I spent many hours in committee meetings, chairing tumor boards, supervising the tumor registry, and in arguing with the COS and with the colleagues who could not understand the essential modern concept of multidisciplinary efforts in cancer. This appeared to be a novel idea to administrators, service chiefs, section chiefs, and medical and nursing personnel. I had to start with establishing tumor boards (also called cancer conferences). These were meetings of physicians and surgeons who reviewed the diagnoses, treatments, and clinical courses of difficult cancer patients. The meeting had to include a pathologist who reviewed the diagnostic material, radiologists who reviewed the pertinent x-ray films, nuclear medicine physicians who reviewed the scans, and the clinicians who presented and discussed the cases. In many such situations, new ideas on diagnostic modalities and treatment may emerge, to the benefit of the patient as well as to the intellectual advantage of the medical personnel in attendance. No such meeting had taken place in many years. Some doctors felt that I was checking up on their practices, and they did everything possible to avoid having their cases presented and discussed in the tumor boards. I responded that we wanted to discuss cases so that we could learn. With great hesitation, they started to like how I conducted the conferences. I was very glad to learn that those conferences continue to take place in full force, even now, after forty years.

It was much more difficult to establish weekly chest conferences. The chief of the Pulmonary Section 'B,' a well-known specialist in pleural diseases, was adamantly opposed to any multidisciplinary review of the patients' clinical problems. In a threatening tone, he asked me: "Are you going to tell me how to treat my patients?" I responded: "If necessary, I will offer suggestions and recommendations to improve the veterans' outcome. Surely, our younger colleagues in training should learn that there is a way to treat lung cancer instead of sending patients home without any attempt to treat them."

There was an active fellowship program in pulmonary diseases, and trainees liked my chest conferences. All concerned disciplines met at these conferences: Radiology, Pulmonary, Medical Oncology, Thoracic Surgery, and

Radiation Oncology. They are still meeting weekly, and I am told that the chest conferences are the best multidisciplinary conferences in the hospital: It was and still is a good work still in force forty years later.

As I already stated, I believe in responsibility and accountability, and it seemed imperative to me to report honestly and regularly on our work, our problems, and our results. This was not only for transparency, but because by recognizing our shortcomings, we might improve on them. This was part of my thinking in writing an annual report on the tumor registry and Cancer Program. I entered all the end-results available in our tumor registry. We had to perform audits and studies on the timeliness of the diagnosis and treatment. We had to report on the survival of our treated patients. The Board of the CoC included representatives from seventeen major medical societies in the US, including the VA. Any new program had to prove sustained activity for two years before being surveyed. In 1980, we passed the CoC survey, with commendations, as a teaching hospital. Historically, our program was the eighth approved cancer program in the VA. We had many triennial CoC surveys and passed them very well. My colleagues on staff elected me the Cancer Liaison Fellow and the Cancer Liaison Physician with the CoC, a function I fulfilled until 2005.

With the CoC's approval of our new cancer program, I started to invite friends and well-known oncologists, surgeons, immunologists, and basic scientists to come as visiting professors and lecture on a large variety of topics in medical oncology. The lectures were well attended and created an academic environment. Dr. Thomas C. Hall came often as a visiting professor. His lectures opened horizons and stimulated new thoughts. We became good friends. Tom Hall was viewed by leading oncologists as the "best mind in oncology" because of his insights and original thinking. I learned very useful facts from our long discussions.

♦

Because of my hard work at LBVAMC, in the first two years I could not do very much for the UCI School of Medicine, except for intense teaching. I taught seven courses. They were essentially courses on the interpretation of the symptoms of diseases, on the pathophysiology of diseases, on how to take a good medical history, how to examine a patient, and how to become a doctor.

I taught the most seminal courses of the medical school. I also lectured formally on cancer, and I served as an attending on service, teaching residents and fellows. I saw patients there once a week and attended various clinical conferences.

I recall my experience with my last group of students: I gave them two patients who had been selected because they were not in pain or otherwise uncomfortable or incapacitated, had obvious signs of their ailments, and, very importantly, were good historians. I introduced my students to them and let the students take their medical histories as they had been instructed. They did their thing and were obviously uncomfortable conducting the first interviews of their careers. I helped them saying by that this was expected and that generations of physicians had felt the same discomfiture. I also said that they had to learn about diseases, their signs and symptoms; I asked them what medical textbooks they used. They replied: "Wikipedia." I could not believe it, but I recovered quickly from my astonishment: Times had changed indeed. It was the last time I taught students.

The UCI employed many excellent investigators in basic science and in cancer research, and many of them had a major interest in developing a clinical cancer center at the medical center in Orange, California. There was no initiative at the local level. There were many on the UCI faculty who criticized the dean of the School of Medicine for not energizing a clinical counterpart in research. In 1981, I was told that word about my work and its results at LBVAMC had spread out, and I was offered the position of Chair of Clinical Oncology at UCI, which I declined. I agreed, however, to serve as Chair of the Professional Education Committee. Among various postgraduate activities, we organized a breast cancer symposium which made a positive impact on the way breast cancer was diagnosed, studied, and treated in Orange County.

I worked very intensively on the UCI Oncology Planning Task Force from 1978 to 1989 as the only medical oncologist. I helped the committee visualize the type of investigator the University needed as director of the Clinical Oncology program. I believed that in view of the limited resources available, we had to recruit a visionary with a passion for developing a cancer center with modest resources. I explained to the dean and to all the parties on the search committee that we needed somebody who had a special investigation project and the ability to establish its research basis. We interviewed many first-class oncologists who declined the position because of the funding restrictions, but eventually the cancer center was created.

♦

In 1979, I accepted invitations to lecture at various universities and meetings in the States and abroad. I made many new friends, especially in Italy. The following year, Professor Georges Mathé, noted French hematologist, invited me to lecture on AILD at the Institute of Cancerology in Villejuif, France. Professor Bernard Dreyfuss, whom I admired for his work on refractory anemia, also invited me to lecture at the Henri Mondor Hospital in Paris. It was a very successful visit. This was followed by lectures on AILD in Israel at Hebrew University in Jerusalem, Tel Aviv University, Ben Gurion University of the Negev in Beer Sheba, and Beilinson Hospital in Petach Tikvah. It was with great emotion and pleasure that I met my former colleagues and the staff of the pathology department I had left fourteen years before. My former colleagues and friends realized that my dreams of years back had become reality due to my perseverance and hard work. We enjoyed meeting friends and family. The cloud over our visit was finding that Mother was not doing well. I observed some clinical signs related to her long-term uncontrolled arterial hypertension. I talked with Father very seriously and insisted that they move to Long Beach and live with us. Huguette was in full agreement with this plan.

My parents came to Long Beach in early 1981. They wanted their own apartment, and we found one in proximity to us and furnished it very nicely. We enjoyed our enlarged family life. My parents came to visit us every day, and we tried hard to interest them in all parts of our daily life. The boys were interesting and funny. I do remember the first Passover we had with my parents in Long Beach. It was highly emotional for me having them with us on such festive occasion.

In the summer of 1983, we made pleasant arrangements for the care and security of my parents, and we went on a long trip to Europe. It was a marvelous vacation with Huguette, Daniel (fourteen), and André (twelve). The boys were at a fine age when we could talk about a great variety of things, including cultural matters. We spent much time together. We flew to Amsterdam and then travelled by train to Copenhagen, Gothenburg,

Stockholm, and Uppsala. We continued by train to Oslo, where we rented a car and visited some of the Norwegian fjords and Bergen. Back in Copenhagen, we went by train to Vienna, where I had to attend an international meeting and present a paper. We visited Vienna well, its art and historical treasures, and the boys were enchanted. We were on the train back to Amsterdam when I suddenly saw from the train window the towers of the Cologne cathedral. Without hesitation, I asked my family to descend from the train, and I shared with them my change of our itinerary. After a nice visit of the city of Cologne, we resumed our trip by car, visiting Aachen, Ghent, Bruges, Brussels, and Antwerp. We came back home full of excitement and carrying in our minds many pleasant memories.

My parents did well during our trip. However, Mother's mental status had slowly deteriorated despite appropriate treatment, and she started experiencing intermittent absences. It was heartbreaking for me to watch Mother, such an intelligent and witty person, losing the function of her most important asset. Father, on the other hand, was very alert, and he wrote many letters to his many friends in Israel. I realized that he missed them and his brothers in the Freemason Lodge, where he had worked with much devotion. My brother and his wife came to be with us on the winter break. On Christmas morning, Mother suffered a stroke that left her unconscious. The CT scan showed a massive hemorrhage that had flooded her brain and impaired most of her physiologic reflexes. There was nothing that could be done. We were devastated. The neurologists at the hospital thought that her days were numbered. We asked Father to stay with us at our house, got a hospital bed there for Mother, and were favored in finding a lady who could take care of her daily. We had a big house, and we made the best arrangements possible. Father was despondent and could not gain any respite. All my support and all my attempts to talk with him were in vain. He asked only how long Mother would live in this condition. When more than one month had passed without any change, the neurologists could not believe that she was still alive. It was a terrible time. After about one year of devoted care during which no known medical complications ensued, Father started talking about committing suicide. This scared me because I knew that he was very depressed and that he could do it. Indeed, he did commit suicide two years after Mother's stroke. He could not endure it any longer. He was eighty-nine years old. The image of my dead father is one of the two mental images of shock that haunts me some nights. Father was an extraordinary man, larger than life. A Yankee in spirit, he exemplified a willingness to take chances on unknown ventures, and he had the determination to succeed. I could not accept his demise. Blessed be his memory. Mother survived for two and a half more years, did not suffer physically, did not develop any infections, and died quietly a total of four and a half years after her stroke. In retrospect, I think that her stroke killed my father first and then herself.

◆

The groundwork for the reestablishment of the Hematology-Oncology section and for the reapproval of the cancer program had been completed and I was proud and happy that I had successfully survived the tribulations associated with those successes. I knew, however, that much more had to be done. The role of cancer programs is to improve the medical practice in hospitals. They are necessary in institutions with any more than two hundred new cancer patients a year. Our daily work, along with the data recorded in the tumor registry and the findings discovered in cancer conferences, revealed severe neglect in the work of some physicians. Some of them were simply ignorant, and their chiefs did not make any effort to educate or reeducate them. There was no internal reporting such as in-service morbidity and mortality conferences. Some physicians thought that without supervision or an obligation to report to somebody with more experience (as is usually done in any responsible institution), they were at liberty to exercise unorthodox approaches without scientific basis. I recall some of the major problems:

We found out that a young thoracic surgeon had operated on a veteran with an advanced lung cancer that had invaded the chest wall, causing severe chest pain. The surgeon removed the cancer with a large part of the lung and part of the chest wall. It was a mutilating procedure without any chance of success. The treatment should have consisted of chemotherapy and radiation therapy and surgery might have been carried out if the patient experienced a regression in he extent of the cancer. When asked why he'd carried out such an operation, he told us that he had treated other cases in a similar manner, and he believed that he used a correct approach. He did not consult with his colleagues or with his chief. We then reviewed all his cases and showed him and his chief that, in fact, all those patients had died a few days after the surgery. There was no comment from the chief of service, a senior surgeon with many years of service. The younger surgeon left soon after his unacceptable operations became known to the medical staff.

I mentioned that we had a very poor relationship with our colleagues on the Pathology service. To avoid conflict, I asked that my staff and the pathologist on call for the week review together all the pathology slides of our new patients at a multi-head microscope. This would have been innocuous and mostly agreeable to any other group of physicians, but our Pathology colleagues felt threatened and hid the slides under various pretexts. In many difficult cases, it was impossible to obtain a review or an outside consultation, which is usually obligatory in any medical institution. At least I helped establish the rule that any change in a reported diagnosis should be communicated to the treating physician and recorded. Many years later, the VA instituted a mandate which required the review of a certain percentage of cases of cancer by a panel of pathologists at the Armed Forces Institute of Pathology.

The most vexing problem was the complete ignorance demonstrated in the documentation of the extent of a cancer (called "cancer staging"). Cancer staging is the most basic determination in cancer management because the treatment of most cancers depends on the extent (the stage) of the disease at diagnosis and te prognosis is directly related to the stage of the disease at diagnosis. The stage of the disease was almost entirely absent or wrong, and this needed immediate correction. The American College of Surgeons and the CoC had defined the stages for each site of cancer, and this is known as the American Joint Commission on Cancer (or, AJCC) Cancer Staging. I lectured, designed staging forms, coaxed colleagues, explained the need for rational diagnostic procedures, and taught the natural history of the cancer of various sites. I reported to the Cancer Committee and to the Clinical Executive Board on the lack of staging evaluations and the consequent incorrect treatments used. It took several years to see the beginnings of improvements and several more years to see correct staging applied in all cases.

◆

Before the introduction of computers to medical practice, it was routine for all services that issued written reports to print them in triplicate. This was the accepted procedure in all hospitals. The original was to be inserted into the patient's medical record, but it did not always make it there because the clerks who worked in the Medical Administration Service often discarded the original copy of the report. The second copy was supposed to be sent to the treating physician, which was a very good practice. The third copy was to be retained in the Radiology service. Due to neglect or incompetence, the clerks in the Radiology service would often say that they were not able to read the name of the physician requesting an X-ray examination and so did not send their findings on to that physician. In this way, physicians often remained uninformed of the findings reported on their patients. It is also true that the doctors did not always recall that they did not receive the report on an X-ray examination they had requested. The consequence of this situation could have a major impact on the patient care. Without knowing that cancer had been suspected on an X-ray examination, physicians could not act properly and were very late in pursuing the necessary examinations. I became aware of this situation when I found out that there was an excessively long period of time between patients' first symptoms and the diagnosis of lung cancer, many times more than four months. All the efforts to make possible the sending of a copy of a radiology report to the treating physicians to alert them on the findings and initiate the necessary work-up were unsuccessful. It took a major effort inside the cancer program to document this situation and its grave consequences.

The medical center's practice of medicine certainly needed urgent and intense supervision and many remedial actions. This was not work that could be done by one man alone. I asked for help, and after I'd sent out many pleas to the Medical Director, the COS, and the Resource Board (on which I served), I received the authorization to hire a nurse for the cancer program. The chief nurse at that time, younger and even worse than the one I found when I came on board, was adamantly opposed to the idea of a nurse working for the cancer program. She wanted to exercise full control on all the nurses. Finally, after some struggle, I was able to offer the position of Nurse Coordinator to a nurse who had worked with me and my staff for quite some time, and we appreciated her.

For the clinical intervention upon detection of abnormalities suspicious of lung cancer, and in absence of regular, direct alerts from radiology to the treating physicians, I thought that we needed to capture these reports. I wanted to code the written reports as "Code 1-T." It took an insurmountable effort to convince the radiologists to use it. We reviewed such reports with the radiologists and the doctors who had ordered the examinations. There was an uproar of critique and negative commentary: "Why does the cancer program need to get involved in our practice?" We had to counterargue, stating that if a diagnosis of lung cancer took more than two weeks, there might be enough reason to intervene. When we were able to document that we could reduce the time necessary for a diagnosis of lung cancer from more than four months to less than two weeks, all the irritated voices calmed down. In addition, major savings (of about $750,000 per year) resulted when we were able to cut down on the long hospital stays needed for poorly planned diagnostic evaluations and the incorrect use of diagnostic facilities (X-rays and CT scans). When the Joint Commission on Hospital Accreditation came for its biennial hospital review, the management asked me to present our work. The commission was delighted and found that our work was exemplary because it showed concern for the sick by identifying a serious clinical problem, devising a method to solve it, and documenting not only that method's success in improving the situation, but its sustainability. With the advent of the computerization of all services in the 1980s, my colleagues realized that it was not a desire to intrude into their relationships with their patients that motivated my efforts, and our work became easier; all the "Code 1-T" alerts were placed online. As I believe in teamwork, we developed a new clinic, the Pulmonary-Radiology Conference Clinic (PRCC) to review the cases coded and initiate necessary diagnostic procedures without delay. The PRCC continues with the work I initiated. It is now thirty-nine years later.

◆

Since the Chicago days, I'd participated in the American College of Physicians postgraduate courses for those preparing for the board examinations in internal medicine; the courses took place in Pasadena, California and Honolulu, Hawaii. In 1990, I took part of my sabbatical at the Armed Forces Institute of Pathology in Silver Spring, Maryland. I wanted to learn more on the molecular biology methods used in the histopathology of cancer diagnosis. Later that same year I spent the rest of my sabbatical in Paris, studying the hematologic changes in refractory anemias of the elderly called myelodysplastic syndromes.

In 1989, I was invited to preside over a meeting of the International Society for Environmental Toxicology and Cancer (ISETC) in Brussels, Belgium. I was asked to serve as an associate editor of its publication, *The Journal of Environmental Pathology, Toxicology and Oncology* (JEPTO). In 1990, I became the Editor-in-Chief of this journal, and, with the cooperation of a fine editorial board, we made the journal into a fine biomedical publication. We published about fifteen articles per quarterly issue, and I personally reviewed each article submitted for publication for its scientific aims and testable hypotheses, methods used, and scientifically valid interpretation of the results as defined by the study plan and objectives. It was great intellectual fun. In 2006 I was already retired from my hospital functions, and I relinquished the editorship of the journal. I was asked to continue as Editor Emeritus.

In 1993, I was invited to teach medical oncology at the new medical school of Uludağ University, which had just been built in the outskirts of Bursa in Turkey. I taught there for two weeks, an almost complete curriculum in medical oncology. My work was helped the medical school, which soon established a new Department of Medical Oncology. Dr. Osman Manavoğlu, who had spent some time in training with me in Long Beach, was appointed Chief of the new Department of Medical Oncology.

The following year, my friend, Dr. Armand Abramovici, who had become a professor and Chair of the Department of Pathology at the Sackler School of Medicine at Tel Aviv University in Israel, asked me to teach hematopathology to the American students at his school. It was a great experience.

A hospital colleague who was member of the Hungarian Academy of Medicine (a US institution) invited me to lecture on the "Management of Prostate Cancer" at the biennial Pannonian Conferences held in the late 1990s at Dunajska Streda in Slovakia and in Romania. The intention of the Academy was to provide an update on cancer diagnosis and treatment to our colleagues in the former socialist republics. I had not wanted to go back to Romania in the forty years since I left the country. I had too many bad memories. But I could not refuse the invitation of the Hungarian Academy of Medicine. At the end of my lecture in Romania, some doctors asked me why it was considered necessary to make a correct diagnosis and staging of the disease. I was surprised by such question. They explained that they didn't have any of the diagnostic modalities I'd reviewed for them...

◆

Real progress in the organization of cancer care in the VA occurred only with the appointment of Dr. Kenneth Kaiser as the Chief Medical Director in 1995. Facing opposition from old-timers in the VA, he was successful in transforming the VA into a modern and energetic healthcare system. Computerization of medical records and superb software were introduced, and twenty-one Veterans Integrated Service Networks (VISN) systems were instituted. Among many other innovations, cancer programs became required functions in the VA and a Chief of Cancer Programs was appointed to the VACO to oversee the cancer programs' activities. I was appointed as the contact person for the cancer program in VISN 22, a role I held until my retirement in 2003. One great satisfaction for me was the VACO's recognition of our medical center as a Comprehensive Cancer Center in the VA in 1997. This was the highest degree of recognition available in the VA. We had built and employed at that time all the functional and necessary parts of sophisticated cancer surveillance: diagnosis, treatment, and a rehabilitation center.

In 1998, the VACO requested that medical centers submit reports on innovations in medical care. The description of our method for early cancer diagnosis and the PRCC work was selected from several hundred papers for presentation at a national VA Conference called "Journey of Change" in Baltimore, MD. Then it was posted on the VA website "VA Intranet Innovations," and on the VA's Virtual Learning Center. I published a short article on the problems we had faced, what we did, and our results. It was the story of major improvements in cancer care in the VA, and many medical centers adopted our program. At the "Journey of Change" Conference, I was invited to participate in a working group of VA leadership to discuss the possibilities of networking. I took the opportunity to develop the idea that cancer education and research offer vast opportunities for collaboration which could, among other benefits, help us avoid unnecessary duplications of effort. The medical directors, associate medical directors, and chiefs of staff in the group asked questions, which I answered in detail, though I thought that all of it would be immediately forgotten. To my surprise, a few days later, Ron Norby, the director of VISN 22, which included LBVAMC, visited me and asked me to develop the ideas I had expounded upon in Baltimore and to make a proposal for a cancer network in VISN 22. I liked the challenge, and I immediately started working, calling colleagues and organizing our first meeting in Long Beach. All interested parties from Loma Linda, West Los Angeles, and San Diego VAMCs, and from the Las Vegas Clinic attended the meeting. There was enthusiasm in the group and agreement on the concept of sharing the resources of diagnostic facilities such as pathology and radiology departments. My proposal to join in clinical research was based on the "Memorandum of Understanding," which the VA had recently signed with the NCI. This interested and made sense to those in attendance. According to the "Memorandum of Understanding," the VA agreed to enter patients into clinical trials designed to improve cancer treatment and survival. The NCI supported these trials with funds for their management. I presented data showing that our VISN could assume a leading role in this endeavor. I summarized our conclusions in a book, the "Blue Book," as we called it. It showed how we could open a new way of networking in cancer care and research. Ron Norby brought the proposal for discussion to the chiefs of staff. Much to our surprise, the COSs of San Diego and West Los Angeles VAMCs opposed any networking without giving us any reason. Ron and I were disappointed, and he said that I was "ahead of the times." About ten years later, networking was introduced to VISN 22.

◆

In retrospect, the 1980s and 1990s were years of intense professional activity with many realizations and successes at LBVAMC as well as at the UCI School of Medicine. I felt many satisfactions after so many well-fought and well-sustained efforts. My most personal solace, in my heart of hearts, came however, from my family life. The boys enjoyed their years of Boy Scouting, something I encouraged them to do, as I had been a Boy Scout in my youth, and I valued those lessons and how they built character. I did realize that the organization and its practice had changed, which was to be expected. I thought that the most important aspect of the organization was how it taught its members to adopt the moral principles of the movement: truthfulness, helpfulness to others, and the virtues of leading a clean life. I think that our sons developed such qualities. Daniel started to show talent for organized work, and his colleagues identified him as a leader. Our boys did very well in school and were chosen for the mentally gifted minors programs. Daniel graduated from high school in the Program of Additional Curricular Experiences (PACE) at Long Beach Polytechnic High School, which was very well regarded, and André was in the fine Signal Hill Academic Research Program (SHARP), also in Long Beach. They were funny, receptive, and adopted the family sense of humor, which pleased me very much. I was not inclined to practice sports, and I regret not having stimulated them in sports activities. They did, however, plaid sports at their respective schools.

I do believe in public education, which I regard as a right of the citizens. However, I felt that the school system betrayed us, the citizens. We entrust our children to the schools daily for more hours than children spend with us, their parents. I was shocked to realize that our public education system imparts so little intellectual curiosity to our children. The official curriculum lacks in many aspects of new knowledge in areas such as history, geography, sciences, and health education. I am referring to new knowledge that parents expect to be taught to their children. This made me think very seriously about what we could do to remedy this failure.

Our boys spoke very well, which I liked. Daniel was very interested in issues of social science and life in general. André was more reserved, a very nice boy. We talked a lot on many social, political, and spiritual topics. I explained countless issues to them, trying very hard to share the ideas and philosophies that are such a large part of our becoming responsible adults and good citizens. One day, close to his graduation, Daniel said: "Dad, I learned more from you than from school." André concurred. "Very nice," I thought, "but do they want to please me or are the schools' curriculums poor?"

André learned some French and participated in a Québecois French immersion program: "Knowing another language is like having a new life," teaches the Talmud. In his last high school years, Daniel went to Oxford University for a summer of studies, and we were happy to make it possible. In the following year, he went to Salamanca University to polish his Spanish. He was curious and bookish. André learned to play the clarinet and made good progress. I loved the way he played Mozart's clarinet concerto in A major.

In the mid-1980s, I got a computer for them because I felt very strongly that they should become computer-literate to succeed in our times. The boys were very surprised when I installed the computer in our home. They rapidly learned the computer programs. I am still very happy about that decision, for it affected their lives most positively, as I had expected.

In 1987, Daniel was admitted to UCLA. He had acquired many advanced placements (AP) credits from high school, which may have served to place him in the a sophomore year, but it soon became known to us that he needed more time for his personal growth. He took a good job using his computer knowledge to help others. He made an excellent income which opened his taste for the expensive things in life. After a few years, he decided to learn digital photography and enrolled in the Brooks Institute of Photography in Santa Barbara, California. He refined his knowledge and experience in computer programs. He joined the Naval Reserve as a photographer. I asked him why he wanted to do this, and his answer was that he wanted to "give something to his country." I liked this. He also became a Freemason, and he took that path in life very seriously. Eventually, Daniel took various jobs that utilized his extensive computer experience. He became a project manager at Boeing in Seal Beach, where he worked for several years, living close to us in Long Beach. He learned the work of project management by himself.

André wanted to learn to play the guitar. I was very happy about that, and we went to a good guitar store where he was shown a variety of guitars. I sensed that he was not interested in them. When I asked him what the matter was, André, a guy of few words, told me: "I am not interested in an acoustic guitar; I want an electric guitar." I didn't know much about amplifiers and high-decibel music, and I had to get educated in this. His interest was in playing rock music with friends. I did not like it because it was so unbearably loud. I saw that they need a place for their rehearsals, and I told them to do it in our backyard until we came home from work. This was a good arrangement for us, but neighbors called the police to report the noise. I thought that our neighbors might have told us that it bothered them instead of calling the police, but they had a different view. Then I let the boys play in the garage until the weather was too cold; then I could not let them down and I told them to use our large family room, with the clear understanding that they would stop their work when we came home. This worked well. Upon his graduation from high school, André took his general college education at the next-door California State University at Long Beach. I talked with him a lot and found it helpful to come home earlier each day in order engage him in interesting conversations — mostly on history and the effect of culture and social events on politics, a topic in which I was always interested. We had a good library of reference books, which he consulted. It worked out very well. I was happy to have had this idea. It bonded us, and I think it helped develop his intellectual sophistication. One day after his second year in college, I asked him what he wished to do in his life. Without hesitation, he said that folk music was his line. I then asked where he could learn it well. He answered that there was a renowned school in Boston, the Berklee College of Music. I asked him if he wanted to go there, and his happiness was evident. And so, he left home and returned in 1994 with a diploma in Music Recording. One year later, he moved to San Francisco, to play music, folk and Americana, but this did not work out well for him financially. He met Noëlle Hampton, a charming songwriter and native of Mill Valley, California. They fell in love and lived there, poor and happy.

Huguette had a quiet life throughout our sons' growth and development. She worked long hours at the Kaiser Permanente clinic in East Los Angeles, where she was well appreciated by the staff and loved by her many patients. She often returned home quite late. That gave me the idea that I might start cooking after I thought for a very long time that I was unable to do it correctly. A senior colleague at the University of Chicago used to say, "cooking is physics and chemistry," and he was correct. My family, as well as invited guests, liked my cooking and baking. It gave me a good feeling to prepare and share good food in a joyous atmosphere.

♦

I served on the Representative Assembly and on the Executive Committee of the Academic Senate of the School of Medicine at the University of California, Irvine for twenty years, and I chaired various committees. I believe that my best work started in the 1990s, when I was asked to serve on the Admission Committee for the School of Medicine. I was very impressed with the quality of the applicants. Clearly, they were devoted to their studies, but I argued that, while graduating from college with a GPA of 4.0 certainly denotes high intellectual achievement, it did not assure us about the human quality for the practice of medicine of the individual candidate. New and younger committee members with fresh views adopted this wisdom in the selection of new students and this view became the new philosophy of the Admission Committee. The result was that we graduated better doctors with a more humane understanding of the profession.

In the late 1990's I was invited to serve on the Curriculum and Educational Policy Committee (CEP), a standing committee of the Academic Senate of the School of Medicine. I started my work by reading up on policies and procedures and the prior activity of the committee. There was nothing interesting, just the rubber-stamping of students' requests to change their rotations at the times of their choosing. I thought that this was not what the work of the Curriculum Committee should be. I was surprised to see that the classes of the first two years (the pre-clinical years) were given in an archaic pattern, with disciplines following one another without any attempt to emphasize the interactions of their subjects and/or their applications to the clinical context. It reminded me of my own curriculum so many years back. It is true that many great doctors graduated from not-very-distinguished medical schools, which means that it is the talent and wisdom of the individual doctor that counts. It became evident to me that nobody ever examined how the school taught its students or how medicine should be taught in general. We could certainly be smarter about it. I recalled some work on possible innovations in which I had participated at the University of Chicago. After a year, I was asked to chair the committee, and I served on the CEP for twelve years, most of the time as its Chair.

I started by inviting the chairs and teachers of all the teaching departments to a big meeting; I showed them a board on one side of which I'd posted small colored tabs representing the classes in the existing curriculum. On the other side of the board, I showed the subjects taught in the order I thought they should be taught. My plan was to make possible and apparent the connections between disciplines, along with their functional interactions and their applications to clinical medicine. I asked the professors attending the meeting: "Do you want to continue in the old way, or would you like my new way?" To my surprise, they applauded. Then I asked why such necessary changes had not been implemented already, and they said: "There was no leadership." They enthusiastically approved my plan. I promised to work with them, and I warned them in earnest that it would be very hard work. Indeed, it took two years to complete the task, an enormous task, with so many discussions, meetings, letters, agreements, and disagreements. At the very end, we'd made a modern curriculum, and the students loved it. It pleased me very much to learn that they were enthused by the new curriculum. It continues to be the curriculum of the School of Medicine at UCI.

While serving on the committee for the Rules and Jurisdiction of UCI School of Medicine, it became known that the By-laws of the school had not been updated for many years. This was not an acceptable situation in an institution like our medical school. I had some experience with the concepts of the by-laws, which were written to protect institutional rights within the university and the community as well as the faculty. By-laws, in general, define in detail the internal organization of an institution and the working of its components. The writing of by-laws is a delicate matter wherein one must keep in mind that the protection of the users should not contradict the interests of other parties related or unrelated to the users. I rewrote the by-laws between 2001 and 2002, and the Executive Committee of the Academic Senate approved them.

I was elected to serve on the Institutional Review Board (IRB), which reviewed all human-based research proposals, and I learned a considerable amount of new information on human rights in research, ethics, and informed consent. I think I also contributed my share, for I had been involved in clinical research for many years. The doctors had some problems with the IRB because the doctors' research proposals were often not well understood, possibly because of the way they were written, and long delays occurred in the review and approval process. Many doctors became discouraged and, blaming the complexities and the delays of the IRB, did not devote themselves to research. This was a loss to the medical school. To improve the record, in 2000 the dean established the Dean's Scientific Review Committee (DSRC) to review all medical school research before it was submitted to the IRB. I was asked to chair and organize the work of this new committee. I wrote its policies and procedures, and, with a fine group of researchers, I was able to expeditiously review all submitted research protocols. We advised on the correct way of writing the background information, theses, objectives, methodologies, results, statistical evaluation of the results, and the significance of the proposed research. It was sometimes amazing and perplexing to see that investigators had excellent ideas but could not formulate them logically and clearly. I do believe that this committee fulfilled a very important function in the UCI School of Medicine's research accomplishments. We overcame the initial local antagonism of those who did not understand our role, and soon it became evident to them that the DSRC was not a nuisance, but rather, a very helpful and effective arm of the research approval process. However, a new dean of the School of Medicine did not appreciate our work and asked for the discontinuation of the DSRC, although many advised him against his idea. It occurred to me that good and necessary work always resurfaces under the same or a different name: The work of the DSRC was reinstated in the UCI Institute for Clinical and Translational Science as the Scientific Research Committee, which I chaired it for four years, a few years after I retired.

♦

In 2003, after twenty-five years of sustained service, I felt that it was time for me to retire from the VA and from my active role on the Academic Senate of the School of Medicine. This would give me the liberty to travel to Ottawa as frequently as necessary to help my brother, who was very sick. I also wanted to have time for other activities. The Chief of Staff and the Medical Center Director asked me to continue as chair of the cancer program, and I agreed. Without much ado, I changed my work schedule, and, without any regret, I became a retiree, continuing my functions, but without any fixed schedule. I recalled that old saying: "Old soldiers never die, they simply fade away."

In Retirement

I wrote in detail about my preoccupation with the time to diagnosis of cancer and the time from diagnosis to treatment. This appeared to be a simple series of medical procedures, but that was not what was happening at LBVAMC. I wrote that it was taking up to four or six months for physicians to make a diagnosis of cancer and about the same length of time to start treatment. On a detailed review, we found that there were numerous and irrelevant reasons for this situation, including the failure of the clerical staff to make the appointments ordered by the physicians and to assure the follow-up. Patients were lost. It was incredible. I reported regularly to the Clinical Executive Board, the COS, and the director, but nothing worked. With perseverance, and with the help of a coordinating nurse acting as a case manager, we improved the situation considerably. It was only much later that the concept of case managers involved in the care of every patient was adopted by the management.

There were many cases of tort claims filed by injured parties. I was asked to review tort claims before and after my retirement, and I found that the VA attorneys were ill-prepared and unable to correctly analyze the medical-legal cases. They didn't take the care to invite expert witnesses for complete in-depth reviews in order to ensure that damages and fines would be paid only if a case warranted the claimed compensation. I reviewed cases in depth, and upon detailed analyses, I made my depositions, and I went to court if necessary. Having witnessed the poor performance of the VA attorneys, I suggested that the COS hold a seminar for the VA attorneys of the Los Angeles VA District Office on the topic of medical reviews of tort claims. I developed a short course for the attorneys, teaching them the correct order of such a medical review, how to assemble and interpret the data, and how to use an expert witness. The idea was to be honest and to review all the data expertly and objectively. I was told that the course helped the attorneys.

◆

The Veterans Health Administration (VHA) and its central office realized that the medical community in the States had become alerted to the cost of health care delivery. The administration rightfully wanted to evaluate the cost of running its hospitals and clinics. Such evaluations were possible using the computer-accessed data of every procedure made by physicians, nurses, and technologists. The Decision Support System (DSS) an invention of VACO, allowed staff to establish the time used for each procedure based on an honor system. In the last year of my service as a retired physician, the medical center's director told me that she appreciated my administrative skills and asked me to serve as a consultant to the medical center. My charge was to review the data held by DSS and examine its authenticity to make possible a comparison with the data of other medical centers in VISN 22 and nationwide. It was quite necessary work. The center's workload was correctly recorded in its huge computer system. By reporting the time used by each employee for each procedure, one could easily determine if a service was efficient or not. I was to report directly and exclusively to a new chief of staff. I worked with each chief of service and his or her business manager to review the work units and the time effort of the employees involved. This showed whether they were within the realm of allocated staffing and expected cost accounting.

In December 2013, I informed the COS that my work had been completed, and I decided to leave my office at the end of January 2014, after ten years of work in retirement. The next day, Huguette and I embarked on a beautiful long voyage to Australia and a cruise around New Zealand, followed by a memorable visit to Vietnam, Cambodia, and Singapore. How refreshing to learn that New Zealand and Singapore were the two countries who formally and severely prohibited corruption in public life and penalized it.

◆

Huguette retired from the Kaiser Permanente Medical Group in 1998, when she was sixty-five years old. That was the rule. After a nice party, she became a retiree. She really liked it. She'd had a good time working in the Kaiser Permanente clinic in East Los Angeles for twenty-two years. She had nice colleagues, and she was appreciated by patients and staff; both miss her now. Huguette has organized her life in retirement quite pleasantly.

Daniel has made noticeable progress in his computer software work and his computer work in general. He had several office jobs, not always pleasant, but he acquired experience and learned program management on his own. He also took special courses and received recognition and certification in that field. In the last several years he has been very gainfully employed. In 2008, he married Berenice Olivas, a lovely mental health specialist. They have twin daughters, Carys and Isla, now seven years old. I was quite enthused when Daniel decided to get an MBA from Chapman University in Orange, California. I think that his new education and degree will support his successful professional progress.

André and Noëlle were happy in Mill Valley near San Francisco. They were socially active but were not making the necessary income. I encouraged André to move to Austin because the local scene wasn't allowing any progress in their careers, and Austin became the center of folk music in the States. It was only in 2004 when André and Noëlle moved to Austin, TX. They got married in spring of 2005. Noëlle composes songs and has made several CDs that have been very well received. André is appreciated in the music industry as a record engineer and producer. He teaches audio engineering at Austin City College. Their careers have flourished in Austin. Recently they formed a band called "The Belle Sounds" which is enthusiastically followed by many who adore their music.

After his marriage to Tilly, my brother established a very nice general medicine practice in Ottawa, Ontario, Canada. He decided that he had worked as a surgeon for many years and that it was time to restrict his practice to general family practice. I thought it was a good decision. With his fine approach to patients, he was much appreciated. However, Tilly missed her native town, Lucerne, in Switzerland, and, after many debates, they moved there. His practice was limited by Swiss law, and I was not sure that he would be able to accept the limitations. I asked him if he thought that the move could be successful, and I remember his answer: "I want to save this marriage." By 1990, he could no longer cover their expenses in Switzerland. Tilly did not want to return to Canada because the "winters were too cold," and they agreed to live separately. Jerome returned to Canada very depressed. I insisted that he spend some time with us in Long Beach, which indeed helped him. He successfully resumed work and reorganized his life in Ottawa. He visited with us as much as possible, and we were in close contact. In 2003, he spent a nice vacation with us. He was planning his return when he suffered a heart attack. No full recovery could be achieved, and he was unable to move to the States because of the health insurance. We thought that the best thing for him would be to move into a good retirement facility, but that did not work well for him, as he was used to being independent. However, he was very sick, and I had to go to Ottawa to see him and take care of whatever I could almost monthly. His heart condition did not improve, and in 2005 he died in his sleep. He was almost eighty years old.

A family picture at home, May 2003. Front row, from left to right: Jerome, Huguette, and me. Back row: Daniel, Noëlle, and André.

♦

"Let's play with mud, Edgar," said Claudia Kaneshiro, my former pharmacist, one day in March 2011. We were both retired. She was a very talented person. I'd never tried my hand at the manual arts, but I had a faint inclination to make things with my own hands. We found that the city of Long Beach had a ceramic arts studio, among many other programs. Registration was simple, and in March 2011 we showed up for the first lesson of a two-month class. Our teacher, the British-born Anita Sinclair, asked what we wanted to learn, "slab" or "sculpture." I could imagine what "slab" work might entail, and I was not interested in it. I was interested in sculpture. Then Anita asked me to do something with a lump of clay. This was a challenge. What could I do? I took home the lump of clay and pondered on what to do with it. I was quite disappointed in myself for not having any idea. I was feeling that I had gotten involved in something that was not within my abilities, when I suddenly recalled that I knew human anatomy very well; I should try to use it in my clay work. I opened a folding table in the garage, and I sat there for a few hours modeling and sculpting a woman's body. It came out quite well. I did not know how to make the hands, and I took the liberty of not making them. I did not make the head either. Next week, I showed it to my class, and Anita asked: "How long did you work on it?" I answered that I had worked a few hours. Anita declared, "You have talent!" This was an encouraging compliment. I had the idea to give a name to my piece, and I called it *Eve of Long Beach*. That opened my desire to express myself through the medium of clay. I proceeded, making *Adam of Long Beach*. I did not like my Adam. He came out quite husky, and I would have liked him to have more harmonious lines. I could detect many defects. My teacher reassured me that all artists are unsatisfied with their creations after they are completed. So perhaps I was an artist deep in myself and I did not know it. After so many years of practicing medicine and scientific research, I thought of myself as a man of science, a so-called left-brain person, and now I had discovered that my right-brain was functioning quite well.

I thought of making a head, and I wanted to make it with my wife's traits. Huguette could not muster the patience to sit as a model, so I was able to get only a general impression, but that was quite enough to help me make a woman's head. At the studio a student said, "That looks like a French woman!" So I called her *The French Woman*. My wife is indeed a French Canadian lady.

I've always admired the work of Constantin Brancusi, the Romanian sculptor, who developed his own original style while working in Paris. His work is highly regarded and may be seen in many great museums. One beautiful piece, *Bird in Space,* is in the Norton Simon Museum in Pasadena. I see his work as representing the elementary features that impress us from our visual experiences. I developed a perennial interest in sculpting heads inspired by the work of Constantin Brancusi. I had to make several heads to get close to my visual idea. The last one I made became elongated in my hands like it was making its own way out of the soft clay. I called it *Thinking of Modigliani*. I participated in three exhibitions in Long Beach from 2012 to 2014, and I received encouraging comments on my work.

Heads à la C. Brancusi (2011-2013)

I admire the harmony and beauty of a woman's body, which has a natural series of peaks and valleys: The head, the torso, and the hips suggest the peaks, while the neck and the waist are the valleys. I made five sculptures on this theme, and I am not yet satisfied with the outcome. However, the last piece in this series had a beautiful head, which I saved when the body broke. It seemed to be like a classic head. I also learned to work with coil and made many vases that I gave to friends. Then I experimented with making sculpted tablets.

A Classic Head (2013)

Daniel and Berenice wanted children very much. In 2013, they had twin girls, Isla and Carys. While waiting for the babies to join us, I had the inspiration for a piece showing the protective hands of the parents and two babies in a heart-shaped basket. I liked my idea, I made the piece, and gave it to the expecting parents at the baby shower.

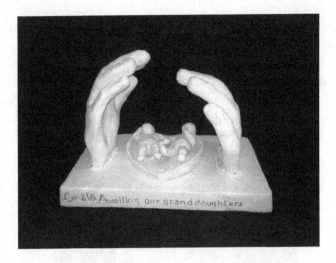

Awaiting our grandchildren. August 2013

At work. Long Beach, 2014

I've created less in the last two years, as I've became involved again in lecturing and teaching. I still love "playing with mud." I feel that it helps me express a state of mind.

♦

I love history because it is man's greatest teacher. It teaches us what not to do. In January 2015, I listened to two lectures on World War I and on World War II on the neighboring University Campus. They were given at the Senior University known as the Osher Lifelong Learning Institute (OLLI) at California State University at Long Beach (CSULB). I learned about Mr. Bernard Osher, a generous millionaire from San Francisco, and his Foundation, which has endowed American universities with grants that make possible for those universities to offer classes to people over fifty years of age, people who desire to continue learning. I found out that the curriculum included various topics, but nothing on life sciences or on the human body. Surprised, I asked the administrator why there were no such lectures in the curriculum, and she stated that there had been a demand for such lectures, but no one had proposed to give them. I had been sincerely displeased with the teaching of health sciences in our high schools, and I had also witnessed the tragedies of otherwise intelligent people who did not know how to manage their health problems. I suggested a course on health sciences, and the curriculum committee approved my plan for a series of eight weekly lectures on *Our Body in Health and in Disease*. I liked to teach the phenomena of biology, such as inflammation, infections, genetics, and cancer. I followed those with a review of the anatomy, physiology, and pathology of our systems. I explained everything in simple terms with excellent illustrations at a college level, and the course was very well received by the audiences. I gave this course several times. The following year, I gave an eight-week course on *Cancer* in which I reviewed the important issues related to cancer epidemiology, its prevention, screening, diagnosis, and treatment. I was lucky to have a very good audience which was eager to learn. Encouraged by those successes, I offered the courses to the OLLI Program at California State University at Fullerton (CSUF-OLLI) and at my university, the University of California, Irvine. The audiences at UCI-OLLI, were large, about a hundred people, and the reception was wonderful. My coordinator at UCI-OLLI was Gary Oberts, a retired geologist with whom I worked very well, and we became friends.

Since my student days I have been interested in the economic phenomena associated with the planet's natural resources. I have read extensively and formed ideas on the distribution of vital resources and how access to those resources has determined the development or the destruction of societies. This access (or lack thereof) has resulted in economic and political issues that in some cases continue to embattle the world. Evidently, it is the access to resources that has determined human existence, the development of civilizations, and possibly of cultures. In fact, the world depends on resources, and the search for more resources is never-ending. I've carried these thoughts for many years, and I've enjoyed talking about them with friends. I had the idea that I might lecture on the topic. I wrote a synopsis for a course I called *The World, its Resources, and Humankind*. The curriculum committees of the OLLI Programs at the three universities approved the course, which was planned as eight weekly lectures. When I started to work on the material for my lectures, writing up my thoughts, I realized that my knowledge of many aspects of the subject of natural resources needed further study and documentation, which took me about five months of intense daily work until it was satisfactorily completed. In the class, I showed how the geography of natural resources (air, water, food, metals, minerals, wood, and the natural resources for various forms of energy) have determined our history and economies by attracting human settlements. I showed how human industry has determined the evolution of societies and their economies, which in turn have dictated political organization, prosperity, and/or destruction; I talked about the importance of coltan and of rare earth elements in the technology of our modern life. I thought that the course gave a great lesson on human history, on how we have evolved as a population of the world, and on who we are as a species. I gave the course at CSULB-OLLI, CSUF-OLLI, and UCI-OLLI, where it was enthusiastically received. I learned so much while preparing the course, and I continue learning about — and feeling in awe of — this course on human evolution.

Recently, an oft-recurring idea came again to my mind: *Why* did this or that event happen? *Why?* Sometimes events occur by chance or things are discovered by serendipity, but oftentimes the cause is there, known or occult, subtle or complex, multifactorial, or just complicated, and it might escape our understanding or require a more fertile imagination than our own.

I decided to give a four-part colloquium on the theme *Why do things happen?* I could answer several *why*'s in biology and medicine, and I added three more sessions for comments on why things happen in our economic, social, and political lives, such as: *Why do we have inflation? Why do we have national debt? Why does humanity go through revolutions, rebellions, and wars,* and the *Why does the death of democracies occur.* In the last lecture, I discussed *Why we have homelessness* and *Why we have immigration problems.* I finished by reviewing the sad chapter of *Why women have suffered injustice throughout history.* I introduced each topic and then invited a free discussion. I thought that for an interested audience, the course and discussion might offer great intellectual stimulation and fun. My audiences agreed with me and responded well. I presume that thinking adults constantly ask "Why?" without realizing how eternally recurrent this question is, and, very importantly, how creative the answers to these elemental questions might become if properly pursued. I gave this course at CSULB-OLLI and at UCI-OLLI, and it was considered very interesting. Lecturing and teaching adults has been a great occupation. I look forward to those lectures with great anticipation, and I feel that the material I present in them meets the interests of my audience.

Last year, I had a rare experience: I was immersed in an interesting conversation with my friend Gary Oberts. I was listening to him. Suddenly, I had a flash: "I must teach about the Holocaust." There was nothing in the conversation I was having with Gary that I could relate to the subject. It was a unique experience that remains unexplained. I quickly wrote an outline of four lectures and submitted it to the curriculum committee, which approved the course. I started working on the lectures without respite; I studied and wrote for five months. I felt it as a moral dictate. After I'd done more than half the work, I had to stop. I felt overwhelmed by the immensity and cruelty of this human tragedy. I took some time to recover and to bring my project to a satisfactory conclusion. I wanted to make the important point that the Holocaust occurred because of unique conditions, which in final analysis can be identified as the badly conceived Treaty of Versailles, followed by the Weimar Republic, the reparations imposed on Germany, and Germany's ensuing economic failure. All this was the canvas, the ground on which the Nazi movement could take hold. The importance of understanding these events lies in the likelihood that similar situations may occur and reoccur; it is our duty to work hard to avoid them. Freedom is preserved though vigilance. As a Holocaust survivor, I experienced many difficult moments while delivering my lectures. The audiences appeared to be captured by my talk. It all went well, and I was asked back to lecture on the topic of anti-Semitism. This may come to pass.

Epilogue

As I explained at its beginning, this book was stimulated by my sons, who were interested in my life stories. They asked me to write about the events of my life. I was reluctant to write my memoirs, but one day I felt compelled to write about that poignant lesson in integrity and generosity that my father taught me in my childhood. I wrote that story under an impulse, and that experience felt significant to me: I just had to write it — and then I liked to read it.

Many other people liked it too. Then I found myself driven by an inner force to write about two more significant stories. Then colleagues prodded me to write more. I did indeed have some unusual stories: A friend said: "Edgar, our boys played baseball at fifteen, the age when you were in the Underground Resistance fighting the Nazis." Another good friend said, thoughtfully, that while reading the stories in the first part of this book, he'd thought that I was "about to be killed three different times." I hope that this record of my stories gives a message of hope to those who read it, in particular the youth.

Readers of the first section of my stories have reported thinking that those stories represent a "sweep of history," and that I must publish them as a record of events that happened to me exactly as I've narrated them. It is not easy to review and write about the years of a life spent bearing the pain of persecution. My life in Israel redeemed my soul, my whole person, and allowed me to come out as myself. I am immensely grateful to have been able to survive — and do some good things — against all odds.

I think that I am a natural storyteller. I love to narrate events, thoughts, and feelings. I know that the first part of this book has in it the special flavor of my growing up, my enthusiastic youth spent in adversity. The second part of the book, which covers my adult life in Canada and the United States, has a totally different flavor and tonality to it. It centers on my professional life and on "attaining my aims." It describes many battles of a very different sort compared to those in the first part of the book. Nevertheless, those battles were intense; for what has been consistently evident throughout my entire life was my battle against adversity — and my perseverance in my efforts to overcome it.

I do believe that man must overcome difficulty, whether it is poverty, hunger, or lack of freedom. I thank the friends and family who helped me toward the conviction that my writing might help those who do not have all the benefits of a happy life in freedom.

Edgar M. Moran
Long Beach, California
edgarmariomoran@gmail.com

Made in USA - Kendallville, IN
1233511_9780578819518
02.15.2021 1307